# Energy, Inflation, and International Economic Relations

Curt Gasteyger
Louis Camu
Jack N. Behrman
foreword by
Pierre Uri

Published for the Atlantic
Institute for International Affairs

# Energy, Inflation, and International Economic Relations

## Atlantic Institute Studies—II

PRAEGER SPECIAL STUDIES IN INTERNATIONAL ECONOMICS AND DEVELOPMENT

**Praeger Publishers** New York Washington London

Library of Congress Cataloging in Publication Data
Main entry under title:

Energy, inflation, and international economic relations.

(Atlantic Institute studies ; 2) (Praeger special studies in international economics and development)
"Part I. The Western world and energy, edited by Curt Gasteyger": p.
"Part II. Spotlights on inflation; report on a meeting of participating members of the Atlantic Institute for International Affairs, chaired by Louis Camu": p.
"Part III. Toward a new international economic order [by] Jack N. Behrman": p.
1. Energy policy--Addresses, essays, lectures.
2. Inflation (Finance)--Addresses, essays, lectures.
3. International economic relations--Addresses, essays, lectures. I. Gasteyger, Curt Walter, 1929- II. Camu, Louis. III. Behrman, Jack N. Toward a new international economic order. 1975. IV. Series: Atlantic Institute for International Affairs. Atlantic Institute studies ; 2.
HD9502.A2E544 1975 382.1 75-19764
ISBN 0-275-01250-6

PRAEGER PUBLISHERS
111 Fourth Avenue, New York, N.Y. 10003, U.S.A.

Published in the United States of America in 1975
by Praeger Publishers, Inc.



Printed in the United States of America

# Foreword

The three Atlantic Papers which are republished in this book have one feature in common: although they were conceived and written in 1973 and 1974, the three of them deal with fundamental economic issues which have not yet been resolved and will continue to be with us for a long time. The energy crisis still deeply affects the economies of industrialized countries, inflation coupled with recession has not yet been overcome, and a call for a new world economic order, however vague the notion, is the cry of the day. The papers differ though, as to their authorship and composition.

The first presents the main written contributions to a conference on "Energy and the Western world" which was held in Tokyo shortly after the ceasefire that put an end to the Yom Kippur war and before the oil embargo that was decided upon by the OPEC countries. It had been planned one year before and brought together some 45 eminent experts from North America, Western Europe, Japan, and Australia. The price of oil had already been increased; nonetheless this advanced planning of the conference testifies to the foresight of the people who had sensed the abrupt turn about from an economy based on cheap energy to one in which it would be both scarce and expensive.

The second paper is based on a conference organized in Munich by the Atlantic Institute for International Affairs for its participating members. Such conferences, which are held twice a year, are devoted to current issues of the highest importance; they are introduced by eminent specialists and provision is made for as much discussion from the floor as possible. The debate is entirely off the record. Thus it is not normal practice to produce a publication from such meetings as undue emphasis on publishing might to some extent limit the free expression of views. However, it was agreed that the papers and discussions were of such high value that, with the permission of the authors and discussants, a permanent record would be a major contribution to the industrialized countries which face, in common, the dual difficulty of fighting rapid inflation and profound recession. The contributions are those presented by the various speakers with one minor difference: the actual wording of the presentation by Ambassador Roberto Campos on "indexation in Brazil" is taken from the statement made by him on the same subject a few days later in London before the Stock Exchange, which has kindly agreed to its reproduction.

The third paper, which has been extensively discussed with a variety of experts, is one man's piece. Professor Behrman has become well known through his work on the growing phenomenon of multinational corporations and the effects of what he calls "international production." He has constantly emphasized that in a world where basic supplies are traded internationally, and where capital and management are increasingly mobile, the industrial policies for which governments are groping—more often than not in an inconsistent manner—exert a more decisive influence on the location of activities than the classical law of comparative advantage.

The contributions on the energy issue are partly descriptive, partly prospective, partly policy oriented. The major data on the over-all situation—that is production, consumption, reserves of fossile fuels, and alternative sources of supply—are presented with great precision and detail in Mr. Sakisaka's paper. The projections indicate what oil consumption would be at alternative future dates on the assumption that growth in the industrialized world resumes its past trend and pattern. The costs, as well as dependence on one particular area of the world, the Middle East, will be formidable. It is a very original feature that analyzes and forecasts have been made by Walter Gumpel and Marcel Toussaint of the energy situation in the major communist countries, the USSR, and China. In the USSR, production of energy has been growing at a fantastic pace, although there is some uncertainty about reserves, which are not clearly distinguished according to whether they are proven, probable or possible. The key problem in the Soviet Union is the distance between the main future sources and the centers of industrial production. In China, energy production has increased but still remains on a modest scale. It is not impossible to imagine that resources there might be even more enormous than those of the Middle East. Even if the new oil situation is rapidly changing the balance of payments of the USSR, technical co-operation from the West will be required, particularly in Siberia; and China will certainly want to accelerate its imports of equipment to push the exploration and exploitation of its vast but largely unmeasurable potential.

Against that background, Wolfgang Hager rightly points out the divergencies of interests as well as the differences of the basic situations of Western and particularly European countries. This warning has been justified by the failure of the European Community to evolve a joint energy policy up to now, as well as by the split between France and her partners at the International Energy Agency. Guy de Carmoy assesses the magnitude of the financial problems created by the accumulation of liquid currency surpluses by oil producing countries, the richest of which have only very sparse populations, and he foretells a necessary redirection of growth in the industrialized world based on a certain austerity. This ties in with the conclusion of Mr. Sakisaka that Japan will have to move away from energy-intensive industries.

Since this conference was held, some action has been taking place to mitigate the difficulties of energy imbalance. The International Energy Agency has begun its work; the International Monetary Fund has set up its special oil facilities; and, at the initiative of Secretary Kissinger and of the OECD, financial arrangements in the nature of a safety net have been agreed upon.

The evolution of the situation confirms the diagnosis and forecast of the Secretary General of the OECD, which are presented as an annex. Addressing the Washington Conference of February 11, 1974, Emil Van Lennep stressed the various factors which might be at work to flatten out the curve of oil import requirements. Policies for economy and conservation have made a limited start. Their advantages in terms of costs as well as of preservation of the environment have also been emphasized in another conference held by the Institute, by Professor Carrol Wilson. But market forces, i.e., price elasticities, make themselves felt; unfortunately the recessionary situation in the industrialized world also makes its contribution to reducing the demand for energy and hence for oil. There is a possibility, given the effect of prices and some action by Governments, that imports of oil from the Middle

East in 1980 will not be higher than in 1973. Thus there are limits to what producers can do without destroying their own markets and harming their own interests. This is the possible basis for a dialogue. It was unsuccessful at the recent Paris Conference but there is now some chance that it might be resumed. In the meantime the OECD and its Secretary General were among the first to stress the dual effect of the abrupt increase in the price of oil—i.e., a major contribution to a cost-push inflation as well as to economic contraction through the enormous transfer of resources abroad, which acts like a suddenly imposed tax on the level of activity. This provides the link with the major theme of the other Atlantic Paper "Spotlights on Inflation".

On such a complicated issue no uniform view or unique recipe was to be expected. However, a strong and convergent emphasis emerges. How does it come that conventional demand management through credit and fiscal policies appears ineffective against price increases, at least internally, whereas they add to recession and the dangerous decrease of employment? There is no question that a steep and synchronized increase in aggregate demand of all of the industrialized countries contributed to the upsurge of prices of raw materials at the same time that droughts pushed up world food prices. But the inflation dates back to more distant periods. Thus structural factors which give it its new character have been mentioned on several sides.

One factor, stressed by a German participant, is that the regional distribution of wages is too uniform to offset regional disparities of productivity, so that unemployment increases from the center to the periphery. A more general remark is that Keynesian economics relied on a stimulation of demand which, as the great economist saw, could lead to bottlenecks and inflationary pressure. When, however, inflation is anticipated, its effects on costs are discounted by the entrepreneur: the stimulus is destroyed. On the other hand, Keynes in his late writings expected that inflation would come to a stop by transferring resources from low to high incomes, from wages to profits and thus come to an end through an increase of savings. With wages anticipating the price increase, this transfer is either nullified or reversed. Inflation itself may lead to a profit squeeze which diminishes the inducement to invest, increases indebtedness, pushes up interest rates and henceforth depresses the stock market.

The structural change may be even more general. The question may be raised whether, by pushing up production, our economies are not reaching the point where decreasing costs give way to increasing costs. This is obviously the case for mineral products as well as for the spreading of the service economy. And even in industry, the extreme diversification and quick renewal of objects and models spurred by fashion and advertising may limit or arrest economies of scale. When this change on the supply side is accompanied by a strong surge of all the claims on supply between countries as well as within countries, the result is a constant upward pressure on prices.

In this connection, the contribution of Robert Roosa is particularly important. Inflation as a long-term phenomenon can only be met by an increase in essential supplies. This in turn requires the setting up of priorities, a euphemism for economic planning. Temporary controls may be necessary to stop the spiral provided they are supported by proper credit and fiscal policies. But the key point is that the investments needed to meet essential needs in productive capacity as well as in communication and housing will provide the necessary and most useful kind of employment in the present recession. A budget deficit financed by borrowing from the oil producers will not be inflationary, as it would just fill the contractionary gap caused by the rise in the price of external supplies.

As was stressed by Nat Samuels, international cooperation, if the diagnosis and type of action are right, is essential to success. As another participant mentioned, there had been hope that fixed exchange rates would limit inflation; this held true as long as the United States' economy was stable. However, when America plunged into inflation, flexible exchange rates—specially, the appreciation of some currencies—appeared to offer a method of insulation from imported inflationary pressure. But flexible rates work in an assymetrical way. Revaluation does not stop the upward movement of wages and may push up world prices; devaluations are soon eaten up. And balances of payments may not react according to text book models: import costs are increased by devaluation faster than exports are made more competitive; the revaluation of a currency may not stop exports if it is coupled with internal deflation.

On the whole one may wonder if governments are not fighting the wrong kind of inflation. Perhaps what is at stake is not excess demand but rising import prices and an internal spiral due to the rigidities of wage bargains and price setting. The upshot of the various analyses presented is that there may be a convergent way out of the present recession as well as the rampant inflation. It would call for a new pattern of growth. The struggle for the fruits of expansion and the social tensions which express it call for more equal income distribution.

Thus again, a link is provided with the very provocative paper written by Professor Jack Behrman. The Research Advisory Council set up by the Atlantic Institute for International Affairs noted how far the present world was departing from strict allocation of resources through the market, be it in the form of concessionary terms granted by some of the industrialized areas to the developing world, or in the form of so-called co-operation agreements with Eastern countries. The Council pointed out the growing importance of security considerations in the broadest sense—that is their importance in policies concerning basic commodities, including agriculture; in the maintenance of employment; in the exercise of control of national economics in the face of the transnational corporations; in the retention of supplies through export controls designed to fight inflation at home as contrasted with import controls prompted by the preoccupation with fighting unemployment.

The piece of work presented by Professor Behrman fits remarkably well into this program. It pulls together apparently divergent phenomena, such as the emergence of regional blocs, the struggle for raw materials, the strategies of multinational firms, the special or generalized preference systems, even the search for a new international monetary system, as so many signs of the recognition that the market is only a mechanism and, under conditions of monopoly and oligopoly, a very distorted one; at best it can serve efficiency in the allocation of goods among those endowed with purchasing power, but it does not answer the fundamental question: is this distribution of purchasing power right? A rational location of activities cannot be determined by current prices but has to take into account future developments and potential advantages. Again the present distribution is largely a function of the past, not only among individuals—by virtue of inheritance—but among countries, many of which, particularly in the developing world, have long been affected by the Colonial Pact, and by a type of free trade in which they provided exhaustible resources subject to wide price fluctuations, whereas the advanced countries shared among themselves the benefits of sophisticated and specialized manufacturing.

Beyond the criteria of efficiency, Professor Behrman discerns in the wake of rapid changes a general quest for more equity, however defined; and, beyond sheer accounting costs, the necessity of paying due regard to all of the social and human costs involved, whether in terms of pollution, or of an unacceptable tempo of change, or of the disintegration of traditional communities. More involvement on the part of governments is inevitable, since market forces by themselves can at best reflect the existing inequalities of power and wealth, but are incapable of redressing them. Professor Behrman's hope is that a return to nationalism by both the developing and the advanced countries can be avoided, through the emergence of a new order of co-operation in which aims, even more than means, can be discussed on the basis of greater equality.

In a time when the vague notion of a new order is largely identified with even more absolute sovereignties over increasingly scarce resources, may this hopeful note be heard.

Pierre Uri

# Contents

## PART III

## TOWARD A NEW INTERNATIONAL ECONOMIC ORDER

Jack N. Behrman

## LIST OF TABLES

# The Western World and Energy

edited by

CURT GASTEYGER

# The Western World and Energy

*By Curt Gasteyger*

If a prize for unpredictability were to be awarded, no doubt the present energy situation would win it. Over the last six months its pace of change has accelerated to a degree that makes yesterday distant history and the present an unreliable guide for tomorrow. The uncertainty is compounded by confusion, and any hint of a possible sense of direction is immediately blurred by multiple contradictions. It takes a considerable amount of courage – or naïveté – therefore, to attempt to write anything which either has not yet been said a hundred times over or will not soon be overtaken by events. The fluidity of the present energy situation – or is it already yesterday's? – is complicated by the fact that it cuts through almost all sectors of daily life, permeates the entire international system, affects rich and poor at the same time, and reverses priorities which have long, too long perhaps, determined national policies and individual preferences. Only one thing is sure: given the extraordinary complexity of the issues at stake there is no ready-made or easy answer to it, no 'quick fix' but rather a 'long mix' of new approaches; there must be different priorities, better institutions and, above all, common objectives aimed at the whole world and not just at a few privileged sectors of it.

## Energy and the international system

It is still too early to assess the overall and undoubtedly lasting impact of the 'energy crisis' on international politics. Such a crisis has been looming on the horizon for quite some time, and was suddenly brought to a climax by the boycott of the oil-producing (OPEC) countries in the wake of the fourth Arab–Israeli war, in October 1973. Everyone would agree, however, that in many ways a *new power constellation* is emerging. The crisis has exposed the great vulnerability of the Western industrialized world, including Japan, while at the same time demonstrating the influence of a small group of countries which has little more to muster than its huge oil reserves. It has revealed the relativity of such traditional notions as military or political power in the age of interdependence, as well as the fragility of such admired manifestations of wealth as staggering growth rates, huge GNPs and fat currency reserves. Japan and, to a lesser but still significant degree, the European Communities face the shattered expectations that they were on the way to becoming the first 'civilian powers' in an era in which an unsurpassed and ever expanding economic wealth would overshadow and finally render insignificant the rôle of military strength. Conversely, the growing scarcity of raw materials may provide those developing countries which possess them with a new and powerful weapon.

This leads to a second related conclusion, concerning the *new distribution of wealth* in the world. Over the next few years, the oil-producing countries will accumulate enormous amounts of revenue. In one way or the other, these vast sums are bound to affect the international monetary system, either as a catalyst of its total collapse or as an opportunity for its overall reform. In either case, the voice of the OPEC countries will have to be listened to in what used to be the exclusive club of the Western countries. At the other bitter end stand the developing countries, for whom this new distribution of wealth means mainly a still longer and dearer way to development. No mechanisms are as yet in sight which would effectively take care of their needs.

Thus, we must conclude, there are *different degrees of vulnerability*. Countries are unevenly affected by the shortage of energy and its rising price. Of all the industrialized countries, Japan is surely the most exposed. Even allowing for a drastic reduction in her energy consumption (with all the ensuing economic consequences), she will to an overwhelming degree remain dependent on external resources, including oil, natural gas and raw materials. Her only assets, though, are important ones – political unity and national solidarity, neither of which Western Europe, even the Communities, will be able to mobilize in any foreseeable future. Europe's vulnerability, therefore, lies less in its considerable dependence on external resources (which may be gradually reduced by the North Sea findings) than in its exasperating political disunity with all its attendant risks of mutual competition and national egotism.

As the strengthening of the dollar shows, the United States in turn has emerged as the Western country with the least vulnerability and greatest capacity for recapturing its autonomy. It possesses both political unity and vast untapped resources. It has, though belatedly, formulated a comprehensive energy policy which will reduce its dependence on oil imports and thus alleviate the strain on its balance of payments. This is bound to reinforce the American position *vis-à-vis* Europe and Japan. They see their newly acquired position of strength, so confidently displayed in recent negotiations with Washington, dwindle as their reserves are eaten up by rising oil prices and inflation. The 'economic triangle' in which Europe and Japan were supposed to play important parts is thus once more getting lopsided. New strains and resentments on the part of the weaker sides, and frustration on the American side, may ensue. This situation is hardly likely to facilitate the evolution of a more balanced and thus more durable Atlantic relationship.

Rather, as the acrimonious proceedings at the Washington Energy Conference in early February 1974 have demonstrated, it re-emphasises the dominating strength of the United States and the excruciating weakness of Europe.

From here it is only one step to the fourth conclusion: the crises in October 1973 have not led to a better management of interdependence: instead of generating more co-operation, they offered the temptation to place bilateral dealings with the oil producers before multilateral negotiations; instead of pushing the Western countries toward a comprehensive internationalism, they revived a narrow 'defensive' nationalism in which short-term national interests provide the easier though hardly the better answer. For the first time in their history the European Communities were drawn together by what appeared to be an external threat, which now looks as if it were going to become an internal one of serious dimensions. This is perhaps so because the previous threats were basically *political* and military in nature whereas the present one is not. Could it be that an economic and monetary crisis instead of drawing the member countries together risks tearing them apart?

Dr Hager is probably right in stressing at the beginning of his paper that the present disunity is not only due to the selfishness or short-sightedness of our statesmen (though they bear a great deal of blame), but also reflects profound and real differences of interest. Be that as it may, the present disarray among the Western democracies and their varying degrees of vulnerability starkly contrasts with the considerably stronger positions of the two major communist powers, the Soviet Union and China. As the contributions by Dr Gumpel and Mr Toussaint show, these powers have vast resources of oil and natural gas, making them considerably less dependent on external resources. Their main problems are that of extraction and transportation over long distances and, at least in the case of the Soviet Union, the rapidly rising demands of industrialization and private consumption. In addition, the Soviet Union must, to some degree at least, supply its Eastern European allies, a political liability China is free of. Up to now, China has been exporting only modest quantities, mainly to Japan. But she may well become an important actor on the international oil market some day. The steep rise in oil prices has come as a windfall to the Soviet Union. No doubt she will profit from it all the more as Western rivalry generates disruption or dissension among the 'capitalist' countries. Moscow and Peking must be aware that their wealth of energy resources helps to strengthen their international position. It is interesting to note that this may considerably influence China's position *vis-à-vis* Japan, and that the Soviet Union's position *vis-à-vis* Europe may come to resemble that of the United States, thus creating a new convergence of super power interests towards the continent.

The sixth point is of a more speculative but no less serious nature. One of the immediate consequences of, first, the oil embargo and then the gradual depletion of oil resources will be a world-wide drive for nuclear power. The scientists assure us that both in terms of explosions and effluence, nuclear reactors pose no unsurmountable technical problems. However, as many experts point out, the problem of how to dispose of radioactive waste is of a different, much more serious nature. Its dimensions will grow as reactors spread over the entire world and increase in numbers. Many of them produce plutonium, a most dangerous poison, out of which atomic bombs can be made. If not properly safeguarded, small quantities of plutonium could exterminate mankind. It could also be relatively easily used (or reused) for military purposes, thus facilitating an uncontrolled spread of nuclear weapons. In ten or fifteen years there will be plutonium-producing reactors all over the world, and the International Atomic Energy Agency (IAEA) will be faced with a staggering task of control .It cannot, however, prevent a country from 'going nuclear' should it be determined to do so; there is no international mechanism in sight which is both sufficiently effective and generally acceptable enough to protect the world from wanton nuclear proliferation.

A final point concerns the security of energy supply and transport, i.e., the political-strategic implications of the flow of energy from its sources to the consumers, mainly by sea and pipelines. A few figures may show the dimensions at stake. Seventy per cent of raw materials and products are transported by sea. The rate of increase is ten per cent. In 1953, the transport of goods amounted to 600 million tons; in 1970, it had increase to 2,500 million tons of which 1,200 million tons were oil products; forecasts for 1980 vary between four and five billion tons. The merchant fleets show a corresponding gorwth: from 97 million cwt and 32,000 ships in 1953 to 230 million cwt and 40,000 ships in 1970. The lion's share is, of course, taken up by the stupendous growth of the oil tanker fleet. The expansion of pipelines is also considerable, though slower and less spectacular. Today, however, there are dozens of pipelines for oil and natural gas stretching over long distances in North America, Europe (including the Soviet Union) and the politically highly volatile Middle East.

Needless to say, both tankers and pipelines are extremely vulnerable – and consequently, so is the fuel they carry. No storage is ever likely to compensate for their blockade or disruption, nor can any military force fully assure their protection. There are more navies than rational governments and the danger of international hijacking descending on super tankers is always present. This does not mean, however, that no precautions should be taken and that military force (naval force in particular) has become redundant.

Yet these are precisely the assumptions a number of Western governments are inclined to make. Faced with what they think has become an impossible task, namely to secure an energy supply from overseas that is vital to their economy, they resign themselves to maintaining symbolic naval forces, counting on American protection or just hoping for the best. The problem is no doubt difficult and a combination of all three attitudes is the only feasible approach under the circumstances, though certainly not the most desirable answer. To rely always and forever on American naval presence in the seven seas betrays a good amount of over-confidence in the durability and extent of American overseas commitments and in an unfailing solidarity among present allies, though solidarity is already overshadowed by a growing competition for energy resources.

## The economic and monetary tangle

The most immediately visible consequences of this rapidly changing international environment are to be found in the economic and monetary field. They raise a lot of questions no one has more than a tentative answer to; they open up entirely new negotiations and shift the emphasis of monetary reform from grappling with balance of payments disequilibria in the Western world to controlling the massive flow of *oil revenues*. The ensuing change in the economic parameters, as Wolfgang Hager points out in a report on the Tokyo conference, is going to upset radically the way governments conduct their domestic and foreign policies. The international economic system which responds to this new situation may therefore look very different from the reformed, liberal trade and monetary system that most people had hoped to see evolving over the next few years.

The following points were discussed at the Tokyo conference. First, the system will have to be much more broadly gauged and comprehensive, in order to reflect the new interdependencies and take into account the new distribtuion of wealth and diversification of monetary power centers. Second, there will be a new orientation in capital spending towards a greater diversification of energy sources; new efforts in export drives to compensate both internally and with the producing countries for the rise of oil prices; energy conservation and the definition of new priorities for the kinds of goods which industrial countries can or should produce and consume (e.g., fewer plastics and more paper, fewer cars and more public transport). Third, there is likely to be an increase in state intervention into economic life for a number of reasons. Thus, shifts in investment patterns of the magnitude required to really matter in the fields of national security and the balance of payments will not come about by the price mechanism alone. Energy, for most industries, represents 5 to 10 per cent of costs. A doubling of these costs would be equivalent to rises in wages which industry has learned to absorb. Furthermore, the market reacts to *private* utility functions, and not to public ones such as security and the balance of payments. Certain sectors of industry will have to be subjected to severe adjustments. They call for state intervention though this time on social grounds. Both developments leading to increased state intervention are almost bound to affect commercial policies (dumping *and* import restrictions in order to ease adjustment). Without a sweeping reform of the monetary system the liberalisation of the capital markets could undergo serious restrictions.

This leads to a fourth point. One of the most urgent challenges to the European countries and Japan is their rapidly slipping balance of payments. Rising oil prices are quickly eating up their reserves and surpluses. The Secretary General of the OECD, in a speech to the Strasbourg Consultative Assembly on 23 January 1974, estimated the import bill of the OECD countries to be $50 billion in 1974. Each extra dollar for a barrel of crude oil means an additional five billion dollars on Europe's balance of payments. In 1972, Japan paid some $4.1 billion for its oil imports; current estimates for 1974 amount to $14 billion, which will absorb more than her total foreign reserves. Even if oil prices should go down, the problem remains disconcerting – for Japan still more than for Europe – and for Europe more than for the United States. But in two respects it concerns them all to the same degree: first, they all will be confronted with the vexing question of how to cope with the fabulous surpluses of some $60–70 billion a year which the oil-producing countries may wish to spend around the world; and second, how to come to grips with the impact which this new situation will have on their commercial policies. Professor de Carmoy, in his paper, deals with the first issue, other papers, in particular Dr Hager's, with the second. Dr Hager argues that, in theory, outflows on the current account represent few problems for the countries concerned: capital flows are expected to redress the balance. Furthermore, even on current account, a rapidly appreciating dollar of an increasingly energy-independent United States will offer new opportunities for manufactured exports from Europe and Japan. In practice, Dr Hager argues that the off-set on capital account will take place under politically 'managed' conditions both on the donor (e.g. the Arabs) and on the receiver side. It may even fall short of matching, dollar for dollar, the current account outflow of the importing countries. On the other hand, it is unrealistic to expect the United States and other more or less energy-independent countries (such as Canada) to let their markets be disrupted by 'cheap' products from countries with depressed exchange rates. How 'cheap' these products can be, in view of the rising energy costs, is yet another question that needs further examination.

At the present juncture one thing seems certain: the position of the United States *vis-à-vis* its allies will be strengthened, as evidenced by the astonishing rise of the dollar, and that this greater strength is bound to spill over into other fields of the triangular relationship, in particular the political-strategic one. It is here that we come full circle and find ourselves back where we started on the stage of international politics. To comprehend, let alone to manage, the innumerable interactions between these various fields and actors is going to be a monumental task. As there are neither adequate mechanisms nor comprehensive concepts to deal with it, one may well wonder whether our present governments will be able to tackle it.

There remain several other important points which should at least be mentioned in passing. The first relates to the future of the (private) multinational oil companies. The papers mention the twilight into which their previous policies has brought these companies. No doubt they have had a bad press in recent times, and their position has become increasingly difficult. They find themselves more and more sandwiched between producing and consuming countries, faced with the prospect of being degraded to risk-taking investors, ill-rewarded advisors, unwelcome tax collectors or simple distributiors, or even with being blamed as reckless profiteers. There are to date no means of effectively controlling them on an world-wide scale, of checking their operations or getting some leverage over their distribution policies. In fact, until very recently, company executives were in a position of making agreements with Middle Eastern producers involving eventual burdens upon the budgets of consuming countries measured in billions of dollars. Companies often acted without any previous, independent study of the overall economic impact of their decisions and no clear definition of the interest they expected to serve.

It was and is the feeling of helplessness *vis-à-vis* this prototype of the 'multinationals' that exacerbated both the governments and the public and prompted them to call for tougher control over their activities. However, as Dr Hager's paper shows, such 'control' is still a long way off. There are doubts whether it is desirable at all and whether it would solve the problem of their future rôle and status.

In the meantime, all the bigger companies have started to move into other sectors of the energy industry, particularly the nuclear field. They are thus following or possibly even leading the trend towards necessary diversification. This may be more easily said than done. The move into the nuclear field is, if not politically then surely technically, as risky a business as oil, or the still less explored sources of energy. On the other hand, it would seem regrettable if these companies pushed their diversification drive so far as to make the energy industry, however central, only one among many of their overall activities. With their huge capital, world-wide organizational network and technical expertise, they are uniquely placed to promote diversification at the producing end, to develop new techniques for conservation and re-allocation at the consuming end, and to contribute to the establishment of more equitable energy distribution between the developing and the industrialized world. By thus making a virtue out of necessity, these companies could indeed play a pioneering role in the reorientation of today's energy policy. For some of them, the process may prove painful. It requires the elimination of time-honoured but often outdated practices and the adoption of new and broader concepts that must go well beyond the specific interests which all too often have shaped their policies.

Above all, there is one fundamental question which tends to be forgotten too easily: what social goal should energy serve? Any convincing energy policy likely to draw the necessary public support will have to answer this question. The answer will determine the outcome of any debate and the nature of any measure relating to energy. It is, of course, the most difficult one to give. There is probably no answer which will satisfy everyone.

But this difficulty should not prevent us from raising the issue, since it brings the energy debate back to essentials. 'Our predicament today is that we are making less, but using more energy' (Freeman). This situation forces us the reappraise the general direction into which a sustainable energy policy should move and to define more clearly its basic priorities. There seems little reason to doubt the prediction of experts such as Professor Sakisaka that for the foreseeable future, the energy situation will get worse and not better. Therefore, it seems high time to decide where the ever scarcer and more expensive energy should go, where it is acually indispensable, where still important and where merely desirable. In other words, the ongoing debate should concentrate not simply on alternative resources but, more importantly on alternative goals.

According to present estimates the United States, with a five per cent annual increase of energy consumption, will need about four times as much energy in the year 2000 as it does today. In view of the disturbing uncertainty about the global energy situation fifteen or twenty years hence, one wonders whether all these 'needs' are, in fact, essential and whether they have to be satisfied come what may. Indeed, what are the criteria by which these needs are defined, and do they apply to all countries in the same way? It seems that a clearer definition and differentiation of such needs are required if serious imbalances in consumption and undifferentiated uses of energy are to be avoided.

The important point is that we are not at the mercy of energy power trends. The above mentioned example of expected American energy needs in the year 2000 is a case in point. By a number of ways, above all conservation, these trends can be reduced, we are told, by one-fourth or even one-third. But even that may not be enough to avoid a further deterioration of the energy situation. If so, this would force us not just to set different priorities within the traditional context of sustained economic growth, but also to look for alternative social goals which are commensurate with, and responsive to, world-wide availability of energy. This is an enormous task to which, quite understandably, little thought has been given so far and for which neither the past nor the present provides us with guidelines and direction. The time has come, however, to raise the issue.

## Towards a comprehensive approach

All these and numerous other aspects of the energy problem beg the question of an overall framework or concept that is capable of dealing with them. As in so many other fields of national and international politics, there is none. While everyone agrees that we are faced with a world-wide challenge transcending political or ideological boundaries, the proposals for new and effective mechanisms to meet it are deplorably scarce. To be sure, an effective conservation policy or a better reallocation of resources need not wait for what might, in a distant future, develop into such an international framework. Rather, its absence seems to serve here and there as a pretext for not taking certain steps at home on the grounds that they make little sense if not properly co-ordinated internationally.

However, there is a growing number of tasks which can be handled much better by, or urgently call for, international co-operation or co-ordination. Professor de Carmoy shows, for instance, that the search for new sources of energy, their management and distribution, their transportation over long distances and through politically and ecologically vulnerable areas has become no less a matter of such co-operation than the handling and absorption of ever growing oil revenues by national and international markets.

It would indeed seem logical to improve first and foremost the co-ordination among the industrialized countries. The formulation of their respective energy policies has so far, to the best of our knowledge, been done on a purely national basis, with a national outlook determined by national interests (the 'policies' of the oil companies are in various ways an exception to this; but they are limited in scope and dominated by private interests). Such international co-ordination, whether informal or institutionalized, need not signal a new kind of confrontation with the producing countries for at least three reasons. First, as many papers show, both sides depend greatly on mutual co-operation; both sides can, in the long run, only profit from a better harmonization of their respective policies. The outbidding among the rich themselves or against the poor is bound to become a dangerously counterproductive exercise for all parties concerned. And incidentally, so is the policy of some Western powers of balancing out their trade deficit with Arab countries by mounting deliveries of highly sophisticated weaponry. These are, at best, short-term (if not short-sighted) measures with potentially long-range effects both for the security of the region on whose stability Western oil supply crucially depends, and for the relationship with other democratic powers who either cannot, or do not wish to enter this kind of competition. Of course, these measures do not solve the problem of oil revenues and their balance of trade effects either.

The second reason has to do with the much feared and criticized cohesion, or rather the lack thereof, of the two 'blocs'. The Washington energy meeting of major industrialized countries proved clearly enough (if proof was needed) that they are far from forming a united front. On the other hand, it would be equally erroneous to see in the OPEC countries a tightly knit unit and to overestimate their bargaining position. Their solidarity also rests on a fragile basis which can crumble at any time either for reasons of external rivalry or internal instability in one or the other key countries.

The third reason why Western co-ordination should not be interpreted as a platform for mere confrontation lies in the fact that over the long haul, it will only work if it embraces more than oil alone. Oil will undoubtedly remain for the next decade the central commodity around which any co-ordination must turn. But it should be seen and treated right from the beginning as an integral part of the much wider and more complex energy issue. As we have seen, this issue encompasses an ever-growing range of political, economic, social, environmental and security aspects. They have become mutually interdependent and have therefore to be dealt with as a whole, lest the entire system collapses. The only sensible and effective approach is a comprehensive one. It is, therefore, no longer acceptable for specific branches of the energy industry nor indeed for individual governments to evolve strategies of their own while neglecting the implication these might have for other sectors or nations. It is in this wider context that the oil issue must be seen if the pitfalls of a fruitless confrontation with the producing countries and an even more costly and self-defeating rivalry among the industriallized democracies themselves are to be avoided.

# The Present and Future of Energy Resources

*by Masao Sakisaka*

## Introduction

The world's energy consumption is expected to keep expanding in the 1970s with the annual rate of growth exceeding that for the 1960s. Petroleum is likely to remain the mainstay of the world energy supply, accounting for about one half of total energy needs. This heavy dependence on petroleum, it is predicted, will continue until the end of the 1980s.

The rising tide of nationalism in oil-producing countries since the early 1970s has been potent in applying increasing pressure on the international oil supply system. Under such circumstances, various restraints on oil supply may well lead to a widespread shortage of this strategic raw material. It is natural that major energy-consuming countries are now trying to secure more stable sources of supply in order to resolve the nagging instability in the world energy situation.

In developed countries, which account for the bulk of the world's energy consumption, the linear expansion of consumption will probably accelerate the trend toward the concentration of energy resource consumption in major developed countries. The growing environmental pollution that has resulted from this now imposes heavy constraints on sound social and economic development. The widely held belief is that one of the most important tasks to be tackled by developed countries in the 1970s is that of devising better ways of saving natural resources and improving the pattern of energy consumption.

Furthermore, long-term prospects for the energy supply and demand relationship are such that most of the problems and dilemmas that now confront the world will be exacerbated in the 1980s. The economic development of developing countries will create an additional demand for energy, thus imposing further constraints on the world's energy supply. Fossil fuel resources will, in the long run, increasingly fall short of demand and eventually become depleted, thus increasing the need to develop new types of energy. In order to cope with these situations it is necessary to ensure optimal allocation of resources and develop new processes for producing different kinds of energy.

In order to set clear-cut goals for energy policies, it is important to start with the problems that are expected to arise with respect to oil supply, and make, on the basis of an analysis of these problems, longer-term predictions for the period up to at least 2000. This article was written for the purpose of reviewing some of the important problems that need studying in the formulation of energy strategy.

## Prospects for energy supply and demand

### *Energy demand in the 1970s*

The world's demand for primary energy is expected to grow at an annual rate of 5.6 per cent in the 1970s. In 1980 the demand is likely to be 70 per cent greater than in 1970, about 8,500 million tons oil equivalent. The demand for petroleum itself will expand by an estimated 6·5 per cent annually in the 1970s, to about 4,000 million tons in 1980, up 90 per cent over 1970. This will account for an estimated 48 per cent of the total demand for primary energy.

In the United States, energy consumption is expected to expand at the rate of 5 per cent a year, compared with 5·4 per cent in the member countries of the Organization for Economic Cooperation and Development (OECD) and 9·1 per cent in Japan. The total demand of these countries in 1980 estimated at 5,400 million tons, accounting for 62 per cent of the world total. The concentration of primary energy consumption in the main industrialised countries represents a trend that will continue into the 1980s. The share of primary energy in 1970 was 63 per cent. In the developed countries mentioned above, dependence on oil is expected to increase in the 1970s. In the United States, however, the rate of dependence in 1980 will remain unchanged at 43 per cent, the same rate that was reached in 1970. In Europe, this rate will

TABLE 1

Per capita energy consumption in developing countries

| GNP Per capita | Population (million) | Gross Energy Consumption (million tce) | Per capita Consumption (Kg) |
|---|---|---|---|
| World | 3,609 | 6,842 | 1,889 |
| Developing countries | 1,724 | 584 | 330 |
| $500 and above | 110 | 181 | 1,650 |
| Between $300 and $500 | 192 | 113 | 590 |
| $300 and below | 1,422 | 290 | 204 |

increase to 63 per cent in 1980 from 60 per cent in 1970 and in Japan, to 73 per cent from 72 per cent. These major developed countries will account for an estimated 70 per cent of the world's oil demand.

Energy consumption in developed countries grew at the annual rate of 4 per cent in per capita terms in the 1960s, registering a 50 per cent increase in that period. Energy consumption in per capita terms in those countries is shown in Table 2.1.

*Energy demand and main resources*

Before going into a long-term forecast of energy demands it will be worthwhile, for the sake of clarifying the points at issue in this paper, to attempt a brief review of the energy situation involving the main resources, such as petroleum, natural gas and natural uranium. However, since quantitative evaluation of major energy resources is not the purpose of this article, attention will be devoted to the so-called resource gap with reference to published data.

1. Petroleum

The world's oil resources at the end of 1971 were estimated at 583,500 million barrels (79,900 million tons) in terms of proved reserves. The ratios of reserve to production in the oil-producing regions (R/P) ranged from 10 to 1 in the Caribbean Sea to 70 to 1 in the Middle East. The world average was 32 to 1.

According to the definition made by a United Nations panel on projection of demand and supply of crude and oil products, the reserves that are technically and economically recoverable include proved reserves, probable reserves and possible reserves. Quantities given by the panel for 1969 are as follows.

| | | |
|---|---|---|
| Proved reserves | 490 | $10^9$BBL |
| Probable reserves | | |
| a | 101 | $10^9$BBL |
| b | 325 | $10^9$BBL |
| Possible reserves | 1,062 | $10^9$BBL |
| Total | 1,978 | $10^9$BBL |

The proved reserves estimated by the OECD nearly equal the sum of proved reserves and probable reserves (a) above. From the standpoint of this paper these figures should be evaluated in terms of (a) geographical distribution, (b) known reserves and future demand, and (c) possibility of developing new reserves.

*(a) Geographical distribution of oil reserves.* The world's crude oil output showed conspicuous changes in the second half of the 1960s. The relative

international position of the United States declined rapidly in that period in striking contrast to the rise of Middle East and African countries. The Middle East accounted for 29 per cent of the world total in 1970 and 35 per cent of the increase in production in 1966–70. It is expected that the Middle East will continue to enjoy its advantage as the outstanding supplier of oil, being capable of meeting 35–40 per cent of the world's oil demand over a long period of time. (5) The shares of crude oil output by region in 1966–70 are listed in Table 2.2.

TABLE 2

The shares of crude oil production

| Year | 1965 | 1970 | Annual growth rate |
|---|---|---|---|
| Gross Production ($10^6$ tons) | 1,569 | 2,352 | 8·5 |
| USA (%) | 27·8 | 22·8 | 4·4 |
| Canada | 2·9 | 2·9 | 8·5 |
| Other Western Hemisphere countries | 15·4 | 11·8 | 2·6 |
| Middle East | 26·5 | 29·3 | 10·6 |
| Africa | 6·8 | 12·7 | 22·8 |
| Western Europe | 1·4 | 1·0 | 0·7 |
| USSR, other Socialist bloc countries | 17·1 | 16·6 | 7·8 |
| Other Eastern Hemisphere countries | 2·1 | 2·9 | 16·8 |

The Middle East accounts for 61·6 per cent of proved reserves, 54·5 per cent of probable reserves and 28·8 per cent of possible reserves. It the reserves in Africa are included, the combined shares of these two regions will be 71 per cent for proved reserves and 66 per cent for probable reserves (Table 2·3). This skewed geographical distribution of known oil reserves puts physical constraints on the world's oil distribution. It is also the cause of various difficulties facing the present distribution system.

*(b) Known reserves and future demand.* Assuming that oil production will expand at the annual rate of 7 per cent in the 1970s, 5·5 per cent in the 1980s, and 3 per cent in the 1990s, then the cumulative totals of production at the end of each decade, based on these assumptions, will be 232,000 million BBL in 1980, 655,000 million BBL in 1990, and 1,300,000 million BBL in 2000. The proved reserves will be depleted by 1986, as will the probable reserves by 1992, if these assumptions prove correct. The ratio of total reserves to annual

TABLE 3

Geographical distribution of petroleum reserves (%)

| | Proved | Probable | Possible |
|---|---|---|---|
| American continent | 17·5 | 17·5 | 29·6 |
| African continent | 9·6 | 11·6 | 12·4 |
| Middle East | 61·6 | 54·5 | 28·8 |
| Asia and Oceania | 2·5 | 4·0 | 11·3 |
| USSR and rest of Socialist bloc | 8·6 | 0·5 | 14·6 |
| | 99·8 | 99·0 | 96·7 |

Source: UN panel

production (R/P), or the number of minable years, will drop to 53 in 1980, when the annual output is estimated at 33,000 million BBL; to 24 in 1990 (56,000 million BBL) and to 9 in 2000 (76,000 million BBL).

If the extraction period of proved reserves in the world is given as 30 years, then 306,000 million BBL will have to be added to the proved reserves in order to maintain the same R/P ratio. This quantity is comparable to the new discoveries (382,000 million BBL) during the past 10 years. Similarly, if the R/P ratio of 30 is to be maintained after 1990 with respect to total reserves, it will be necessary to discover 350,000 million BBL in 1990 and 1,600,000 BBL in 2000.

(*c*) *Possibility of new discoveries.* The above statement seems to show that it is almost impossible to maintain the same R/P ratio over the next 30 years. It is clear, of course, that the possibility of discovering new reserves depends on the capacity to develop oil resources on the continental shelf or in the seabed.

Of oil production in 1972, 18 per cent was produced from off-shore oil fields. Estimates of reserves show that off-shore reserves represent 18 per cent of the proved reserves, 25 per cent of the probable reserves, and 49 per cent of the possible reserves. Of the known reserves 35 per cent are off-shore reserves.

The off-shore reserves of ultimate potentially recoverable petroleum as estimated on the basis of physiographic studies are as follows: Continental shelf reserves are estimated at 1,344,000 million BBL and ultimate reserves including those in the slopes and rises as well as natural gas reserves at 2,272,000 million BBL.

2. Natural Gas

The world's natural gas consumption expanded at the average annual rate of

9 per cent from 1946 to 1972, in which it reached $1{,}100 \times 10^9$ m$^3$ compared with the $120 \times 10^9$ m$^3$ in 1946. The share of natural gas in primary energy supply increased from 8 per cent to 17 per cent in 1972. Many estimates indicate that natural gas consumption will double by 1985, to about $2{,}000 \times 10^9$ m$^3$. In other words, consumption is expected to grow by 4·5 per cent a year on average, accounting for 16 per cent of the total energy consumption in 1985.

Meanwhile, natural gas reserves are estimated at $53{,}000 \times 10^9$ m$^3$ (about 330,000 million BBL as oil), according to an estimate made in 1972. The R/P ratio for that year's consumption was about 45. In terms of thermal units, natural gas reserves account for one-third of hydrocarbon resources including petroleum.

The geographical distribution of these reserves in the world is indicated in Table 2.6.

The United States and the Soviet Union account for 77 per cent of the world's total consumption. It should be noted here that the supply-demand gap of natural gas in the US is responsible, if not directly, for the so-called energy crisis. Of course, natural gas is being supplied from one region to another, as from Canada to the United States, from the Netherlands to European nations and from the Soviet Union to European countries. Transfer of natural gas also has been accomplished between Libya and Italy/Spain, between Argentina and Britain/France, between Alaska and Japan, and between Brunei and Japan. But these natural gas supplies to individual countries remain marginal in relation to each country's total energy supply markets. Considering increasing natural gas imports from Alaska, Africa and the USSR to the US, from the Middle East and Siberia to Japan, and from South-western Africa to Europe, it is estimated that consumption in the major industrialized countries in the 1980s will reach somewhere between $110 \times 10^9$ m$^3$, or about ten times the level in the 1970s.

However, despite the growing public concern over environmental pollution caused by energy consumption in developed countries, the international supply of natural gas is expected to play only a marginal role in resolving the present energy problem.

### 3. Natural Uranium

The development of natural uranium resources was pushed primarily for military purposes, as shown by America's Manhattan Project in 1942–43. The military emphasis on uranium development continued until 1957–58 when the US and Russia engaged in a nuclear arms race. The major regions that supplied natural uranium were the United States, Canada, South and Southwest Africa. As is noted in the distribution of resources in Table 2.4 these regions still account for 75 per cent of the known low-cost reserves of natural uranium. France (including Gabon and Niger), which embarked on uranium development after World War II, and Australia together account for 20 per cent. It was not until the 1960s that open uranium markets for civil demand were developed. Recently, the total annual volume of trade in natural uranium for the needs of nuclear power exceeded the peak volume of military procurement.

TABLE 4

Uranium reserves and requirements

| Requirements through 1985 | Thousands of tons $U_3O_8$ | % |
|---|---|---|
| United States | 474 | 47 |
| Japan | 106 | 10 |
| United Kingdom | 92 | 9 |
| West Germany | 65 | 7 |
| France | 40 | 4 |
| W. Europe Other | 107 | 11 |
| Foreign Other | 116 | 12 |
| Total | 1,000 | 100 |

| Reserves – \$10/LB$U_3O_8$ | Thousands of tons $U_3O_8$ | % |
|---|---|---|
| United States | 330 | 29 |
| South and Southwest Africa | 300 | 26 |
| Canada | 236 | 20 |
| France, Gabon, Niger | 124 | 11 |
| Australia | 92 | 8 |
| Others | 68 | 6 |
| Total | 1,150 | 100 |

It may be unreasonable at this time to consider the availability of uranium resources in definitive terms. Yet, as will be described later in this article, it will be necessary to clarify the characteristics of uranium resources, in view of the potentially important role of nuclear power generation in the long-term distribution of energy.

It is assumed that nuclear power generation will follow a sharp upward curve in the period up to 2000. Of the reasonable reserves, an estimated 1,150,000 short tons of low-cost reserves which cost about \$10 or less per pound are expected to be used up before 1985. Reserves costing a little more, or between \$10 and \$15 are expected to be depleted before 1990. Total reserves including those additional reserves, which cost more than $15, estimated at 3,600,000 short tons, will likely fall short of demand before around 1995. Requirements of individual countries in the period up to 1985, which are more or less established, are indicated in Table 2.4.

Such comparisons are not to be taken as direct constraints on uranium resources. Development is likely to expand as marginal costs are reduced. Moreover, additional supplies can be hoped for through the extension of techniques for treating low-grade uranium ores. Prospective areas in which uranium may be produced in the future include Brazil and Sweden. Information on communist countries is not available. From the fact that uranium resources are concentrated more or less in Western industrialized countries arise certain major economic features that are distinctly different from those of petroleum, for example. The technical condition that now limits nuclear power generation – the fact that natural uranium must be processed into enriched uranium before it is used as a fuel – is another important factor that must also be taken into consideration.

### Energy consumption in 2000 and balance of resources

Many imponderables are involved in any attempt to consider the allocation of resources needed to meet energy requirements in the period up to 2000. Examples of energy consumption in the period up to 2000 are few. Distinctly different approaches have been suggested as to ways in which such energy demand will be met in the period under review.

TABLE 5

Energy demand and composition of primary energy in 2000 (%)

| No. Case | Total $10^9$ tons | Petroleum | Coal | Gas | Hydro | Nuclear |
|---|---|---|---|---|---|---|
| No. 1 (1970) | 25 | 32 | 20 | 16 | 4 | 28 |
| No. 2 (1971) | 25 | 59 | – | – | – | – |
| No. 3 (1968) | 30 | 26 | 24 | 23 | 5 | 22 |
| No. 4 (1971) | 36–39 | 55 | 11 | 30 | 4 | |

Table 2.5 indicates, with reference to four different cases, the levels of energy consumption in 2000 and the primary energy compositions in that year. With the exception of case 4, consumption is estimated in all three cases at 25,000–30,000 million tons as coal. It is agreed that consumption will grow at the annual rate of 4 per cent after 1985.

TABLE 6

Forecast of regional distribution of energy consumption (%)

| | Communist bloc | Developing countries | Industrial countries |
|---|---|---|---|
| Total energy | 40·0 | 30·4 | 29·6 |
| Petroleum | 32·0 | 35·5 | 32·5 |
| Natural gas | 29·0 | 40·5 | 30·5 |
| Coal | 66·0 | 14·0 | 20·0 |
| Nuclear | 35·0 | 27·0 | 38·0 |

*Energy consumption by area*

A regional breakdown of energy consumption is a major factor in the consideration of the level of consumption in 2000. In this respect, cases 3 and 4 in Table 2.5 are of interest. In case 3, it is assumed that as a result of the economic growth of Socialist nations and of developing countries in general, the gap between per capita consumption in industrialized and in less industrialized countries will be eliminated in the next 35 years. The expectation is that the shares in total world energy consumption of the developing and Socialist blocs will expand to 30.4 per cent and 40 per cent, respectively, in the year 2000. The proportion of the populations of these regions to the global total in that year will be 45·7 per cent and 35 per cent, respectively. By comparison, the industrialized countries will account for 29·6 per cent of the total in 2000, and will represent 19·1 per cent of the world's population. On the basis of this assumption – that the geographical distribution of energy consumption will be drastically altered – the allocation of energy resources is predicted in Table 2.6. It is worth noting that dependence on nuclear energy will reach a high level in the Socialist and industrialized nations.

In case 4, it is assumed that per capita energy consumption in the developing countries will expand rapidly. If the per capita GNPs of developing countries grow at the rate of 3·5 per cent (compared with the world average of 2·5 per cent as in 1950–68) the disparity between developed and developing countries will narrow to 1 to 12, compared with 1 to 18 in 1968. As a result, the world's energy consumption will increase from an estimated total of 36,000 million tons to 39,000 million tons. The possibility of a large increase in energy consumption in the developing countries is very likely to have a great impact on the distribution of primary energy resources.

*The pattern of energy consumption in developed countries*

In view of such probable trends in the developing world, the pattern of energy consumption in developed industrial nations must be reviewed. Here predictions will be made with respect to consumption in the US and Japan in 2000.

According to the estimate of energy consumption in the US by the Department of the Interior, the GNP growth rate is estimated at 4·3 per cent in the period up to 1980. The IIP in the same period is expected to rise by 5 per cent annually. After 1980 the GNP will grow by 4·0 per cent a year and the IIP by 4·4 per cent. On these assumptions, the level of consumption in that country in 2000 is estimated at $191 \times 10^{15}$ BTU ($6{\cdot}9 \times 10^{9}$ tce).

In Japan's case, the Institute of Energy Economics estimates that the GNP growth rate in the period up to 1980 will be 8·8 per cent and after 1980, 5·1 per cent. Thus the energy demand elasticity with regard GNP will be reduced from 1·17 at present to 0·88–0·80. On this assumption, the level of consumption in Japan in 2000 would be $51 \times 10^{15}$ BTU ($1{\cdot}8 \times 10^{9}$ tce).

Long-term estimates in developed countries cannot be made without taking account of changes in their energy consumption patterns. Notable changes are expected to be the expansion of power and energy consumption in the non-industrial sector. In the US for example, the share of power consumption in the total energy consumption will probably expand to 50 per cent in 2000 from 24 per cent in 1971. This means that per capita power consumption will increase 4 times in the period up to 2000, exceeding the rate at which total energy consumption is expected to grow 2·03 times. This can be said to be a trend common to Japan and the European countries.

In the United States also, energy distribution by sector (industrial, household and transport) remain almost unchanged, as will be noted below:

| | Industry | Household | Transport |
|---|---|---|---|
| 1971 | 40 | 30 | 30 |
| 2000 | 41 | 28 | 31 |

The similarity of consumption patterns among developed countries will contribute to increasing the conversion loss between energy input and output. In the household and transport sectors many restrictions will be imposed on the improvement of energy consumption efficiency. For these reasons, the possibility of energy conservation will be reduced.

### *The composition of the energy supply source*

Many imponderable factors are also involved in the distribution of resources needed to meet these energy requirements. As is noted in Table 2.5, the most important factor is the possibility offered by nuclear energy development in the overall picture of long-term energy supply. Utilization of nuclear energy will take the form of power generation in the initial period of development. In order that the world may rid itself of its tendency to depend on petroleum, it is necessary to promote the incorporation of nuclear power generation into the energy supply structure and thereby reduce the rising demand for oil. This is considered the only way to achieve a break with the traditional dependence on oil.

As for nuclear power generation, estimates are made in Table 2.10. The world total of nuclear power generating capacity in 2000 is estimated at $3{,}260 \times 10^6$ kw. Of this total, 37 per cent will be consumed by the United States, 19 per cent by the Socialist nations, and 44 per cent by other regions. The other regions include Western Europe ($870 \times 10^6$ kw; see Table 11) and Japan ($200 \times 10^6$ kw). The total nuclear power output mentioned above is equivalent to about $7 \times 10^9$ tons of coal. The contribution to total energy consumption $25 \times 10^9$ tce, as mentioned in Table 2.8, will be 28 per cent.

The composition of energy consumption by resources in 2000, based on the nuclear power output estimated above, can be assumed as follows:

| | | | |
|---|---|---|---|
| (a) | Nuclear power | 28% | $7 \times 10^9$ tce |
| (b) | Other | 40% | $10 \times 10^9$ tce |
| (c) | Petroleum | 32% | $8 \times 10^9$ tce |
| | Total | 100% | $25 \times 10^9$ tce |

The share of coal, natural gas, hydraulic power and other types of energy sources may be given as about 40 per cent; dependence on oil will naturally hinge to a large extent on the level of nuclear power generation. At the same time, this will determine the extent to which oil consumption in major industrialized countries will be reduced.

TABLE 7

Forecast of nuclear power capacity up to 2000 ($10^6$ kw)

| End of year | USA | Other | Communist Bloc | Total |
|---|---|---|---|---|
| 1980 | 132 | 141 | 20 | 293 |
| 1985 | 280 | 303 | 56 | 639 |
| 1990 | 508 | 578 | 146 | 1.232 |
| 2000 | 1,200 | 1,460 | 600 | 3,260 |
| | (37) | (44) | (19) | (100) |

Source: US Atomic Energy Commission – Nuclear Power 1943–2000-WASH-113p

TABLE 8

Western Europe: forecast of nuclear capacity ($10^6$ kw)

| Country | 1975 | 1980 | 1985 | 2000 |
|---|---|---|---|---|
| Austria | – | 1·2 | 2·4 | 9·2 |
| Belgium | 1·5 | 3·5 | 6·0 | 14·7 |
| Finland | 0·5 | 1·7 | 3·7 | 16·5 |
| France | 3·0 | 6·2 | 18·3 | 80·0 |
| West Germany | 6·9 | 25·8 | 51·0 | 175·0 |
| Great Britain | 12·6 | 29·0 | 49·0 | 208·0 |
| Greece | – | 1·0 | 2·5 | 18·0 |
| Ireland | – | – | 0·5 | 4·0 |
| Italy | 1·4 | 8·0 | 24·0 | 140·0 |
| Netherlands | 0·5 | 1·1 | 3·0 | 40·0 |
| Norway | – | 0·6 | 1·6 | 22·0 |
| Portugal | – | 0·5 | 1·5 | 5·0 |
| Spain | 1·0 | 5·5 | 14·0 | 69·0 |
| Sweden | 3·3 | 8·0 | 14·0 | 42·5 |
| Switzerland | 1·0 | 2·7 | 4·3 | 13·5 |
| Turkey | – | 0·5 | 2·0 | 11·0 |
| Total | 31·7 | 95·3 | 198·3 | 868·4 |

Source: Stanford Research Institute – IP 71

Two predictions may be cited here with respect to the balance of energy resources in the year 2000. One is the estimate by the United Nations Committee on Natural Resources. As shown in Table 2.9 cumulative energy requirements in the period up to 2000 are set against the known reserves. With the exception of coal, long-term demand for oil and natural gas is expected to reach 2·5 times the known reserves in 2000. The proved reserves plus probable reserves calculated in 1969 prices correspond roughly to this estimate. Another estimate (Table 2.14) has been made by the UN Economic Commission for Europe, which calculated the ratios of cumulative consumption in the years up to 2000 to the ultimate reserves of individual resources. Oil and natural gas are estimated to account for 87 or 75 per cent of the ultimate reserves. In this case, the volume of oil resources given as $350 \times 10^9$ tce is equivalent to about $1{,}600 \times 10^9$ BBL. Therefore, the cumulative consumption which would account for 87 per cent of this would be about $1{,}400 \times \times 10^9$ BBL in the period up to 2000.

The break with the traditional heavy dependence on oil and other conventional types of energy represents a challenge which the world must accept in order to overcome the looming energy crisis.

## TABLE 9

Resources demand – reserves balance (1968–2000)

| Energy resources | Cumulative demand as a percentage of present world reserve at 1969 prices |
|---|---|
| Coal | 2 to 3 |
| Natural Gas | 176 to 264 |
| Petroleum | 158 to 256 |

Source: ECOSOC: Committee of Natural Resources

## TABLE 10

World energy reserves

A. Reserves expected to be used on a large scale under technical and economic conditions predicted to prevail up to 2000

| Energy source and type of recoverable reserves | Reserves in 1970 | | Percentage consumed by 2000 |
|---|---|---|---|
| | $10^9$ tce | Percentage share | |
| 1. *Conventional forms of energy* [(a)] | | | |
| (a) depletable: | | | |
| Petroleum (proven, probable, possible reserves, ocean beds excepted) | 350 | 4 | 87 |
| Natural gas (proven and probable reserves) | 233 | 3 | 73 |
| Coal (proven, probable, possible reserves) | 7,600 | 93 | 2 |
| (b) renewable: | | | |
| Hydropower potential ($22,856 \times 10^9$ kWh/year) | 3 | – | 34 |
| | 8,186 | 100 | 8 |

2. *Nuclear fission*

Uranium (proven and probable reserves) at

| | | | |
|---|---|---|---|
| (a) extraction costs below $30/kg:[b] | | | |
| used in thermal reactors | 50 | | 100[c] |
| used in breeders | > 3,750 | | very little |
| (b) extraction costs up to $200/kg:[d] | | | |
| used in thermal reactors | 1,150 | | very little |
| used in breeders | > 86,500 | | very little |

B. Reserves whose technical and economic viability, on a large scale, cannot as yet be assessed

| Energy source and type of recoverable reserves | Reserves in 1970 | | Percentage consumed by 2000 |
|---|---|---|---|
| | $10^9$ tce | Percentage share | |
| Oil shale (reserves whose organic content is greater than 5 per cent of weight)[e] | 825,000 | | very little |
| Solar energy (1 per cent of solar energy falling on land surface)[f] | 300 | | very little |
| Geothermal energy from high temperature fields[g] | 7,000 | | very little |
| Tar sands[e] | 621 | | very little |
| Fusion of deuterium isotopes[f] | unlimited | | |

Sources for Table 2.10:

[a] United Nations, *World Energy Requirements and Reserves in the Year 2000*. Paper presented to the Fourth United Nations International Conference on the Peaceful Uses of Atomic Energy, Geneva 1971, No.A/CONF.49/P//420. 'Possible' reserves are as yet unknown reserves which are expected to be used under technical and economic conditions predicted up to 2000. The final column is based on projected consumption levels. The hydropower potential is converted at 1,000 kWh=0·125 tce.

[b] 2·6 million tons $U_3O_8$: *Nuclear Energy in Electric Power Production* ST/ECE/EP/62, p. 8.

[c] ENEA/IAEO report to the Fourth United Nations International Con-

ference on Peaceful Uses of Atomic Energy, Geneva, 1971, No. A/CONF. 49/P. 678.

(d) 60 million tons, including uranium extracted from ocean water, excluding the Soviet Union and China; see H. Mandel in *Atomwirtschaft*, May 1970, p. 222.

(e) United Nations, *World Energy Reserves, Supply and Demand.* Note by the Secretary-General to the third session of the Committee on Natural Resources, New Dehli 1973 (E/C. 7/40/Add. 1), p. 9.

(f) *Ibid.*, p. 18.

(g) *Ibid.*, pp. 13 and 19.

(h) Whereas fusion between lithium and deuterium is limited ultimately by the availability of lithium isotopes, fusion between deuterium isotopes is unlimited.
*Ibid.*, p. 19.

**Structural changes in the oil industry and the impact of resource problems**

In the 1970s the world oil industry is about to undergo significant structural changes. The direction of such changes will have great impact on the world's resource economy. In any study of energy resources and of the problems involved it will be difficult to provide an explicit answer to the question of what the right resource policy should be unless a careful analysis of this impact is undertaken.

The impetus to structural change came from the offensive launched by the member countries of the Organization of Petroleum Exporting Countries (OPEC). As the study in the preceding section suggested, the continued expansion of world energy consumption, the continued dependence on oil, and the widening supply-demand gap in the United States, the largest energy market, have all combined to strengthen the position of OPEC countries. Under such circumstances, the OPEC countries find a realistic basis for their policies, which often lead to rational changes in the international oil situation.

Major developed countries of the West continue to depend on the Middle East for many of their oil requirements. This heavy dependence on Middle East oil is considered essential to meeting both short-term and medium-term oil demands in the period up to the mid 1980s. Moreover, the oil supply system is now changing to one in which the oil-producing countries are assuming leadership. There is no denying, given this situation, that major oil-consuming countries are increasingly concerned over instabilities in the future prospects for the continued flow of oil producing to consuming regions. In some cases, considerable friction in the oil supply system may develop. Needless to say, changes in the oil supply system are closely linked to future trends in the international situation. For the present, the primary condition for stability in the world oil situation will be an equilibrium that can hold in check potential factors contributing to friction.

*Oil-producing countries' participation in oil industry*

The world's crude oil output reached about 49,600,000 B/D in 1972, of which 35 per cent was produced in the Middle East, 11 per cent in Africa, and 9 per cent in Venezuela and Indonesia. Estimates of oil supplies based on production plans and each oil reserve in major regions indicate that the world's crude oil production will total about 90 million B/D in 1980 and about 110 million B/D in 1985. The shares of the above three regions will be 42 per cent, 10 per cent, and 6 per cent respectively in 1980, and 43 per cent, 9 per cent, and 5 per cent respectively in 1985. Thus, oil production is expected to become increasingly concentrated in the Middle East. This means that future expansion of oil supplies depends largely on the capacity and willingness of Middle East oil-producing countries to supply their oil to the rest of the world. Specifically the countries that will hold the key in this region are Saudi Arabia and Iran, which together account for 70 per cent of the region's oil supply capacity.

As is well known, OPEC countries are trying to assert their interests in foreign oil projects either through nationalization or through direct participation. They also intend to participate in the downstream operations of consuming countries. Participation in oil production shows its effect, for example, in the expansion of the right of the producing countries' national oil companies to dispose of their crude oil. Crude oil at their disposal can be sold directly to consuming countries. Through these direct deals some OPEC countries can reserve the right to control oil prices and dictate certain terms of trade. Thus oil-producing countries aim to take the initiative in bringing about certain changes in their industrial structures.

Under the present terms of the Riyadh treaty (new consortium agreement and nationalization), national oil companies of OPEC countries are expected to hold a 16 per cent share in the crude oil market in 1980 and a 23 per cent share in 1985, with the exception of the so-called phase-in crude. In the near future, the agreement is expected to be revised so that the share of oil-producing countries will be further expanded.

Participation in foreign oil operations serves the purpose of establishing the sovereignty of developing countries over their natural resources and fulfilling their nationalistic aspirations to a certain extent. It also provides a springboard from which they can launch their economies on a take-off course through increased oil revenues and joint ventures with oil consuming countries. Indeed the assertion of sovereignty by producing countries in the developing world and their participation in the development of their resources will be a general aspect of the world's resource economy.

### *Decline in the role of international oil companies*

The extension of the control exercised by oil-producing countries over the production and marketing of oil has led to a weakening of the traditional market control that international oil companies have enjoyed in the past. As a result, the role of the majors in the world oil industry has declined. The combined share of the seven majors in the global oil supply is expected to drop from 60 per cent in 1972 to 53 per cent in 1980 and to 48 per cent in 1985. And in 1980–85 the volume of crude at their disposal will show almost no increase.

The decline in the functions of the majors has reduced the supply elasticity in the world oil market which they controlled in the past. The result has been to increase the feeling of instability regarding the global oil supply system. Since such a situation will inevitably bring about a worsening in the financing capability of the majors, their capacity to raise funds will weaken accordingly, thus placing constraints on their ability to develop new reserves.

Development of new reserves is not only the function of the majors but also a matter of global concern since this is essential to the continued expansion of oil supply and stabilization of the oil supply systems. However, new projects, whether they be on the continental shelf, on the seabed or in the polar regions, require enormous investments. How to raise funds, therefore, is now a question of strategic importance to all consuming countries.

### *Changes in oil money flow*

The situation described above is expected to bring about changes in the flow of oil money in the oil industry. The accumulation of huge oil revenues in the oil-producing countries will probably be a major factor influencing the structure of the international financial market. The increase in oil revenues is a strategic means of achieving the economic take-off of oil-producing countries. However, the concentration of crude oil in certain producing countries is most likely to produce massive foreign exchange surpluses in those countries far exceeding the amounts actually required for their domestic development.[1] The existence of this enormous pool of funds, if used for speculative purposes, will pose a great threat to the stability of the international monetary situation. But, if any oil-producing country limits its oil production in order to avoid an accumulation of oil money, it would impose a direct restraint on the possibility of expanding the world's oil supply.

*Optimization of oil resource distribution*

The excessive accumulation of oil revenues, however, will provide an opportunity to take stock of the dilemmas facing developing countries that possess oil resources. As mentioned earlier, the possession of oil reserves, and for that matter, any other important natural resources, is an effective means of assuring them an early economic take-off. In countries that do not have oil resources, however, opportunities for economic development are greatly limited. And so, also, are the opportunities for participation in the international oil market. This means that they will have to accept all the disadvantages arising from the rise in oil prices and from the constraints imposed by the oil market. It also means that the economic gap between countries that have oil resources and those that do not will widen.

In order to avoid such difficulties and dilemmas it is necessary for the par ticipants in the oil market to curb the excessive increase in oil prices and ensure more equitable distribution of oil resources. This makes it necessary for the oil-consuming countries to develop substitutes for oil so that oil can be diverted to those developing countries which do not have natural resources.

Optimization of the distribution of resources in the developing world is a question of great importance to the present international economy. If the energy policies of developed countries do not take this into account, countries that hold resources will be compelled to follow rigid policies in an attempt to expedite the accumulation of benefits from their resources. If this happens, the difficulties and dilemmas facing the world resource economy would be exacerbated.

## Long-term targets in resource and energy policy

The focus of short-term energy policy, as described in the preceding chapter, is on the stabilization of oil supply. But the fact remains, as has been made clear in the above discussion, that the world cannot continue to depend indefinitely on conventional fossil fuel resources. The responsibility for establishing a strategy for coping with such long-term constraints rests primarily with the major consuming countries.

The purpose of this section is to discuss some of the questions that need to be studied in order to establish a common goal for the resource policies of those advanced countries, and thereby provide a certain degree of uniformity in the application of their policies.

*Conservation of energy resources*

Restriction of energy consumption is now a question of vital importance in developed countries, one of the major reasons being environmental pollution. There is also a need to curb energy consumption from the stand-point of resource conservation.

The question of conservation in developed countries has two aspects in macro-economic terms. One is the certain prospect that the loss between energy input and output will increase, given the actual and expected pattern of energy consumption. For instance, in the case of the United States the ratio of conversion loss resulting from power generation will increase every year because electric power will account for a growing portion of energy consumption. The total loss is estimated at 27 per cent in the year 2000, including the loss from synthetic gas production, compared with 17·3 per cent in 1971.

Another aspect of the conservation question is the fact that the composition of energy consumption imposes certain inevitable constraints on the use of resources (Table 2.2). In developed countries excluding Japan, more than 50 per cent of the total energy supply is consumed in the household and transport sectors in which there are limits to the improvement of energy consumption efficiency. In Japan's case, consumption in the industrial sector accounts for the bulk of energy consumption. In terms of consumption efficiency, however, there is little room for improvement in this sector. The present situation is such that direct restraints on energy consumption cannot be imposed except by holding down the level of production in industries where large quantities of energy are consumed.

In the long run it is certain that Japan will be forced to shift her industrial structure from high energy-consumption industries to energy-saving industries, and to diversify or relocate her heavy industry to other parts of the world.

The oil-consuming countries must in the future follow a policy of reducing, by direct means, the consumption of fossil fuel resources. To do so, however, will inevitably result in a changed pattern of energy consumption and an altered industrial structure in each country.

### *Possibilities of nuclear energy*

Brief reference was made in the first section to the possible role of nuclear energy in the overall energy supply system. Some major issues remain unresolved, however, with respect to the utilization of nuclear energy. Two reasons may account for this. One is that utilization of nuclear energy is confined to nuclear power generation. Nuclear power generation as a substitute for conventional thermal power generation is an effective way of reducing the incremental demand for fossil fuels. This is because power generation in the developed countries will continue to expand. Assuming that the estimates in Tables 6 and 7 are correct, 50–60 per cent of power generating facilities in the United States, Japan and many Western countries will use nuclear power in the year 2000. The contribution of nuclear energy to the primary energy supply in individual countries will probably reach nearly 30 per cent.

However, in order to expand further the contribution of nuclear energy it will be necessary to accelerate the commercial application of the high temperature reactor and promote its multi-purpose use. There are already plans in Japan, West Germany and Britain to use the high-temperature reactor for steel-making. In the United States, the idea of using reactor heat in the gasification of coal has been advanced. Multi-purpose utilization of nuclear reactors involves latent possibilities for the materialization of a new energy system through the development of high-temperature technology and the realization of hydrogen economy. Therefore, multi-purpose use of the nuclear reactor is considered a promising way of reducing dependence on oil and thereby effecting a break with the traditional oil-oriented energy system.

Utilization of nuclear energy, however, presupposes the resolution of safety and environmental problems which now confront the effort toward stepped-up nuclear power generation. In certain developed countries the construction and operation of nuclear power stations is subject to a number of limitations. In those countries public criticism has been directed against the safety and environmental aspects of such nuclear power plant projects. Without resolving this situation it will be hardly possible to achieve the goal of nuclear power development ranging from fast breeder to thermonuclear fusion, and including multi-purpose use of the nuclear reactor.

Establishment of safety and environmental standards for nuclear power generation, examination and monitoring of the implementation of such standards, and research and development work on safety engineering are the functions of the governments of the individual countries concerned. These functions are being carried out in most cases in compliance with international standards. In the present circumstances, research and development work on the disposal of radioactive waste (including its final disposal) and on other aspects of the fuel cycle should also be conducted within the framework of international co-operation. And in setting development goals, individual countries should try to promote their co-operation instead of engaging in an international race for nuclear development.

*Development of new energy resources*

The conversion of energy resources involves not only nuclear energy but also reuse of coal, gasification and liquidization of tar sand and oil shale. In addition, geothermal and solar energy, and tidal energy—all three of them grouped as cyclical resources—are involved. Development and utilization of these resources is a question of long-term importance to the conversion of energy resources.

As has been noted in Table 2.10, the recoverable reserves of tar sand are almost equal to those of fossil fuel resources excluding coal. The reserves of oil shale containing more than 5 per cent (by weight) organic matter are 10 times those of conventional fossil fuel resources including coal. It is certain that the world is now moving toward developing these vast reserves of potential energy in the context of long-term energy consumption.

Of course, development of new energy resources is predicated on the evaluation of economic and technical feasibility of development projects, development of new energy utilization and consumption techniques, and study of effects such new energies will have on the conventional fossil fuel resources. This is essential to the effective allocation of development efforts. In view of the present state of the resource economy greater effort should be made to develop such under-utilized resources as coal, tar sand, and oil shale. It is also necessary to devise an international system whereby multilateral co-operation can be promoted in order to resolve common problems facing the developed countries, e.g., reduction of dependence on conventional resources and diversification of resources.

*Development of new oil resources*

The oil discoveries in the world in the period from 1961 to 1970 amounted to 63,700 million kilolitres. The regional breakdown is given below, It is notable that that the Middle East accounted for 53 per cent of the total.

| | | |
|---|---|---|
| | TOTAL | $637 \times 10^9$ kl |
| of which: | Middle East | $338 \times 10^9$ kl (53%) |
| | Africa | $77 \times 10^9$ kl (12%) |
| | USA | $60 \times 10^9$ kl ( 9%) |
| | Eastern Europe | $86 \times 10^9$ kl (14%). |

Development efforts are being directed to continental shelves around various countries, to the polar regions or to the seabed. Naturally, this involves an additional burden in terms of exploratory and development costs. According to an estimate by the Chase Manhattan Bank, the total investment by the world oil industry in the period from 1970 to 1985 is estimated at $600,000 million, of which $35,000 million will be invested in the development of new reserves. The decline of majors in the oil industry or changes in the flow of oil money indicate, however, that the some $40,000 million needed annually for new investment will be too heavy a burden for oil companies to bear, and that the burden of initial investment will be particularly onerous.

The promotion of joint oil ventures and multinational projects is an important means of resolving this financial problem. Also dispersion of supply sources, establishment of a new energy distribution system and securing of additional reserves are other objectives for the stabilization of the world's oil supply.

### Toward world cooperation and a new order

Finally, I would like to discuss the situation we are faced with in and beyond early 1974. The crude oil price hikes carried out by the OPEC nations exceeded the amount which the world energy economy and society were capable of absorbing without severe dislocation.

Not presuming to assail OPEC's grounds for effecting price increases, the spiraling price of crude oil not only places a great cost burden on the oil-consuming nations, but is detrimental to the rational distribution of oil throughout the world. As I mentioned before, one of the primary objectives of our long-range energy policy should be to attain optimal distribution of energy resources throughout the world. In the case of the high energy-consuming countries, this will require cuts in energy consumption and development of new sources of energy that will substitute for fossil fuels. At the same time, however, great care must be given to provide those developing countries which do not possess energy resources the opportunity to achieve a reasonable rate of economic growth.

Another effect of the crude oil-price rises has been to accelerate the inflow of foreign currency into the oil-producing countries. In fact, these nations are expected to accumulate massive sums of money surpassing any previous estimates. While this process is going on, the high energy-consuming nations will be forced to spend so much for oil that they will experience deteriorating international balances of payments. This situation is quite likely to prolong, and even worsen, the many problems that already plague the world's currency and financial systems. Furthermore, if each oil-consuming country were to follow its own independent policy for procuring oil, this would not only be injurious to a stable world oil situation, but would act to hinder the smooth functioning of the world economy as a whole.

As I mentioned in the third section, the world's structure of oil economy will undergo increasingly rapid transformation, in particular the policies of the OPEC countries will have a decisive impact on the world economy. In other words, the oil-producing countries will play a determining role in the economic relations that will prevail in the next decades.

In normal times, resource and energy policies are based upon long-range forecasts and future strategies. However, it is quite evident that at present the energy situation is in a state of flux, and its outcome will have a direct bearing upon the stability of both the world's political and economic stability. For this reason, our resource and energy policy objectives, and the actions we take to realize these objectives, must be rooted in a broadly based form of international cooperation between the members of the international community, i.e. the industrialized nations, the natural resource-possessing nations and the developing nations.

### Note

1 cf. the contribution by de Carmoy.

# The Energy Policy of the Soviet Union

*by Walter Gumpel*

With the long-established policy of intensive industrialisation which the USSR stepped up sharply after the second world war, her consumption of primary and secondary energy has mounted rapidly. The result is that Soviet energy policy, like everybody else's, is now primarily dictated by the difficulty of securing a sufficiency of supplies. Whereas, however, energy policy in Western Europe is largely framed in terms of the replacement of coal by oil and natural gas – in other words in terms of a competitive process – the main energy policy problems of the Soviet Union (and of the other socialist states) involve overcoming the general shortage of all forms of energy. Not that the USSR does not have the substitution problem as well. For one thing, the Soviet Union has become increasingly involved, from 1960 onwards, in the division of labour at world level and therefore needs to keep production costs as low as possible. Added to this, there are the obvious compulsions of the changes taking place in modern technology. The Soviet planned economy system, however, enables the substitution process to be controlled from the centre, which means there is no competition between the different forms of energy and no running down of the coal industry.

In the USSR and the other socialist states the substitution process in the energy economy is a slow one, for two main reasons. First: the USSR did not begin any large-scale exploitation of her oil reserves until the 1950's, her energy policy up to then being based on coal. The substitution process in her energy economy, therefore, got off to a very late start, and the backlog of demand at the present time is considerable. The only way to satisfy it is to open up new deposits, for which large-scale capital investment is required. The amount of capital available is limited so that the rate of progress can, at best, be only moderate. Second: converting heat and power generation from coal to oil and natural gas means converting the plant and equipment that burn the fuel – another capital-intensive operation. Conversion is, therefore, going steadily forward – but not at too fast a pace. The extent and timescale of the conversion process depends not least upon the country's resources and the degree to which they can be exploited.

## The energy resources of the Soviet Union

The primary energy resources of the USSR are extraordinarily plentiful, but assessing them accurately is not easy because of the difficulty of interpreting Soviet statistics: they invariably err on the high side. The explanation is that USSR figures include many reserves that cannot be qualified as more than 'probable' or even 'possible'. In her resource estimates, oil, natural gas and coal are put into four categories: A, B, $C_1$ and $C_2$. Only those in categories A and B are fully prospected deposits and it is only for these that the figures may be regarded as reliable. Categories $C_1$ and $C_2$ apply to 'probable' and 'possible' reserves respectively. Official reports and figures on the country's underground wealth, however, always include the $C_1$, and often the $C_2$, reserves, a practice which even Soviet experts frown upon.[1]

Unfortunately, Soviet statistics rarely specify the categories to which they relate. In addition, the figures differ considerably from author to author. Further, the recoverability factor, though varying from area to area, is generally very low. For natural gas it is said to average 50 per cent; for oil it may in some cases, depending on the permeability of the rock formation, be very much lower. In the future major oil production area of Samotlor, in the West Siberian Plain, recoverability does not exceed 26–35 per cent. Thus, only a small part of the reserves that are actually available can be extracted and used. Transit losses are particularly high in the case of coal because of the poor condition of rolling stock and the fact that theft assumes very large proportions.

Statistics on Soviet primary energy resources are, therefore, not very enlightening. It is certainly true that the energy resources of the USSR are very considerable indeed but, to take coal as an example, the total of 8.700,000 million tons applies to 'geological' reserves. In other words, not only is the figure itself uncertain but it disregards the matter of whether the coal can be mined or not. A large proportion of these resources lies in inaccessible regions. Soviet sources put 'only' 240,000 million tons under the 'industrially workable' heading and this figure includes lignite as well as coal. What is more, some of the reserves are of low quality (high water and ash content) and would be uneconomical to ship out from the mines.

In any assessment of Soviet resources, whether coal or other fuels, it is essential to look carefully at their geographical location, because transport costs are a very important factor. It is highly relevant, for example, that out of the 8,700,000 million tons of geological coal reserves, 7,500,000 million (over 85 per cent) are in the Siberian fields. Of the coal suitable for mining on an industrial basis, 70 per cent of the whole of the Soviet Union's workable reserves lie in the two biggest Siberian fields, the Kuznetsk and Kansk–Achinsk basins.

This highlights one of the main problems for Soviet energy policy, namely the enormous gap between where energy is found and where it is to be used: 90 per cent of primary energy deposits are in Asia, whereas 76 per cent of the population and 80 per cent of industrial production are located in Europe. Vast quantities of coal and other fuels therefore have to be shipped across to the European part of the USSR with the result that transport costs are a disproportionately heavy burden on the Soviet economy. 140 million tonnes coal equivalent (tce) were ferried from east to west in 1970 and this figure is likely to rise to 350 million by 1975. By 1980 only 32·5 per cent of Soviet coal will be produced in USSR Europe. Her European output of coal will increase in absolute terms but at the cost of a heavy input of capital because the seams left to be worked lie deeper and deeper underground. At all events, production in some fields in European USSR, the Moscow basin in particular, is already falling.

To sum up: because of their natural situation, their generally poor quality and the high transport costs involved, the coal reserves in the Asian part of the USSR have nothing like the importance that one might be inclined to attach to them in view of their extent; the Kuznetsk basin is the only exception to the rule and coal production in the Asian part of the country is incapable of providing any real relief for the tightly-stretched energy balance of the USSR. Regarding reserves in European USSR, it is clear that they are fast becoming depleted – the direct consequence of the higher quality and easier accessibility of the coal and the better infrastructure. The fuel deficit of USSR Europe, which accounts for 15 per cent of the national fuel demand at the present time, is thus mounting. The Energoset Project Institute has calculated that this deficit will increase by five or six times in absolute terms in the coming decades.

Because of the very conservative Soviet energy policy the production of *oil and natural gas* has, up to the early fifties, been extremely small, but since then output has risen steeply. The 1972 production figures are $221 \times 10^9$ m$^3$ of natural gas and 394 million tons of oil. In the first half of 1973 the output of natural gas was already $117 \times 10^9$ m$^3$ and that of oil 203 million tonnes, indicating that the trend is still upwards.

Estimates for the USSR's oil resources vary between 10·8 and 40—45 $\times 10^9$ tons; these potential reserves must be among the largest in the world. As a producer of crude oil the Soviet Union is second only to the USA. Thus, her energy policy problem is not a matter of shortage of reserves but of the difficulty of exploiting them, particularly in view of the major changes that have taken place over the last thirty years in the regional pattern of oil production in the USSR. With the increasing depletion of the Baku reserves, this traditional oil-producing area is steadily losing its importance and production is on the wane. Even in the Volga-Ural region (the 'Second Baku'), which is currently the largest oil area, production is declining in the Bashkir part and increasing only very slightly elsewhere (Tatar, Kuibyshev). Oil output could certainly be stepped up in other fields, but none with anything like the importance of these two areas.

One of the most vital tasks of Soviet energy policy is therefore to open up new oil reserves to join the ranks of the older oil-producing areas. The choice has fallen on the West Siberian Plain where there are vast fields of top quality oil and natural gas, but opening up this as yet practically uninhabited region presents serious difficulties because of the highly unfavourable climate and terrain. The area is remote from existing lines of communication and the low winter temperatures cause above-average wear and tear to machines and plant, resulting in higher capital investment. Another serious drawback is the permeability of the rock formations. Samotlor, the prime oil production centre, is sure of a high rate of output for only five to six years; after that production will begin to decline appreciably. All the same, an output of 230–260 million tons is forecast for the West Siberian Plain in 1980.

Another project relates to the Mangyshlak peninsula in Kazakhstan but the oil in this field presents a whole series of recovery, transport and refining problems because of its high paraffin content.

To sum up the oil situation: whilst the USSR may reasonably be said to possess extensive reserves, oil quality in some cases leaves something to be desired. But, above all, providing access to the oilfields seen as the source of future supplies is difficult and costly. Some fields are approaching the end of their potential and for this reason the opening up of new and remote oil reserves has become a matter of primary importance for the national economy.

The country's utilisable reserves of *natural gas* are estimated at $15{,}500 \times 10^9$ m$^3$, of which $12{,}500 \times 10^9$ m$^3$ are located in the eastern regions. Whilst the increasing rate of extraction is depleting these reserves at a rapid pace (by 1980 about $4{,}680 \times 10^9$ m$^3$ are expected to have been used) other discoveries are likely to have been made meanwhile. However that may be, deeper and deeper drilling is becoming necessary in some fields, in Ukraine and North Caucasus for example, which increases extraction costs. On the other hand, prospects for natural gas in the West Siberian Plain are promising: the hope is that some $600–700 \times 10^9$ m$^3$ will be brought to the surface in the next few years. The plan for the future is for the West Siberian Plain to cover 40 per cent of the USSR's fuel demand, although opening up natural gas reserves involves the same difficulties as oil.

USSR *water power resources* make a considerable contribution to the country's energy balance. Converted to tce their share of total national energy resources is put at 14·1 per cent. Unfortunately, only a small proportion of this figure is harnessable since the rest is in East Siberia and the eastern extremity of the country, remote from industry and located in inaccessible or nearly inaccessible regions. For these and other reasons recourse to these resources is difficult and costly.

Consequently, it is the hydro-electricity generated in the European part of the Soviet Union that is more important at the present time; hydro-electric power stations here generate from 16 to 17 per cent of the power produced in the whole of the country. Energy policy-makers in the USSR are planning further extensions to the existing facilities in order to ease the situation of the country's energy balance. However, the opportunities offering the most economical generation costs and most favourable locations for industry have already been taken so that new hydro schemes generally require a high input of capital, thus necessitating higher prime costs per kWh. The power generated in USSR Europe is, therefore, considerably dearer than that produced in USSR Asia.

## Focal points of Soviet energy policy

Soviet energy policy, based on the country's resources and the characteristics of those resources, hinges primarily on the following factors:

1 *The continuous process of industrialisation* is creating an ever-increasing demand for primary and secondary forms of energy. The increase in the consumption of electricity is particularly high. Compared with the industrialised countries of Western Europe, where energy consumption is assumed to double every ten years, the figure for the Soviet Union is every seven to eight years. Electricity consumption is escalating so rapidly because the USSR is not only aiming at greater economic expansion, but is also determined to modernise her production facilities and rationalise production processes in order to improve productivity – which is far below the western level – and thus improve her competitive situation on international markets. Investment on rationalisation is also made necessary by the difficult situation on the manpower market, particularly in the development areas and industrial conurbations.

2 *Productivity in Soviet agriculture* is also lagging behind that in comparable Western countries in terms of yield per acre, and capital and labour input per acre, and at the same time the industrialisation process is placing greater demands on the agricultural sector. The process itself can be speeded up by making more foreign currency available to buy imported machinery and plant and this would be possible if agricultural imports could be cut. This, however, means mechanising Soviet agriculture and implementing electrification schemes which, in turn, imply higher consumption of fuel and power.

3 *The increasing importance of the individual* as a consumer, which has grown in the recent past and will continue to grow in the future, is resulting in higher private consumption of energy and fuel, and of electricity and petrol in particular (the latter mainly in the future). By western standards the equipment of households with electrical appliances is only in its infancy. Production of these goods has already developed considerably and will continue to increase. It is not just that consumer demand is becoming more insistent and sophisticated; there are other reasons bound up with the labour market situation. If the very last of Soviet housewives are to be mobilised for industry or other work and their productivity improved, then they have to be relieved of some of their household tasks; this can be done by greater use of labour-saving appliances. The arrears to be made up here represent a very considerable demand.

4 For the reasons set out in the above paragraphs the Soviet Union is pressing on with the *expansion of the tertiary sector* (services), implying a further increase in energy demand.

5 *The increase in the number of vehicles* in use, which applies in the USSR just as it does elsewhere, is having its impact in the hydrocarbons sector. Conditions in the country, particularly the inadequacy of the road system both in quantity and quality, rule out any likelihood that motor vehicle use in the Soviet Union will parallel that in Western Europe or America, even in the long term, but the increasing number of private cars will undoubtedly have repercussions on the country's energy balance.

6 Fuel, particularly oil and, from 1973 onward, natural gas, is important to the USSR as an *export*. Her main customers are the COMECON countries which she supplies with their fuel requirements. Soviet exports cover 98 per cent of their oil needs. The USSR is concerned to maintain this state of affairs since it helps to secure the adherence of these countries to her leadership. She has also taken on extensive commitments with regard to natural gas exports. Despite high prices, the COMECON countries find the arrangement advantageous since they do not have to pay in 'hard currencies' which, like the Soviet Union, they lack. A further advantage is the high degree of security of supply. The Soviet Union also exports considerable amounts of energy to Western European countries. Her exports of oil and oil products to Western Europe in 1971 totalled 42·06 million tons (compared with 47·62 million tons to the COMECON countries). Oil and natural gas are extremely useful earners of foreign exchange for the Soviet Union since the possibilities of exporting industrial products are now as ever severely limited because of the quality hurdle. Even labouring under a general shortage of energy in its own country, the Soviet government is therefore very much concerned to

continue exporting oil and natural gas to the West, since on these exports depend the expansion of Soviet industry and, not least, the opening up of the urgently needed reserves of fuel in peripheral locations.

All the above considerations indicate that the present tensions in the Soviet energy economy are likely to become even more acute in the future. If the USSR fails to increase oil production to levels above those that are planned, she may well find herself having to cope with a shortfall of about 100 million tons of oil in 1980 which will have to be made good from imports.[2] Since the forecasts for natural gas production to 1980 have had to be revised – downwards – there is no help to be expected from that quarter.

## What the Soviet Union is doing to improve the energy situation

Soviet energy policy measures have primarily to be directed towards increasing the flow of supplies, to reducing waste and losses and promoting the more rational use of energy. The main features of Soviet policy are therefore as follows:

1 *Provision of a broader fuel production basis* by the opening up of as yet untapped reserves of primary energy. As has already been shown, this is attended by considerable difficulties since the largest reserves are located peripherally in areas with bad climatic conditions. The capital investment required is high and the Soviet Union is in no position to finance the projects from her own resources alone. She is already availing herself of the financial help provided by various COMECON countries (Czechoslovakia and the German Democratic Republic in particular) and is raising loans on the COMECON investment bank. She is also seeking finance from the western industrial countries that are richest in capital (USA, Japan and the Federal Republic of Germany).

2 As a corollary to these measures there is the need for *building up lines of communication*, in other words the transport infrastructure whereby the fuel won from the earth may be shipped to its users. This means constructing pipeline networks and railways. Considerable difficulties are presented in both cases since ground conditions (particularly in tundra areas) present obstacles in the way of laying the necessary tracks and roads, etc. The West Siberian Plain is particularly hostile territory as far as communications are concerned and the laying of pipelines, railway track and roads demands conciderably higher capital outlay than would normally be required. A further financial burden is the development of the East-West links that will be necessary to cope with the flow of fuel exports.

3 In order to relieve the load on lines of communication and to reduce the burden of transport costs on the national economy, measures are also being taken with regard to the *location of industry*, efforts being made to have industrial plant located near the fuel production centres. So far, however, the climate of Eastern USSR and the absence of ancillary industries have severely limited the possibilities. The policy also needs to be accompanied by more intensive manpower migration. Efforts are being made in this direction (in particular, by offering material incentives) but for years now more people have been migrating away from, than into, Siberia. Experience shows that in practice the Soviet authorities give preference, in their investment decisions as far as location is concerned, to the industrial areas of the west of the country that have already been opened up, in spite of the fact that this increases the acuteness of the energy problems of USSR Europe. A further point is that locating industry near sources of energy implies new or extended transport infrastructure requirements and, once again, high capital expenditure.

4 Thus the Soviet Union's future action with regard to her energy economy will centre primarily on the *hydrocarbons sector*. This will bring about major changes in the production side of her energy balance as can be seen from the following table showing trends to 1975 (in per cent):

TABLE 11
Soviet energy balance

| | 1960 | 1970 | 1975 |
|---|---|---|---|
| Coal | 53·4 | 35·7 | 29·5 |
| Oil | 30·5 | 41·1 | 44·4 |
| Natural gas and oil gas | 8·4 | 14·3 | 22·9 |
| Peat | 2·9 | 1·7 | 1·6 |
| Oil shale | 0·7 | 0·7 | 0·7 |
| Wood and other fuels | 4·1 | 1·5 | 0·9 |
| | 100·0 | * | 100·0 |

Source: Energetika SSSR v 1971–1975 godach, Moscow 1972, p. 35.
* The figures in this column do not total 100 – probably a printing error in the Soviet source.

These changes in the energy balance are mirrored in the pattern of fuel consumption by thermal power stations, which will increasingly burn natural gas and liquid fuels in the future, with natural gas gaining the most ground; by

1975 it will account for 26·8 per cent of thermal power stations' fuel requirements.

5 An effective tool for improving the situation of the energy economy is to make *more efficient use* of the fuel extracted from the earth and to reduce production and transport losses. In 1969 about $12 \times 10^9$ $m^3$ of oil/gas (37 per cent of total production) were lost at the production stage alone. This is equivalent to 17·5 million tce and it is obvious that there is considerable room for saving here. The corresponding figure in the USA is 7 per cent.

6 Further help for the energy balance could be found by *generating electricity with the low-grade coal* in the eastern areas of the country or harnessing the water power in the Asian rivers and sending the power to USSR Europe. Unfortunately the difficulties involved are so great and the cost so high that projects on this basis are not going to materialise in the near future even though they are already on the drawing-board. The problems arising are not only technical (long-distance transmission of high voltages), a question of raw material is also posed. By Soviet calculations, eight transmission lines measuring a total of 250,000 to 300,000 km would be needed to cover the energy deficit of the European part of the country by 1990. The quantity of aluminium this would use amounts to some 3·8–4·5 million tons. Even so, although electricity cannot be a substitute for oil and natural gas in every case, this is one long-term way of easing the energy supply situation, particularly since, apart from the rising demand for electricity for power purposes, requirements for technological and chemical processes are also climbing.

7 Another plank of the policy is to press on with the *construction of nuclear power stations*. Out of the 65–67 million kw capacity to be created in USSR by 1975, 6–8 million kw are to be generated by nuclear plant. However, the economics of nuclear stations can be compared with those of thermal stations only in certain parts of the Soviet Union, that is to say in Europe, west of the middle course of the Volga.[3] For the time being this is the only area where it pays to build them. One of the 'urgent tasks', therefore, is to increase the economic efficiency of nuclear power stations by reducing construction costs and the cost per kw of the current that is generated. It is not surprising, then, that the planned capacity of Soviet nuclear stations for 1977 (4,855 MW installed power) is far below the corresponding figure for the German Federal Republic. The USSR is not in a position to speed up the development work involved and is therefore seeking to acquire capital and know-how from the West. Just as she pays for her pipeline imports from the Federal Republic with supplies of natural gas, so she wants to finance the building of nuclear plant by supplying electricity to Germany. Nuclear power stations built in the western regions of the Soviet Union would have the advantage

of being suitably placed to supply not only the west of the USSR but also Poland and Czechoslovakia. The Baltic would be the ideal location.

8 *Households* in the cities and in most medium- and small-size towns are to be converted to natural gas in order to save on coal transport and thus take some of the load off the railways.

9 The ninth package of Soviet energy policy measures has been hinted at in what has already been said. These are the steps being taken to obtain *Western capital* and know-how, under agreements on technical and economic co-operation, in order to speed up the expansion of the energy economy. Here the USSR would like to benefit from American experience in opening up the territories of the far north and from the techniques that were developed in the process, because in this field she has a considerable amount of leeway to make up. From the Federal Republic she is hoping to acquire new know-how in nuclear engineering and in pipe-casting.

10 As far as her *foreign trade policy* is concerned, the Soviet Union is anxious to keep her commitments to the COMECON countries within reasonable bounds. The oil requirements of the countries of Eastern Europe will have risen to 170 million tons by 1980 since the substitution process is going forward in their case too, although restrained rather than urged on by the governments concerned. The USSR is in no mind, and in any case not in a position, to take on supply commitments of this magnitude. She is, therefore, encouraging her partners in the COMECON to step up their purchasing in the Near East in order to relieve her own situation although, for political reasons, she will doubtlessly continue to meet part of the demand from East Europe. The burden on the USSR represented by her commitments to the COMECON countries can be measured from the frequency with which the Soviet financial and economic press carries articles in which it is argued that the USSR would be better served if she concentrated on expansion in the engineering industries rather than in fuel production.

There can be no doubt that future economic growth in the Soviet Union depends largely upon the success of the measures described, for the danger of development being arrested by energy difficulties is already present. The USSR will have taken a very appreciable step towards solving these problems if she succeeds in ensuring a greater inflow of Western capital to finance her projects.

The Soviet Union will also be affected by the world energy crisis, but in a substantially different way from most of the Western industrialized countries. The chief consequences will derive from the increase in the price of oil on the world market.[4]

TABLE 12

USSR energy production (total and by area)

| | USSR (absolute figures) | | | in % | |
|---|---|---|---|---|---|
| | Total | Europe | Asia | Europe | Asia |
| Coal (Million tons) | | | | | |
| 1965 | 578 | 351 | 227 | 61 | 39 |
| 1970 | 624 | 355 | 269 | 57 | 43 |
| 1972 | 655 | 355** | 300** | 55** | 45** |
| 1973* | 665 | 359** | 306** | 54** | 46** |
| 1975* | 688 | 351 | 337 | 51 | 49 |
| Crude oil (Million tons) | | | | | |
| 1965 | 243 | 226 | 17 | 93 | 7 |
| 1970 | 353 | 288 | 64 | 82 | 18 |
| 1972 | 394 | 293 | 101 | 74 | 26 |
| 1973* | 423 | 294 | 129 | 69 | 31 |
| 1975* | 496 | 337 | 159 | 68 | 32 |
| Natural gas ($10^9$ $m^3$) | | | | | |
| 1965 | 128 | 110 | 18 | 86 | 14 |
| 1970 | 198 | 139 | 59 | 70 | 30 |
| 1972 | 221 | 150 | 71 | 68 | 32 |
| 1973* | 238 | 151 | 87 | 63 | 37 |
| 1975* | 320 | 169 | 151 | 53 | 47 |
| Electricity ($10^9$ kWh) | | | | | |
| 1965 | 506 | 483 | 123 | 76 | 24 |
| 1970 | 740 | 546 | 194 | 74 | 26 |
| 1972 | 858 | 626** | 232** | 73** | 27** |
| 1973 | 915 | 656** | 259** | 72** | 28** |
| 1975 | 1,065 | 746** | 319** | 70** | 30** |

* Planned

** Estimate

As the Arab states hold such an important share of world supplies they can safely put up their prices without needing to fear a short-term falling off in demand. The other producer countries are only too glad to acknowledge Arab leadership in this respect (while prices are rising) with the result that the world market reflects the terms they lay down.

The USSR will likewise adapt to the new conditions. In its case, with exports which amount to more than 107 million tons of oil and petroleum products, the higher prices will signify a considerable increase in revenue from trade. The additional inflow of currency from the Western industrialized countries will allow more goods and equipment to be imported than under the agreements hitherto and thus help to speed up the USSR's schemes for modernization.

Soviet trade with Eastern Europe will also provide an additional income, because the exchange of goods among the socialist countries operates according to prices based on a world-market average which is taken over a given number of years, though, with certain ups and downs, prices stay at this level for quite a long period. Negotiations to determine the new prices have been in process since the beginning of 1974 and there is every likelihood that the Eastern European states will have to cut heavily into their reserves.

Even though the USSR is paid chiefly in machinery and industrial plant and not currency for the raw materials and fuel it delivers to these countries, it will still derive some benefit from the increased prices. If the Eastern European countries wish to go on being supplied with fuel in the next few years, they will have to augment their exports and Soviet industrialization schemes will be aided again.

In any case the present situation is bound to worsen the position of the Eastern European countries because the current shortage of energy sources in the USSR will oblige them to fall back more and more on the Near Eastern states and reduce their scanty reserves even further. (Iraq has proved an exception in this respect so far by allowing payment in the national currency). In view of their present output, the Eastern European countries will have to restrict their not very extensive exports of industrial equipment to Western Europe in order to pay for their fuel from the USSR. The consequent drop in the inflow of foreign currency will cause a setback in the industrialization process, which is still a very long way from completion in these countries, and inevitably strengthen their ties with the Soviet Union.

It would be practically impossible for the Eastern European countries to reduce their imports of oil, as their energy substitution process is far less advanced than in the Western industrialized states. Oil is used because it is urgently needed. The substitution process in force at the moment will have to be slowed down in any case and this in turn will curb the rationalization scheme so indispensable for increasing incentive and productivity.

Thus, the Eastern European countries have at least as many urgent grounds for adopting strict economy measures as Western Europe and the United States, although so far they have imported comparatively little oil from the Near East.

For the Soviet Union, as I mentioned above, the situation presents a different picture, although it too will have to economize. The fact that oil is scarce and likely to become scarcer (for reasons I explained elsewhere) will prevent the USSR from taking full advantage of its export outlets, but there is every reason to expect that it will try to increase its deliveries to the Western industrialized countries. Under the present circumstances, these states are valued customers because they pay for their fuel in currency. But in order to make the necessary quantities available, severe restrictions in home consumption would have to be introduced, involving a slowing-down of the energy substitution programme. It is also doubtful whether, at the present rate of development, there will be enough coal for a brake to be put on the consumption of oil without causing a corresponding drop in growth. Another open question is whether or not the present system of transport could cope with the additional quantities, which would chiefly affect the already heavily congested exchanges between East and West. But as the planned economy of a totalitarian state allows private consumption to be restricted without serious risk of opposition from within, it is to be supposed that a certain amount of reserve supplies can be mobilized effectively. If the Soviet Union were to increase its oil exports by temporarily slowing down the replacement of coal as a source of energy (as I indicated earlier), it would not only be able to procure additional materials for its industrialization process but also seize the opportunity to develop new oil deposits.

In their endeavours to diversify their sources of supply as far as possible, several of the Western industrialized countries will no doubt feel inclined to see their position in respect of Soviet wishes for capital investment in a different light. This is particularly obvious in Japan's case where, though the attitude towards the West Siberian lowland remains fundamentally unchanged, there is a readiness to co-operate in the development of Soviet resources on the east coast shelf. Once again the trend is working in the favour of Soviet targets and the strengthening of Soviet economic policies.

The possible drawbacks arising from the world energy crisis will be comparatively slight for the Soviet Union and will affect it only insofar as it too is an importing country. Unless the Arab states allow the USSR preferential tariffs she will also have to pay more for its crude oil and its petroleum products. Compared with the volume of its exports, which amounted to 7·8 million tons in 1972,[5] this does not weigh very heavily in the balance, but it is nevertheless a sum which cannot be ignored. It seems legitimate to suppose that the Arab states will regard their oil deliveries to the USSR as a means of payment for

Soviet arms. This applies especially to Iraq and Syria, both of which could theoretically use their oil to clear their substantial balance of trade deficit in respect of the Soviet Union. Algeria, which exports crude oil to the USSR, is in a different position with a surplus balance. The interesting feature about these relations is that, with the exception of Algeria, the oil supplies from the Arab producer countries fail to appear in Soviet foreign trade statistics. This can presumably be explained by the fact that they were placed straight to the account of the arms deliveries. But if the Soviet Union has to import increasing quantities of oil from the Near East on a long-term basis,[6] it will cease to derive the same advantages from the business as it will have to share the consequences of the world shortage and at the same time be urgently required to re-assess the use of its oil at home.

This places a very different emphasis on the question of substituting oil for coal, although there remains the possibility of introducing secondary development methods to carry through the increasingly costly scheme in the Volga–Ural area and help to raise the comparatively low yield of many other resources (often only 28–35 per cent). The temptation to open up peripheral deposits would thus be all the greater.

There is no doubt that the energy crisis will affect the Soviet Union politically as well as economically. The question of the distribution of Soviet oil supplies has been a frequent source of friction among the Eastern European countries, especially in connection with Hungary, and it seems highly likely that the rise in prices will encourage some countries to cease to take full advantage of their contracts with Iraq and Iran and to demand more oil from the Soviet Union in order to avoid having to pay in currency. In the present circumstances these requests will have to be refused, although the Soviet Union has already stated its intention of augmenting supplies of gas to ease the energy situation in the partner states and forestall political repercussions. The USSR has apparently agreed to deliver 25cbm. (billion cubic metres) of gas to the Eastern European countries if they undertake to build 500 kms. of the 2500 kms.-long pipeline themselves.[7]

The Soviet Union has also been able to increase its political influence elsewhere in the world. By delivering weapons to the Arab states it has succeeded in strengthening their allegiance and developed its political role in the Near East which, in view of its own precarious energy situation, is by no means negligible. Its offer to find outlets for unsold Arab oil shows in which direction the new way is leading. The embargo on deliveries to the US and the Netherlands and the restrictions in supplies to the Western industrialized countries will mean that the economic growth of these countries will be temporarily undermined and their military strength weakened as a result. When everything is added up, the assumption that Soviet agents have been active behind the scenes seems more and more justified. Apart from one or two minor inconveniences which she too will have to share, the Soviet Union will be the one country to benefit politically and economically from the world energy crisis.

## Notes

[1] Cf. M. M. Brenner, in 'Ekonomika neftjanoj i gazovoj promyslennosti SSSR', Moscow 1968, p. 86.
[2] Cf. W. Gumpel, *Energiepolitik in der Sowjetunion*, Cologne 1970, in particular pp. 275 ss.
[3] Energetika SSSR v 1971–1975 godach, Moscow 1972, p. 138.
[4] Cf. detailed account by W. Gumpel, 'Sowjetunion: Erdöl und Nahostkrise', *Aussenpolitik*, No. 1, 1974.
[5] This oil is directly transferred from the Arab fields to several Eastern European countries, where it counts as Soviet delivery. Cf. *Novoe vremja*, 1973.
[6] Cf. *Aussenpolitik*, No. 11, 1971, p. 679.
[7] Cf. *Neue Zürcher Zeitung*, No. 298, 1.11.1973.

# China's Energy Policies

*by Marcel Toussaint*

When discussing China's oil and energy development – or, for that matter, any other economic activity – it must be remembered that the People's Republic of China (PRC) publishes almost no meaningful statistical data on its economy. The economic development plans are kept secret, as are other important figures. Whenever figures are released, they are normally percentages of some unknown absolute figure or they refer to some other data that are not public knowledge. As a consequence, the analyst is forced to piece together different data from different sources, to make conjectures, to resort to speeches and comments made by Chinese officials, and to relate all these bits of information to the few known facts. Fortunately, the results can occasionally be cross-checked against newly emerging informational sources. Yet, the final estimates are of necessity only approximate, and must always be taken with a dose of caution.

## Basic assumptions

With this in mind, a number of basic assumptions can be made in the fields of 1) electric power, 2) coal, 3) water-power resources, and 4) petroleum.

*Installed electric capacity*, which totaled 1·85 million kilowatt (kw) in 1949, had increased about ten-fold by 1970. The estimate for 1972 was about 22 million kw. By 1973, it may have reached about 25 million kw. A very large portion of this capacity consists of thermal power plants. According to best estimates, at least 70 per cent of the PRC's installed electric capacity is produced by thermal plants. Almost all of them are coal-fired, the remaining ones are water-powered.

*Electric power production* has about tripled in the past 10 years, rising from 30 billion kilowatt-hours (kwh) in 1962 to 95 billion kwh in 1972. It is estimated that some 15 billion kwh of this has not been available for consumption because of internal plant use and transmission losses. Of the remaining 80 billion kwh, more than 83 per cent were consumed by industry, slightly over 7 per cent by agriculture, less than 1 per cent by transportation, and the remaining 9 per cent half by construction and half by residences and commercial facilities. The largest industrial consumers were, and are, in the fields of chemicals, non-ferrous metals, as well as iron and steel.

*Coal reserves.* Estimates of the PRC's coal reserves vary widely. It is however practically certain that the country possesses some of the world's largest deposits. Proven reserves are probably in the neighbourhood of 80 billion metric tons (MT), and total reserves, according to Russian estimates, may be as high as 1,500 billion MT. Apparently a full survey of the nation's coal reserves has not been made recently, although some sporadic prospecting for coal as well as new mineral deposits seems to have taken place. Some of China's large older mines are likely to become depleted in the not-too-distant future, yet there has apparently been no concentrated effort to open up new ones on a large scale. Until about two years ago, there was a movement to build small mines. It seems that these efforts were abandoned.

*Coal production* has soared – with considerable fluctuations and disruptions – from under 30 million MT in the early thirties, and considerably less in the late thirties and during the forties, to over 200 million MT in the late fifties. During the sixties, such events as the withdrawal of USSR experts, economic downturns, the Cultural Revolution, and changing plan targets as well as policy readjustments provoked wide variations in the coal output. It may be assumed, however, that annual production occasionally surpassed 400 million MT and averaged an annual 300 million MT. Last year's production probably amounted to approximately 340 million MT.

*Water resources* are plentiful in the PRC, but the extent of this potential is uncertain. Prior to 1949, the Kuomintang regime estimated the existing hydroelectric potential at 137 million kw. The United Nations' ECAFE later put the figure at 109 million kw, but this estimate excluded Northeast China, Tibet and Sinkiang. In 1955 and 1958, PRC sources, on the other hand, claimed resources as big as 540–580 million kw. While the latter figure appears exaggerated, the earlier estimates could well be overly conservative.

*Oil reserves.* In the 1950s, confirmed oil reserves in the PRC were put at just under 6 billion MT. More recently, these estimates have been upped by experts to over 10 billion MT. However, estimates vary widely. For example, one estimate (by Shell) mentions established, recoverable crude oil reserves of 2.7 billion MT, while another speaks of the possibility that offshore reserves of more than 50 billion MT exist. The lower figure is admittedly an extremely conservative one taking only the established oil-bearing areas into account. The higher figure, on the other hand, is somewhat speculative. Including the six major producing centers, the areas with different degrees of oil prospect are known to approximate four million square kilometers. This amounts to almost one third of China's total land area. Until this area has been fully explored, any prediction as to the amount of oil reserves must remain incomplete and speculative. Whatever the actual amount of oil reserves, the quantities are large, and the prospects for further finds are favorable. In addition, large known deposits of oil shale exist in the provinces of Kwangtung, Hopei, and particularly Heilungkiang in Manchuria. According to an estimate of the Ministry of Petroleum Industry in 1959, the total deposit of shale found up until then amounted to about 360 billion tons as the average of 6 per cent oil content. This alone would yield as much as 20 billion tons of oil.[1] Altogether, there can be little doubt that China could multiply its current crude production many times without running out of reserves for many decades.

*Oil production.* In 1958, the PRC still had to import some 2·5 million MT of petroleum products (mainly crude, diesel oil and gasoline) from the USSR. In 1962, such imports still amounted to 1·9 million MT. Since then, no imports have been noted. It can safely be assumed that the PRC is today self-sufficient in petroleum and probably has been so since as early as 1963. According to the best estimates, the PRC produced between 18 million and 20 million MT of crude in 1970. Production probably increased by 28 per cent in 1971 and rose another 16 per cent in 1972. Hence, the output in 1972 should have been between 26·7 million and 29·7 million MT, with the higher figure the more likely one. Since late 1971, China has been exporting some kerosene to Hong Kong, and this year exported some crude oil to Japan. The PRC hopes to export in 1974 about 3 million MT of crude to Japan. This oil is of low sulphur content and high viscosity.

## Geographic distribution

The largest coal reserves are located in the Shensi Basin and the Szechwan Basin, with smaller ones in the Northeast around Kirin and the far Northwest of Sinkiang province. However, there seem to be deposits spread all over China, with some in almost every province. More than half the country's coal is mined in the North and Northeast. Some of the coal production is close to the industrial concentration of southern Manchuria, but other large mines are in the farthest North of Heilungkiang province, near the Soviet border.

Oil production is roughly in the same geographical areas where coal is concentrated, i.e. in the Shensi Basin, the Szechwan Basin, in the Northwest of Sinkiang province, and in the Northeast, where at least half of China's oil is produced. Fortunately, it is also close to the country's main industrial area. The same is true of the Sheng-li oilfield, which is somewhat north of Sheng-li and close to Tientsin. More removed from industrial centers are the crude production centers of the Shensi Basin (at Yen-chang) and the Szechwan Basin (near Nanchung). The other major oil fields, however, are very far from any industrial activity.

The largest hydroelectric resources, on the other hand, are located in South and Southwest China, especially the provinces of Yunnan, Sikang, the western part of Szechwan, and eastern Tibet. This means that the largest hydroelectric potential exists in the country's least populated and least industrialized parts. It also means that coal-oil and hydroelectric resources approximately complement each other regionally.

The greatest amount of installed power-generating capacity is of course situated in the industrial areas, i.e. in the southern part of Manchuria, in the Peking–Tientsin area, in the Shangai–Nanching region, and, to a lesser degree, around Chu-chou in Hunan province and near Chung-ching in the densely populated Szechwan Basin.

Major refineries have been located near the large consuming centers or close to the producing areas. Those close to the oil wells are Ta-ching in the Northeast, Tu-shan-tzu and Karamai in the far North Northwest, Long-hu and Mang-yai in Chinghai province's Tsaidam Basin, Nan-chung in the Szechwan Basin und Yumen in the central northern province of Chiu-chuan. The refineries at Fu-shun in the Northeast and at Mao-ming in the southern province of Kwangtung are close to shale oil production sites. The refineries serving the surrounding consumption centers are located at Peking, Dairen, Chin-hsi, and Chin-chou in the Northeast, Shangai and Nan-ching in the East. One refinery, at Lanchou, is neither close to a production area nor to a population or industrial center. It was in fact, installed by Soviet technicians prior to 1960 because Lanchou is about halfway between the remote northwestern oil fields and the eastern industrialized areas. It is also a railway hub.

## Policies and outlook for development

The figures show the PRC has large coal, oil, and water resources which are more than sufficient to back an industrialization programme of major proportions. Obviously, there is no need for the country to deviate from its principle of self-reliance in the field of energy. The electric power industry, too, seems to be able at this time to meet the demands of the country. This does not mean, however, that China faces no energy problems.

First, the electric power industry is rather inefficient and not very advanced technologically. Power plants tend to be relatively small, many of them are old, and there is probably no excess capacity left. Also, progress in building hydroelectric stations seems to have been surprisingly slow.

Next, coal production has been beset by various problems, many times resulting in shortages. Even now the supply situation is tight, at best. In view of the importance of coal to China, the modernization of existing mines and the opening of new ones are imperative, especially since it takes about three to five years to build a new mine. Rapid mining expansion, however, requires mining equipment in large quantities that may not be readily available in the PRC. It is also doubtful that China produces the modern types of equipment necessary for sophisticated exploitation.

Furthermore, while oil production at present is sufficient for the nation's needs, and oil reserves are potentially huge, the absolute amounts produced are still comparatively insignificant. For example, in 1970, the PRC's output of crude amounted only to about 4 per cent of production in the United States. What is more, the expansion of refining capacity has not kept pace with the expansion of output of crude. As a result, there exists now a small gap between output of crude and refining capacity. It is possible that this is the reason why China has agreed to sell some crude oil to Japan this year – and it is also possible that the quantity exported to Japan is more or less the excess crude production that cannot be readily refined domestically. Based on this assumption, China's shortage of refining capacity is about one million MT this year, and in 1974 it will be about three million MT.

Another difficulty is the question of transporting the fuels in China. Any major expansion of oil production would require a major expansion of railroad and/or road facilities, or the construction of long-distance pipelines.

In brief: while China's energy resources are plentiful, their development, processing, and transportation are other matters. Yet there is no doubt that such development is called for lest the country's economic progress be jeopardized.

Although the details of China's fourth Five-Year Plan (1971–75) are a state secret, it is known that fuel and power supply as well as mining (which would most certainly include coal mining) are given priority. This is in fact highly necessary, since the plan also emphasizes the development of three fuel consumers – rail transportation, road transportation, and water transportation.

In addition, the PRC's industries are becoming increasingly mechanized, and industrial expansion is heaviest in the energy-intensive areas. It has been estimated that at the current rate of progress, China's industry will require between 7 per cent and 14 per cent more energy each year, and that most of this requirement will be in the form of electric power.

This need poses several problems. For one, China will soon be unable to produce domestically the quantities of generating equipment required. Even after expansion and streamlining of existing capacity to produce generating equipment, the industry is unlikely to be able to supply more than 3 million kw of power generating equipment per year. Yet it has been estimated that 3 million kw of generating equipment will have to be installed as early as

1975, followed by 3·2 million kw in 1976, and 3·5 million kw in 1977. By 1985, equipment for the generation of 7·6 million kw will have to be installed per year. But for another matter, the PRC will need much larger and more sophisticated equipment than is currently being produced inside the country. Large gas turbines are one example. The past slowness in completing large hydroelectric power plants also suggests that the industry has some problems in turning out large quantities of the required equipment.

Fueling the additional power plants poses another problem. Based on the expected increase in the PRC's industrial production, it has been estimated that the output of coal will have to increase by as much as 30 million MT annually for the next decade. By 1985, annual coal production would have to reach more than 640 million MT. For this reason – and because of the better efficiency and convenience of oil-fired power plants as well as the increased availability of oil – it is quite likely that China will not only shift increasingly to oil-fired new thermal plants, but also convert some of the existing ones to oil fuel. At the same time, however, more petroleum will be needed by the increasing number of boats, ships, trucks, diesel locomotives, and agricultural implements such as tractors and pumps. This rising demand for oil products in turn will necessitate both more refinery capacity, and equipment for exploration, production, and transportation of oil. China may find it difficult to produce this needed equipment, or at least to produce it fast enough in sufficient quantities.

The chances are that the PRC, realizing the situation fully well, will stress the rapid development of oil production, refinery capacity, coal production, power generation facilities, and transportation/transmission facilities for electricity, oil and coal. As all this will have to be done more or less simultaneously, the country is faced with a daunting task.

## Cooperation

Under these circumstances the PRC will probably turn abroad for assistance. Despite the country's firm policy of self-reliance, it will not hesitate to import whatever is required to achieve self-sufficiency in the longer term. Much has been written and said about possible cooperation in the exploration and exploitation of off-shore oil reserves between the PRC and other countries, such as Japan or the United States. But while such a cooperative effort cannot be ruled out, it seems at least improbable and contrary to current Chinese philosophy. However, China is not averse to importing the needed equipment and/or technology.

Therefore, we can speculate at this time that the PRC will purchase abroad such equipment as drilling rigs, refinery equipment and conceivably entire refineries, coal mning machinery and equipment, and power generation equipment or even entire power stations. Furthermore, China may turn to foreign countries for assistance in building pipelines, transmission lines and equipment, and sophisticated technology in all these fields. She will do so, however, only to support her own operations. To obtain the foreign exchange needed for the purchase of such equipment and know-how, China can be expected to export part of the country's oil production.

There is already evidence to support the above assumptions. Thus, it has become known that Peking requested technical information from a Japanese firm concerning the construction of a long-distance pipeline that would probably stretch from the Ta-ching oilfield to a Gulf of Pohai port and possibly go as far as Peking and Shangai. It has also been reported that China ordered a number of drilling rigs, as well as suction dredges, from Japanese and Dutch firms.

The question arises whether or not China will in the foreseeable future become a large-scale exporter of crude oil. After all, if the most optimistic estimates should turn out to be justified, China's oil reserves would surpass the deposits of the Middle East. Also the pipeline to the coast, whose construction is apparently being contemplated, would facilitate the crude's transportation not only to China's industrial center in the Northeast and on to the Shanghai industrial agglomeration, but also the shipping of oil overseas.

Attempting to answer the question at this time would be futile and premature. Intriguing as the idea may be that China could become one of the world's large oil exporters, replacing the Middle East in first place of importance, and in the process being freed of all foreign exchange anxieties, the matter is to a large extent dependent upon China's economic development and her future political-ideological outlook. Both may be subject to considerable adjustments or alterations.

## Note

[1] Cf. Choon-ho Park, Oil Development in the People's Republic of China. Unpublished paper.

# A New Challenge to the European Community

*by Wolfgang Hager*

Few things are more difficult than discussing public policy in a revolutionary era like the one going on in the field of energy. The analyst is tempted to restrict himself to the firm ground of known policies though the assumptions on which these policies rest are being challenged by new events almost daily. And when the subject is international cooperation, the temptation again is to argue within an intellectually consistent framework, stressing the advantages of unity over the risks of competitive chaos. But the real task before us is probably to deal with a disunity whose cause, while not simply the short-sighted selfishness of statesmen, reflects profound and real differences of interest.

## New dimensions in the American-European-Japanese triangle

A European government wishing to intervene in the internal or external oil market can do so on three or four levels: the nation-state acting on its own; the Community level; cooperation (collectively or separately) with the US and Japan; or through the OECD; and, for some purposes, action within a world-wide forum perhaps under UN auspices.

The problem, of course, is not to choose between any of these levels to the exclusion of others, but to allocate certain economic, political, and quasi-diplomatic tasks among these different levels. There are difficulties with any cooperative action in that prospective partners must all make fairly similar choices as to the distribution of tasks, as well as agreeing to specific lines of conduct. It is not surprising, therefore, that while the oil situation lends itself admirably to an application of the cooperative rhetoric of post-war internationalism, concrete reactions have led to confused unilateralism.

## The oil companies

Since the Teheran agreements of 1971 there has been a muted debate in Europe as to whether the clearly weakened position of the oil companies require direct consumer-producer links at the government level. The problem was (and is) that any attempt to by-pass the oil companies might further threaten the remnants of their contractual rights. Although the oil companies could do little but acquiesce in the successive increases in their taxes (through raising posted prices) and in the share of production they had to cede to the host governments (participation oil) there was little assurance that government-to-government deals would be cheaper or more secure. Indeed, by the end of 1973, the companies supplied crude to their European customers at a considerably lower price than that demanded by government monopolies in Venezuela and Iran, or for the participation oil sold in the Gulf. Furthermore, sceptics could cite the example of France's attempt to establish special oil relations with Algeria which ended in the debacle of 1971.

Yet the evidence is not conclusive. Companies have now very little bargaining strength at all. Consumer governments would not have much either, but could perhaps do marginally better by providing incentives for contractual, more stable relations. In the past, the argument rested on a false dichotomy: whether companies or governments should be the customers for OPEC oil. In that context, producer countries were likely to prefer the companies with their much larger marketing outlets.[1] On the other hand, consumer governments could profit from the diversified sources of the companies, plus their sophisticated production, shipping and downstream operations.

Now that much of the OPEC oil is nationalised or about to be nationalised, and shipped by companies and independent agencies on the basis of what amounts to service contracts (just as the production of this nationalised oil is often carried out by the companies as service operators[2]) it is logical for the consumer countries to speak with the principal rather than his agents. The government-to-government relationship is thus complementary to, rather than exclusive of, a continued role of the companies.

Secondly, and this is another major consideration of a consumer oil policy, this agent – in a non-interventionist, free market context on the consumer side – disposes over allocative powers which touch the essence of the oil-based economies of the consumer countries. These powers cover not only the ability to allocate supplies in a crisis, but equally importantly, they include the design of long-term geographical supply patterns of investment and exploration strategy. For example, whose offshore fields should get priority in the allocation of not only scarce capital, but even scarcer rigs and manpower? There is also the question of the pricing ('windfall profits') and allocation of oil products in what may remain times of recurrent short-term bottlenecks and at least minor crises.

A greater government role, both in the domestic oil market and in direct consumer-producer contacts seems necessary in order to satisfy the national interests of both parties which go beyond the simple supply of oil for monetary payment. The consumer side is concerned to cope with the monetary problems associated with oil purchases. The binding of short-term assests into crisis-proof long-term investments is one of these problems and the off-set of the massive current account outflows through the scale of goods and services is another. Successful cooperation on both these fronts might by itself increase the security of supplies. On the producer side, broad economic development goals which can not be solved by money alone, as well as even broader diplomatic goals, also argue in favour of direct consumer-producer contacts on the government level.

*National vs. private companies*

One instrument of direct consumer-producer contacts can be an oil company – provided it is 'national'. This, of course, has long been central to French, and to lesser extent, Italian policy (for Britain it is more true to say that diplomacy served its major oil companies perceived primarily as economic assets rather than vice versa).

The original aim of Franco–Italian efforts to gain 'control over crude' is becoming rapidly outdated – no one but the producer government has such control. Yet in today's world it is hard to escape the conclusion that a national company is one very important asset for any government wishing to engage in oil diplomacy. The United States, though never neglecting the interests of its companies in the Middle East, indirectly served the general interest of the oil consumers. Now, however, given the new import dependence of the US, its own national interests are much more directly involved.

This compromises the hard-won 'international' image of American[3] companies. Europeans shuddered when they heard of Mr Connally's visit to Saudi Arabia as the representative of Occidental. Though the State Department seems to have successfully resisted the conclusion of a formal agreement such as that suggested by Sheik Yamani – long-term supply guarantees in return for investment access to the US – such an agreement is really not needed. (On the other hand, European countries have now used the compromised position of the US to conclude formal agreements with trade, not investment access, as the counterpart).

Furthermore, the US government has a choice, when exercising its diplomatic influence, to compromise, say, on price in return for assurances concerning the legal or commercial position of its companies. Its cost-benefit analysis in encouraging a 'boycott' of its companies in Libya may differ from that of, say, the Federal Republic which depends substantially on this source. In a period of shortage or genuine crisis, the US, if it came to the crunch, has a greater capacity to influence the behaviour of its companies than any other government except Great Britain. (There were press reports according to which the British Government faced the summer of 1973 shortage calmly, since in the North Sea concessions it possessed adequate means of sanctions should oil companies step out of line on price and quantity. This same power of sanction failed however in the late autumn 1973, when the companies pro-rated the British market on a non-preferential basis).

*Between cooperation and competition*

This does not mean that Western cooperation on energy matters is no longer possible. It does mean, however, that the pursuit of such cooperation will occur simultaneously with competition. Obviously, the latter will constantly interfere with the former. Western Europe (and Japan) are bound to challenge the 'middleman' role of the US companies. At best, this will result in a cautious jockeying for position with the producer countries. The automatic restraint, however, is the overwhelming importance which US companies continue to hold in most of our countries. There can be no question of pulling the rug from under the feet of the companies, e.g. through the creation of a unitary European company, but rather only of reducing the size of the rug.

It is thus the difficult task of intra-OECD diplomacy to cope with this process, though it will be partially at the expense of the US whose imperial services are no longer outweighed by post-imperial liabilities, while at the same time pursuing cooperation in energy matters. For in terms of international politics, the (foreign) nationality of the companies on which the bulk of Europe's oil supplies depends is both an asset and a liability.

It is an asset, as long as the United States can continue to insure through its considerable diplomatic resources a modicum of secure tenure (and production) to 'its' companies. Only the United States can provide an essential service to the conservative regimes of the Persian Gulf: the provision of security against possible internal subversion and external threat. At the same time it is also the only Western country which could hold out with some credibility the threat of an ultimate sanction of some kind of intervention. The fact that vital US interests are now engaged in safe oil supplies, rather than just company assets, must enter into the calculation of any government contemplating extreme measures of curtailing supplies. One does not have to accept the gory scenarios, described by Mr Fulbright in recent Senate hearings, of punitive proxy wars by unleashed Israelis, to conclude that the enormous resistance of civilian-minded electorates to military adventures of any kind might find a limit if normal life styles were endangered by the 'irrational' acts of minor princes. In this sense, Europe and Japan may continue to benefit from a US 'oil umbrella' almost as vital as the nuclear umbrella.

By the same token, relying on US companies represents a liability for Europe and Japan. It is now likely that the next phase of the Arab–Israeli conflict will shift from the battlefield to the oil fields of the Middle East. It is as yet uncertain whether this will be a long drawn out struggle marked by many 'minor' and major crises or whether it will end quickly with a weakening of US support for Israel and an enforced settlement. Even such a 'settlement' would probably usher in a period of further revisionism. There is an incentive for European governments to begin to establish a network of supply which runs parallel to that of the oil companies, though that network may be more costly.

## The energy policy of the EEC

Community policy as proposed by the Commission contains a multitude of elements: some burden–sharing on high cost coal, higher mandatory stock levels, a machinery for crisis allocation of oil,[4] etc. But its most interesting and controversial element is the suggestion to create a single oil market for the Community. This would of necessity be a managed market, its purpose being to serve as a means of bargaining with both oil-producing governments and the oil companies.

The Community together represents the most important single market for imported oil (and virtually anything else) in the world. In order to play a role, this market must be surrounded by a fence. This fence could take the form of what amounts to a publicly-organised cartel[5] of importing companies. These would be 'accredited' to the Community on condition of abiding by the rules set by the Community authorities. Among these rules would be an obligation to furnish data on the economics of their operations, and to observe 'orientation prices'[6] set on the basis of this information.

At times of scarcity in certain refined products, such as that caused by the 'phony' energy crisis in the summer of 1973 due to insufficient refining capacity in the US, discipline on prices would be imposed to prevent companies from making windfall profits. (It would almost automatically have to be accompanied by export controls to prevent 'distortions' of normal supply patterns). In normal times, however, prices would be set at a certain level to ensure adequate profits to the companies with which to fulfill greatly increased investment needs. The system of Community 'accreditation' could furthermore be used to bargain with OPEC national companies wishing to establish downstream operations in the Community.

### *The commission's proposals*

Such an arrangement could serve as the thin end of the wedge of direct producer – consumer deals which both parties are cautiously talking about. Once the dialogue is opened, more complex elements of agreement might be brought into play. This would involve what the Commission calls 'establishing relations of confidence', a policy which meets with both scepticism and resentment by critics inside and outside the Community. The language of the Commission's proposals is both ambitious and vague. Thus it is argued:

> The economic and social cooperation between the two groups, i.e. EEC and oil exporting countries in all areas of common interest and based on mutual advantage could facilitate the industrial and economic development of the oil exporting regions and the establishment of a desirable stability in the relations between equal partners.[7]

And

> The Commission considers it necessary:
> (1) to create a mechanism for a dialogue with the exporting countries; the mixed commissions which are to be established with some of the countries could be used for this purpose;
> (2) to send, at the same time, groups of industrialists from the Community to the exporting countries, and vice versa, to examine concrete possibilities for economic cooperation;
> (3) to negotiate cooperation agreements which should observe the following principles:
> - an undertaking by the Community to favour the economic and social development of the exporting countries by making available technical and perhaps financial assistance, as well as to open its markets for the industrial and agricultural products of these countries
> - an undertaking by the exporting countries and the Community to observe certain rules and guarantees for commercial transactions and industrial investments.[8]

It is easy to argue that this line of thinking is both ineffective and harmful to harmonious relations in the West. Ineffective, because we live in a seller's market for oil; because market access for other kinds of goods is at present of limited relevance for most of the countries involved, the same being true for financial assistance; and because visits by industrialists are not very effective compared to the more solid advantages which the US can offer. Harmful, because both geographically and as regards the means (market access, investment cooperation), this oil policy merges with the Mediterranean policy of the European Community, which is known to be a bone of contention between Europe and America.

As usual, the Community can argue 'they started it'. Algeria, wanting to get better terms on market access to the Community, offered long-term supply guarantees for both oil and gas. Iran certainly has an interest in assured markets as it enters the next stage of its economic development. Most

Arab countries might have an interest in negotiating access to the European capital market for long-term investment, not because that market gives better returns than the US market, but because they wish to spread the risk of a retaliatory freezing of assets.

The talk of cooperation and financial and technical assistance is partially a euphemism for non-monetary payment for oil. Such forms of payment – petrochemical plants, port installations and other oil-related infrastructure in a first phase, and perhaps other kinds of social and industrial infrastructure investment in a second stage – are indispensible; they keep alive the interest of producers in production, and achieve some balance-of-payments offset on current account. Buying what amounts to a package of expertise in production, initial management, and market access from as many sources as possible is economically and politically attractive to oil-producers. Japan seems to base its strategy on just such a broad view of consumer–producer relations.

While Europe has no particular advantage as regards expertise or funds available to engage in such a policy, the diversification argument and the proximity of its market would make it an acceptable partner among others.

### *Divergent national outlooks*

The preferential opening of markets (both ways?) strikes a particularly sensitive cord with those who argue that a non-discriminatory 'one world' is preferable to one of contending spheres of influence. This is not the place to argue why an absolute adherence to this concept is probably no longer practicable or indeed practised in today's world (are Phantoms sold on a MFN basis?). What critics of the Community approach should understand, however, is that market power is virtually the only instrument the Community has (just as investment power is the chief Japanese asset). To deny it the use of this instrument may mean denying it the means of any independent action at all.

There is no doubt, however, that this programme brings to the fore difficult problems both on the national and on the international levels. Grappling with the national level, the proposals mean in fact that the rest of the Community should take over what are essentially French practices of economic management of the oil market. This is not surprising since France (and Italy) are the only countries which have an intellectual concept for such management. Moreover, the concept has been tested in practice.

For Germany, and especially the officials of the economics ministry, the 'French' concept poses theological misgivings. The setting of orientation prices for oil products, for example, may lead to serious maladjustments and/or to quasi-permanent intervention as to quantity of production (in order to ensure that even low-yield products are produced) and intervention into intra-Community and third country trade (strict export licensing).[9] On the other hand, opinion on these matters is changing so fast in Germany that prediction is very difficult. It should be clear, however, that divergent models of internal market management are no longer possible in times of scarcity. In the autumn of 1973, companies in countries with controlled product prices (France, Belgium, Italy) seem to have stepped up exports of oil products to Germany. The alternative to common rules is therefore the imposition of export controls within the Common Market.[10]

A different sort of national problem raised by a Community oil policy relates to the contract-making powers with producer countries implicit in such a policy. The broad kind of cooperation envisaged by the Commission is precisely the kind being vigorously pushed by national ministries. Every country wants to ensure for itself a substantial share of 'technical cooperation' (which means ultimately sales of goods and services) and investment flows from the oil producing countries. Moreover, to the extent that this 'technical cooperation' involves military matters, the Community as a whole cannot play a role.

### *Conflicting interests*

Thus even a cursory look at the behaviour of European countries during the second half of 1973 shows that the 'scramble for oil' is a very complex affair even within the Community. Once non-monetary payments for oil are the chief instruments for competition, control and supervision become very difficult, even if the willingness to be controlled existed. How can such diverse elements as diplomatic support, military supplies, technical assistance, market access, and upstream and downstream investment-cooperation be measured against a common yardstick? Is it of interest to Britain to incorporate imports of refined products in a joint production scheme, such as that worked out between Germany and Iran, since it will be hard put to handle its own North Sea oil in a few years? Would the Netherlands be interested in devoting scarce investment capital to laying a giant gas-pipeline from Iran to Germany and Italy? Can one blame Denmark, deprived of virtually all other independent market power, for joining its small Scandinavian partners, Norway and Sweden, in forming a purchasing pool outside the EEC?

Even more intractable than divergent economic interests, which in theory at least can be incorporated into a balanced bargain, are the present and future political dimensions of a special relationship with the Arab oil producers. The political nature of an EEC-Arab investment/development cooperation, advanced by French foreign Minister Jobert and welcomed by the Secretary General of the Arab League, Mahmoud Riad, was symbolised by the presence of a number of Arab ministers at the EEC summit of December 14–15 in Copenhagen. It would be a mistake to think that the diplomatic component of such 'cooperation' could remain limited to the kind of, ultimately innocuous, verbal support of the Arab position such as that given by the Nine in the famous November 6 declaration. The Arab summit in Algiers, whose 'secret' resolutions were published in the Beirut press,[11] made it clear that support for UN Security Council resolution 242 is only the first demand that will be made to the West. Further demands may include a total embargo of arms to Israel, the abandonment of restrictions on arms sales to the Arabs, the break-off of air and sea links with Israel and what amounts to an economic blockade and so on. Going beyond these published sources, it is now clear the Arab world is poised to regain its traditional role of leadership in Africa, where it possesses not only economic carrots and sticks, but the means to advance African political objectives (Rhodesia, South Africa) through pressure on the West. European compliance in such a strategy would of course be an asset.

A complacent attitude to the stakes becomes even more untenable when we view the very strong military component of Arab demands. Both Britain and France have concluded agreements for long-term supplies of crude oil in return for arms[12]. The new element in this trade is not only the replacement of a monetary payment for oil by a straightforward, COMECON-type, barter deal between governments. More serious in the long run is the greatly weakened capacity of arms-supplying governments to control the effectiveness of the arms in question. What if Israel were to be faced with offensive weapons like the Chieftain tank as well as excellent defensive weapons from the Soviet Union? One thing is clear: ultimately no European country will be able to satisfy escalating Arab demands for arms; but before the final 'no', relations with fellow member countries, with the United States and with Israel will have been subjected to very great stresses. For there is no upper limit to these demands: Mr Heykal, when still editor of Egypt's *Al Ahram*, called for the acquisition of nuclear arms 'at all costs', and the subject is already said to have been raised by 'several Arab leaders' in recent conversations with the French government.[13]

### *The political rôle of the Community*

A European policy of systematic friendship towards the Arabs is thus a slippery slope which is bound to lead to major conflicts all round. Judgments on how far it should be pursued will differ among Community member-states; those who, through a distorted industrial structure, are prisoners of the need to export arms will be willing to go quite far. A 'political' Arab-energy policy ultimately involves fundamental choices as to the world role of the

Community: will it be a traditional power using elements of military force to further its interests (major arms procurement projects constitute alliances of sorts); or will it be a civilian power,[14] dully plodding along establishing contractual relations based on civilian economic and welfare interests?

In the short run, the choice has been suspended. Clearly, member countries are acting independently. They follow their particular preferences as to the mix of economic, political or military components in the contracts which all of them are seeking with the Arab world. Much of the scope for a European energy policy has thus been effectively pre-empted. In the slightly longer run, however, with or without a deliberate European arms policy, there will be very few weapons systems in Europe which are purely national. If, moreover, a formal military procurement agency emerges from the work now being done by the Eurogroup in NATO and the WEU, a policy on arms exports must be developed.

As to Arab demands of economic warfare, the somewhat schizophrenic division of Community business into economic and political sectors for which France has always pleaded could be put to some use in this context: a mere EEC Commission cannot be asked to deliver anything but 'civilian' quid pro quo. It cannot support Arab diplomatic efforts in the Near East, Africa or the Islamic world[15] unless these include constructive long-term solutions of economic problems. In the complicated bargaining with individual countries for long-term economic arrangements under the Community's Mediterranean policy, grandiose plans for economic boycotts against Israel have no place.

The question of Community diplomatic support of a more verbal kind cannot be easily avoided. Arab diplomats insist that they value positions taken by the Nine more highly than those of member-states separately. As Community foreign-policy making emerges from the obscurity of the political directors to the ever more frequent meetings of foreign ministers and heads of governments, a policy of tergiversation will be hard to follow. This is shown by the apparently unsolicited presence of Arab ministers at the December 1973 summit of the Nine.

So far the Community has been able to stick to positions which had the formal backing, if not of public opinion, then of that 'world opinion' which is embodied in UN resolutions. Should the US publicly harden its attitude towards Israel in the course of what must be ,at least to some extent, an enforced settlement of the Arab-Israel dispute, the Community may be spared worse humiliations than those already suffered (and the same applies to Japan). In all likelihood, however, the next moment of truth will be the issue of Jerusalem; and Saudi Arabia, the leader of the oil coalition, feels strongly about it. No American administration (and few European governments) could accommodate Arab demands in this respect.

## The issue of Western solidarity

Many of the problems connected with EEC energy policy and oil diplomacy are raised in the context of a joint Western approach. The following considerations argue for a joint approach by the industrial countries to the challenge posed by Arab policy:

(a) competition for Arab goodwill drives up the price of oil;
(b) a joint and firm foreign policy stance is the only effective answer to escalating Arab demands;
(c) in times of boycott an agreed policy of allocation of available supplies is the only alternative to competitive outbidding;
(d) long-term solutions to the energy problem can best be found by a rational use of scarce financial, capital and technical resources;
(e) the North American continent contains very significant reserves of hydro-carbons (coal, shale, tarsand) which could be developed for mutual profit;
(f) the consequences for world economic and monetary relations of high oil prices require a joint approach by the key industrialised countries.
The general case for cooperation was well put in President Nixon's letter of invitation to the consumer countries' meeting on 11 February 1974:

> Developments in the international energy situation have brought consumer and producer nations to an historic crossroad. The world's nations face a fundamental choice that can profoundly affect the structure of international political and economic relations for the remainder of this century. Today the energy situation threatens to unleash political and economic forces that could cause severe and irreparable damage to the prosperity and stability of the world. Two roads lie before us. We can go our own separate ways, with the prospect of progressive division, the erosion of vital interdependence, and increasing political and economic conflict; or we can work in concert, developing enlightened unity and cooperation for the benefit of all making producer and consumer countries alike.

### *Different time perspectives*

At the best of times, one of the principal handicaps for enlightened action by governments is the predominance of short-term over long-term considerations. In the field of energy, the long-term begins in a matter of months as far as the international economy is concerned, but the short-term is so desperate that it is bound to prevail.

In the very short run, as has been suggested above, different diplomatic postures between the US of the one hand, and Japan and Europe on the other are more efficient than a common showdown. They do not significantly weaken the American negotiating stance in the Middle East (though the US government is highly irritated that it has been weakened at all). They also avoid the choice between a collapse of our economies and armed intervention in the Middle East. The process of concluding the long-term barter deals described above has led to an immediate improvement in the allocation of oil to the countries involved; this probably meant that the total of internationally traded oil has increased as well.

In the medium and long-term, Europe and Japan are likely to be outbid by the United States in a strictly competitive situation. Not only does the US have a broader range of economic and political services to offer than any of the other major consumers, but it will eventually be able to pay almost any price for imported oil. For as the US strategy of self-sufficiency by 1983 progresses, imported quantities will have an ever decreasing impact on total energy costs.[16]

But barter sales as such raise important questions of principle for the international economic order. It can be argued that such sales have a built-in guarantee of stable real prices, since unilateral price changes of one party can be reciprocated by a similar action by the other party. But if growing proportions of the balance of payments are managed in this way (and with capital flows equally managed) the assumptions of a liberal world monetary system are greatly weakened. Equally, those of a liberal world trading system for two reasons:

1 the goods specified in barter deals are usually those in short supply in world markets: scarce investment goods, and such commodities such as steel and cement;

2 to the extent that investment goods which give rise to export industries are involved, re-export agreements will form part of the deal. This, incidentally, may lead either to significant breaks in the Community common trade policy, or a Community involvement in the barter deals themselves. Ultimately, accommodation to economic demands made especially by Iran, Algeria, and Saudi Arabia, involves fundamental choices of industrial policy in the largest sense: the deliberate and agreed transfer of industries from the North to the South.

In this context, the differing time scales of the oil problem for the US on the one hand, and Europe and Japan on the other, come into play. US officials stress the need to find ways of encouraging production, to counter the attractions of letting oil appreciate 'in the ground'. But they think of it as a relatively short-term problem which can essentially be solved through politically and economically attractive investment opportunities for the new oil revenues of the producers. Europe, however, must calculate in terms of decades. Nothing short of a tight web of mutual interdependence on a broad basis can ensure long-term security of supply. This interdependence is based on an exchange of petroleum- and energy-intensive products for capital goods and services. In order to achieve it, the Community will have to accommodate its style of 'trade policy' to that preferred by its prospective partners. That style includes a preference for contracts over the free play of market forces, and hence a further derogation from the liberal, GATT system on which we continue to place our hopes for Western harmony.

*The coal alternative*

There is of course, a major alternative/source of long-term supplies: the immense hydro-carbon reserves of the United States. Certainly, every effort should be made for Western cooperation in know-how and investment to develop the US and Canadian reserves as soon as possible. This is an attractive policy, if only to reduce pressure on the international oil market generated by US requirements. But at present it seems difficult to conceive that the US will slow down its plans for self-sufficiency by the early 1980s through a significant increase of its exports, in the first instance coal, and later oil derived from shale, to European (and Japanese) consumers. Moreover, a democratic government like that in the US is not entirely sovereign in the matter of insuring long-term supplies: as the example of the Alaska pipeline has shown, the courts, and the environmental lobbies which initiate litigation, create serious uncertainties.

Assuming that Europeans converted a significant number of power stations to the use of imported coal, and began to produce synthetic oil and gas from such coal, the ensuing US monopoly power to raise prices would be a constant threat. The steep rise in imported coal prices of recent years giving US producers scarcity rents not unlike those levied by OPEC, and the experience of the sudden increase in the price of enriched uranium by the US government as the monopoly supplier are cases in point. Obviously, European governments and/or utilities will seek to participate (i.e. invest) in possible export-related developments of coal production, transformation, and transport in order to avoid a purely seller-customer relationship. Investment participation was also a feature in the ill-fated 1972 US proposals for new enriched uranium contracts. But the formula of advance payments chosen does not satisfy the control requirements.

Nevertheless, American coal is the one alternative fossil fuel in the West which can be developed most quickly. Although it can not significantly affect Europe's dependence on Arab oil by itself, it could be one of a number of measures which together would make a difference.

Even more significant is the potential importance of the relative US wealth in indigenous resources in times of scarcity. Secretary of State Kissinger's generous offer, made to the consumer nations assembled in Washington on February 11 may not be taken up owing to the churlish response given by one of the potential beneficiaries, but it deserves to be quoted:

> The United States declares its willingness to share available energy in times of emergency or prolonged shortages. We would be prepared to allocate an agreed portion or our total petroleum supply provided other consuming countries with indigenous production do likewise. As we move toward self-sufficiency, our ability for sharing would of course increase. Building on the earlier work done in the OECD, definite recommendations should be submitted to governments including:
> - a sharing formula;
> - criteria to determine when a supply shortage exists;
> - a mechanism which would implement and terminate the sharing arrangement; and
> - complementary programs such as stockpiling and standby rationing schemes.

The last-mentioned elements are of course not so much technical as political in nature. Accepting US aid would imply solidarity on the issue which caused the supply crisis. Since such solidarity could vary according to the issue, it might be useful to work out a number of different schemes beforehand. They could be matched with the diplomatic realities at the time the next crisis occurs. The unwillingness of one member country of the Community to go along at all, may, however, turn the US offer into a present and future divisive element for the Community. One recalls Mr Kissinger's earlier offer of oil to the Netherlands as a reward for its political stance over Israel. The emergence of an Anglo/German/US coalition willing to press for lower oil prices as opposed to a policy of accommodation also shows that a Community solidarity which limits itself to rhetoric could lose out against the more solid advantages which some member-states may find in Atlantic ties, which thus would not complement Community policy, but replace it. Given the close interrelationship between energy policy and ultimately all progress in Community development, such a trend has far-reaching implications. Exactly the same general point applies to cooperation in R & D on long-term solutions like advanced nuclear system.

*Common monetary management*

The main area of joint Western action probably lies in the field of monetary management. It is the West's collective system which is going to be affected most strongly. It will have potentially grave effects on employment and inflation – the two variables of economic management on which governments are judged above all. One approach which has been tried, and has failed, is that of understanding among governments[17] on the principle of moderation in seeking to correct current account balance of payments deficits either by deflation (which hurts the export markets of others) or by aggressive export drives (e.g. through a devalued currency) which does the same.

Theoretically, the general interest is best served by such moderation. In the present conditions, however, no single power is willing to suffer economic damage in the uncertain expectation that moderation will be rewarded by equivalent action by others. Moreover, mere understandings are usually based on principles which are to be followed by everyone. However, very different lines of conduct, provided these are agreed to, may be more likely to provide optimum and realistic solutions.

## Possible approaches

In order to give concrete expression to the interdependence of both the general and the particular interest, and to allow differentiated but concrete policy commitments by the principal participants of the international economic system, a body like Working Party 3 of the OECD might be charged to establish a five-year plan for balance-of-payments equilibria. It should take into account, for instance, the expected improvement in the British and US balances as domestic oil resources are developed, the different reserve holdings of Germany and Italy, the relative adaptive capacities of the French and Japanese economies, etc. As a counterpart to refraining from beggar-my-neighbour policies, countries would receive assurance on similar action by others. In addition, they would get specific undertakings on either official credits or the management of long-term capital flows to benefit those countries for whom medium improvement on current account seems excluded (e.g. through undertakings on interest rate differentials). A package which included all these diverse elements simultaneously would be a more solid incentive for moderation than a sectorial approach. Some seemingly insoluble problems, like that of the dollar overhang, could find a solution in a planned, rather than rule-based, approach to international adjustment in a period of exceptional dangers to the world economy.

Such understandings would also improve possibilities of common Western approaches to the OPEC governments regarding the management of enormous liquidities produced by the recent price rises. It is thus conceivable that some of the annual $70 billion or so would be placed in a common fund, which would issue high interest bonds guaranteed against exchange rate losses.

These funds could then be re-lent (invested), in a deliberate fashion, to those countries, whose economic collapse threatens world prosperity as a whole. As an intermediary between OPEC governments and firms, such a fund would also help to solve the problem of foreign government ownership of significant shares of national wealth. Furthermore, such a fund could have a 'soft loan window' for aid to developing countries, though additional real transfers from both oil producers and industrialized countries are unavoidable if the bankruptcy of resource-poor LDCs is to be avoided. Such 'burden-sharing' directly involves the preservation of markets and hence employment. For the industrialized countries, it is only feasible within a broad context of economic cooperation such as suggested above.

To conclude, this point can be made in a more general way: there is no hope of agreement either within the Community, or in the Western world, or between it and the oil producers, if problems are tackled one by one. It is a fact that interests diverge on every single issue. It is also a fact that global interdependence will cancel out gains made by unilateral action, but that the sum of such actions would result in a significant decrease in welfare and security. In order to move the notion of interdependence from the theoretical to the political level, a series of very comprehensive negotiations seems to be required. Their result ought to be new international institutions charged with the management of the new, more complex world economy. For the Community, this probably means a choice between a real European government or joining a reinforced Atlantic system in dispersed fashion. On a global level, the short-cut to the UN level proposed by France will certainly not be sufficient to create a more disciplined international system.

## Notes

1 And a residual capacity, now probably gone for good, of starving non-compliant countries of outlets: Iran in the 1950s, Iraq in the early 1970s.

2 In Kuwait, with 51 per cent participation in capital and taxes on the rest of production, the government receives about 85 per cent of the benefits of oil production, and the companies 15 per cent.

3 One objection to the talk of US majors is of course that Shell and BP are European (not to mention CFP). But both, in terms of capital, markets, and joint consortia are closely linked to US companies.

4 It must be noted that for the immediate situation of spring 1974 the Commission did not go so far as to suggest a 'sharing of oil', but preferred as a practical alternative to set common standards for curtailing consumption, which, together with a common system of export licensing to third countries

and the abolition of such licensing within the Community would have an equivalent effect.

[5] A cartel of companies for oil products is inevitable, if companies want to realise the projects upstream which they are no longer able to make downstream. The question is therefore only which form it will take.

[6] Each government could set prices 10 per cent above or below the orientation price for each product, so that price relationships among products could vary nationally to reflect different industrial priorities.

[7] Translated from 'Notwendige Fortschritte auf dem Gebiet der Gemeinschaftlichen Energiepolitik', Bulletin der Europäischen Gemeinschaften, Beilagen 11/72.

[8] Idem.

[9] A milder form of export licensing on oil products, designed to allow the Commission to gather information forms part of the latest (January 1974) proposals.

[10] The UK, Belgium, Italy and Holland have taken powers to control exports of refined products, not in order to disrupt traditional flows but to prevent sudden 'distortions of trade'. *Financial Times*, 11 December 1973.

[11] *An Nahar*, 4 Dec. 1974.

[12] According to the *Financial Times* of 2 January 1974 Britain was said to have concluded an agreement to furnish 'modern weapons' in addition to civilian aid in exchange for 30 million tons of crude a year for 10 years, while France is said to have agreed to build a 'sophisticated' arms industry in Libya in return for long-term petroleum contracts. (*Orient Pétrole* no. 118, Dec. 1973, p. 5). France was seeking to conclude a contract with Saudi Arabia for 800 million tons over 20 years. At the time of writing, the price of a first three–year contract already concluded is set at 93 per cent of posted prices at the time of delivery, companies are not involved in the deal, and such weapons as the AMX tank and Mirages III-E were reported to be part of the deal (*The Times*, January 8, *Le Monde*, January 9). Even Germany is said to be including arms in her dealings with the major non-Arab source of crude, Iran (*The Times*, January 9).

[13] *Orient Pétrole*, loc. cit.

[14] See François Duchêne: 'The European Community and the Uncertainties of Interdependence', in *A Nation Writ Large?* ed. M. Kohnstamm and W. Hager, Macmillan, London 1973.

[15] An example of non-civilian European support for a policy of increased Arab leadership in the Islamic world is the proposed construction by France of a Mirage assembly plant in Pakistan with financial help 'from several Gulf states' (*Le Monde*, 9 Jan. 1974). This effectively undercuts the policy of arms limitation in the subcontinent pursued by the US since 1965.

[16] The operation of this principle was demonstrated in 1972 in the purchase

of Algerian LNG by El Paso at very high prices, since the quantities involved had little impact on total costs.

[17] E.g. the meeting of the Committee of Twenty in Rome on 17 January 1974 followed by the floating of the French franc on 19 January 1974.

# The Economic and Monetary Implications of the Oil Crisis

*by Guy de Carmoy*

The rapid increase in oil consumption in all the industrial countries, the stepped-up oil imports to the United States, the steep rise in the price of crude, the participation in or nationalization of the international oil companies by the oil-producing countries, the reluctance of some of these countries to meet ever-increasing demands – such are the factors of the present oil crisis. The continuation of these trends over succeeding years would lead to a major balance-of-payments crisis with serious economic and monetary implications, especially for the industrial countries. It is necessary, therefore, to assess the changes in the balance of payments of the oil-producing and the oil-importing countries that are likely to take place until 1980 in order to analyse the ways and means of correcting the imbalance of the suppliers and the purchasers.

## Changes in the pattern of the balance of payments

Oil is the largest traded commodity and the increase in oil trade has brought considerable change in the balance-of-payments pattern of the countries concerned. The operations linked to oil affect the importing countries not only in their trade balance but also in the balance of services (taxes, royalties, freight, consulting), and in the capital balance (investments in upstream operations by the international companies). The oil-exporting countries register return flows in the form of purchases of consumer goods and equipment goods and in portfolio investments and short-term deposits.

Detailed statistics broken down by major items and by country are lacking for the balance of services and for private overseas investment (with the exception of those of the United States). Therefore, analysis of balance-of-payments change related to oil must rely mainly on trade statistics. These statistics should be considered from the point of view of imports of energy and the trade balance between importing and exporting countries. During the 1960s, the United States remained practically self-sufficient in energy whilst Western Europe and Japan drastically increased their imports of oil.

Between 1970 and 1972 the cost of energy imports has risen as follows in billion of dollars:

TABLE 13

| | United States | OECD Europe | Japan |
|---|---|---|---|
| Energy imports | | | |
| 1970 | 1·7 | 11·2 | 3·3 |
| 1972* | 2·9 | 16·9† | 4·8 |
| Oil imports | | | |
| 1970 | 1·4 | 9·8 | 2·2 |
| 1972* | 2·4 | 13·7† | 3·6 |
| Oil imports as percentage of total imports | | | |
| 1970 | 4·7 | 7·3 | 13·9 |
| 1972 | 5·2 | 8·6 | 20·6 |

* 1st semester on an annual basis
† Estimate.
Source: OECD Trade by Commodities, Jan.–Jun. 1972.

The rise in the cost of oil imports is due to an increase both in quantities and in prices. The oil-producing countries account for over one-half of the increase in prices due to their higher fiscal income between the 1971 Teheran and Tripoli and mid-1973 agreements, whilst the rest is related to an imbalance between import demand and export capacity.[1]

The bargaining power of the oil-producing countries in price fixing and the use of their oil reserves (i.e. the volume of authorized exports) has become much stronger as a result of nationalization of the assets of the international oil companies (in Algeria, Iraq, Iran and to a large extent, Libya) and of participation in these assets (in Saudi Arabia and in the Sheikdoms). Another new factor is the emergence of the United States as a major importer. Her imports of oil have almost doubled in two years and she will be competing with Western Europe and Japan in tapping reserves from the Middle East.

The trade balance between the oil-importing and the oil-exporting countries has evolved as follows since 1970, in billion dollars.

The trade balance of the United States with the Middle East is still running a surplus because of arms sales. The deficit of Western Europe and Japan with the Middle East is increasing fast. Western Europe is running a deficit with North Africa as well. For geographical reasons she is almost the sole importer from this area.

The question arises of how the importing countries will adjust their trade

TABLE 14

| Trade Balance | United States* | OECD Europe | Japan |
|---|---|---|---|
| (a) With the Middle East | | | |
| 1970 | +0·6 | —3 | —1·7 |
| 1972 | +1·2 | —5·4 | —2·4 |
| (b) With North Africa | | | |
| 1970 | +0·1 | —1·5 | +0·1 |
| 1972 | +0·2 | —1·8 | +0·1 |
| Total | | | |
| 1970 | +0·7 | —4·5 | —1·6 |
| 1972 | +1·4 | —7·2 | —2·3 |

* US trade balances (f.o.b.–f.o.b.)
Source: OECD, Overall Trade by Countries, Series A, June 1973

deficit in energy. One method is to build up surpluses with other trading partners. In this respect, the devaluation of the dollar *vis-à-vis* the European currencies (by an average of some 25–30 per cent) and the yen (40 per cent) will increase the competitive position of American exports. The traditional European trade surplus *vis-à-vis* the United States disappeared in 1972, and the large Japanese surplus *vis-à-vis* the United States is expected to be reduced by half in 1973.

**Balance of payments prospects for 1980**

According to the OECD,[2] oil imports in 1980 will amount to 934m. t.o.e. for Western Europe, 400m. t.o.e. for North America and 464m. t.o.e. for Japan, representing respectively 53 per cent, 15 per cent and 73 per cent of the total primary energy requirements of the three zones.[3] These estimates are based on the assumptions that the industrial countries will undergo economic growth rates somewhat similar to those of the 1960s and will therefore increase in almost the same proportion their rate of total energy consumption. They also assume that the supply of oil will come from the same group of countries and that rising prices will not slow down the use of energy. The question is whether the export capacity of the producing countries and trends in prices will allow the importing countries to satisfy such projected import requirements.

Because of the lead time for the development of other sources of oil (Alaska, Canada, Siberia, off-shore drilling in deeper waters, extraction of oil from bituminous shale and asphaltic sands, etc.) and other forms of energy (nuclear power plants), the extra supply of crude will have to be delivered by the present suppliers. Amongst them, those who are able to step up their production (assuming they are willing to do so) without depleting their reserves over a period of several decades are the countries situated around the Persian Gulf (Iran, Iraq, Abu Dhabi and above all Saudi Arabia). The geographical concentration of a large part of the world's proven reserves in the Middle East (54·2 per cent) gives these countries a strong bargaining power.

The contractual system for fixing the price of crude oil which had been established by the Teheran and Tripoli agreements in 1971, and revised so as to take into account the depreciation of the dollar and of other major currencies, broke down after the 1973 Arab–Israeli war. On 1 October 1973, the posted prices of crude oil were in the range of \$3/bl. for the Gulf countries and \$5/bl. for Libya. They were increased twice, on 16 October and 23 October 1973, their present level being around \$11·6/bl. for the Gulf countries and \$18·7 for Libya. These figures correspond to market prices of around \$8 and \$13·3. The prices reached at tenders arranged by the producing countries for the crude oil they own directly have reached much higher figures. Each individual producing country decides its own price.

On the basis of the quasi-quadrupling of the posted prices, the OECD has calculated that the oil import bill of the major consuming countries (USA, Western Europe and Japan) would be increased by \$50 billion in 1974. It is difficult to assess at this stage the amount of the trade surplus of the oil-producing countries with their main industrial clients. One would have to take into account the reduction in supply imposed by the producers to 'neutral' and 'unfriendly' countries and also the self-imposed restriction that some countries might decide for monetary reasons. But the overall surplus might well be in the range of \$30–40 billion in 1974. As for deliveries, several Arab countries, including Saudi Arabia, are reducing them by 5 per cent per month until Israel agrees to withdraw its troops from the territories occupied after the 1967 war.

In the circumstances, it is impossible to make reasonable forecasts as to the price/quantity mix in the forthcoming years except that prices are bound to increase and quantities are likely to be reduced. The estimates of the US Department of Commerce are therefore as good as any other for giving an idea of the magnitude of the balance-of-payments disturbances in the near future. Any increase of \$1/bl. in the cost of crude to the consuming countries at the pre-war production level means an increase in imports of \$5 billion a year for Western Europe and \$1·25 billion a year for Japan.

## Balancing the trade and payments of the oil-producing countries

Several means are available to the oil-producing countries to reduce their balance-of-payments surplus to manageable dimensions: limiting oil exports, developing imports, increasing domestic investments, expanding foreign aid and proceeding to foreign investments.

The policy chosen will depend on population density and natural resources (in oil and other commodities) of the countries concerned. Scarcely populated countries tend to limit and even reduce their output of oil to the level of their financial requirements. The more densely populated countries intend to devote a sizeable part of their oil reserves to imports of equipment and to domestic investments so as to develop their economy and reduce its dependence on oil in the future. They consider that oil revenues are not a truly disposable income and should help create a modern agro-industrial economy.

Libya and Kuwait have chosen the first course of action. Libya has reduced her production of oil by 25 per cent since 1970. Saudi Arabia and Abu Dhabi have the capacity to implement the same policy. An economic factor in the decision is the opportunity cost of the marginal barrel of oil – whether it is sold or remains in the ground. Today, the interest earned on a barrel sold is high, but the up-valuation of the crude in the ground, considering the trend in prices, is probably higher. The political factor for limiting production has already been mentioned. Iran and Algeria have set up ambitious development plans. Iraq, assuming political stability, will probably follow the same path. Iran, with a population of 30 million, expects to double its imports over the period of the five-year plan, 1973–77.

Imports of the oil-producing countries fall into three parts: consumer goods, equipment goods, armaments. Iran and other Gulf States are engaged in a crash armament programme. The hardware is bought from the United States, and to a lesser extent, from Britain and France. The devaluation of the dollar favours the United States, which is backing the political status quo in the Gulf area. Like all developing countries, the producers of oil in the Middle East and Africa have a structural demand for industrial equipment and technical know-how. The price elasticity of such imports is generally high. But the importing countries may offset this pattern because of the strong competition between American, European and Japanese goods and services in comparatively small markets, which are becoming buyers'markets.

The imported equipment will help the oil-producing countries to expand their activities in the oil business. Thanks to nationalization and participation, the national oil companies will become more and more involved in downstream operations such as transportation, refineries, petro-chemicals and fertilizer plants. The Shah of Iran expects the West to buy oil finished products from his country.[4] Such a flow of trade would not alleviate but aggravate the trade balance between sellers and buyers of oil. Products and fertilizers should preferably be sold, once the domestic markets are being served, to neighbouring developing countries. Another move now under consideration would involve attracting some energy-consuming capital intensive industries to the oil-producing countries, such as steel and aluminium smelting.

Some of the oil-producing countries are already devoting a part of their oil revenues to help other Arab or Moslem countries. Such is the case for Saudi Arabia, Kuwait, Abu Dhabi and Libya. Egypt is the largest recipient of this aid. The extension of such aid to countries neither Arab or Moslem may be limited by lack of an ideological motive. A possibility to be explored would be to induce the oil producers to accept that a part of their oil revenues should be paid by the industrial countries in the form of World Bank or regional development bank bonds.

The last possibility of reducing the surplus is already used to a certain extent. Several London and Continental banks are entrusted with the management of part of the oil revenues. The question is whether much larger amounts of revenues could be invested either in downstream operations in the oil industry (as the Saudi Oil Minister proposed in 1972 to the United States) or in other major business ventures in the industrial countries. On the first count, the national oil companies in the Middle East and Africa could become the partners of the international oil companies for their operations in the industrial countries. On the second count, the agents of the oil-producing countries could expand their direct or portfolio investments through purchases in stock markets. The dimensions of the New York and Tokyo (after the revaluation of the yen) markets are such that sizeable foreign investments could be made before becoming politically dangerous for the home country. On the other hand, Arab authorities have made clear that no discriminatory restrictions should be imposed on their prospective investments.[5] The amount of capital likely to be accumulated by the oil producers might lead at the end of the decade to the setting up of a financial market somewhere in the Middle East.

The oil-producing countries have a great flexibility in the choice of the means of balancing their external accounts and a strong leverage *vis-à-vis* the oil-consuming countries, i.e. the threat of reducing the extraction of oil. The three key countries in this respect because of their productive capacity and reserves are Iran, Saudi Arabia, and Kuwait. The only way in which the industrial countries can contribute to the balancing of the accounts of the producer countries is through the acceptance of foreign investments – short of measures on the domestic front which are discussed below.

## Balancing the trade and payments of the oil-consuming countries

Of the four economic objectives of the major industrial countries – growth, full employment, stability and external equilibrium – priority has been generally given to growth, and substantial growth records have been registered, thanks inter alia to the availability of increasing quantities of cheap energy. These countries are suddenly faced with high cost energy and risks of shortages. Their main political concern, in their present plight, is to maintain the possibilities of economic growth. Unable to change the trend in prices, they try (a) to induce the producing countries to supply ever greater quantities of oil, and (b) as a matter of security to promote the accelerated development of oil-fields in 'safer' areas and higher cost alternative fuels. The drain of oil imports on foreign-exchange reserves might be offset in part by an export drive. As a last resort, the industrial countries will consider, reluctantly, the reduction in total energy demand which would entail a reduction in the growth rate. To summarize, the industrial countries should engage in an export policy, an energy-oriented investment policy and a policy of energy consumption limitation. The question then arises of the feasibility of these policies – subsequently or jointly – in conjunction with the main economic objectives mentioned above.

### *Policies*

#### EXPORTS

The limits of an export drive of equipment goods to the oil-producing countries have already been mentioned; the potential market, though bound to enlarge, is relatively small. The competition will be fierce, as exemplified by the Suez pipeline project, which the Americans with a cheap dollar are about to take over from the French and Germans. The oil-producing countries will be in a position to choose according to the best mix of price and quality. Building a large trade surplus with the underdeveloped countries is not a commendable goal at a time when the economic gap between the rich and the poor countries is widening. Spreading aid money to developing countries for them to channel back into world trade should fall on the 'new rich', i.e. the suppliers of oil.

#### INVESTMENTS

Planning and implementing a sound energy investment policy will be a great challenge to the industrial countries. The scope of such a policy is very large. It covers all the existing industrial branches: oil, natural gas, coal, conventional and nuclear electricity. The basic goal is to reduce dependence on the Middle East oil suppliers. The oil companies will have to expand their exploration, drilling and transportation activities in areas considered politically safe but involving harder physical and geological conditions. The utilities will have to increase the number and size of nuclear power plants. Comprehensive R & D programmes will be required to promote the production and marketing of untapped resources (shale-oil, tar sands), to develop new processes (coal gasification) and to draw on renewable sources (solar energy). Lastly, all new investments in the field of energy will have to take into consideration environmental problems.

The volume of investments will be considerable. It has been estimated before the present crisis that the capital requirements of the larger American oil companies over the 1970s would amount to $350 billion.[6] The requirements of the European companies have been estimated to be $150 billion, and a simulation game has shown that if the European oil companies passed on to the consumer of petroleum products no more than the increase in the price of crude they would make no profits after a couple of years and would be obliged to borrow $80 billion per year on the financial markets. The recourse of all the sectors of energy in Europe to the markets would have to be increased from 5 per cent of public issues to 13 or 14 per cent. Can such large amounts of capital be raised in the countries concerned? And what of the location of these investments? The bulk of the money will be spent on the national territory but a sizeable part, especially in the oil sector, will be spent overseas with a possible drain on the capital account of the balance of payments. These considerations should lead the industrial countries to accept some of the requests of the oil-producing countries concerning their participation in business activities in the United States, Western Europe and Japan, either in the form of joint ventures (e.g., in downstream oil operations) or in sizeable portfolio investments.

### CONSUMPTION LIMITATION

Industrial countries have been wasting energy. They considered the resources unlimited and ignored the political risks of shortage. They now have to become thrifty. One of the obvious means is higher prices, though the price elasticity of energy is low at present levels. This would probably change anyway with the much higher energy prices to be expected. A move to compensate price rises by a reduction in taxes would be counterproductive. Economies in energy should be applied to the four main users: industry, transportation, domestic use and production of electricity.

High-energy-consuming industries should be carefully scanned. Are all plastic materials extracted from oil indispensable? Could not the uses of aluminium be reduced? Smelting of non-ferrous metals should be located only on hydro-electric sites consuming renewable energy. Recycling scrap metals and recuperation of paper should be given special incentives. Prestige lighting in retail trades should be drastically cut. Large savings in the industrial use of energy can be expected with proper incentives over the next ten years.

The private car is largely responsible for the waste of energy in transportation. The proportion of Net Energy Input taken by cars is 16·1 per cent in the United States, and 9·4 per cent in Europe. The proportion of oil consumption by cars is respectively 33·3 per cent and 17·3 per cent. But the energy efficiency of the various passenger transport systems expressed in passenger-miles/gallon in the United States varies as follows: large car 8, small car 40, commuter train 120, microbus 360.[8] This points to the energy-saving value of collective transportation systems – and also of the bicycle.

Thermal insulation of houses and collective heating in urban districts are two obvious means of reducing domestic energy consumption. Utilities industries are not always interested in efficiency. They tend to reduce the price of energy so as to satisfy the market. They should be induced to substitute progressive for degressive tariffs.

Conversion of primary energy in electricity involves a considerable loss of power. We should improve thermal output of power plants and perhaps reconsider the trend toward increasing the proportion of secondary energy consumed out of total energy.

To summarize, a systematic drive in energy consumption limitation would amount to a new industrial and social revolution. But such a drive would probably constitute a strong argument in favour of the industrial countries in the negotiations with the oil-producing countries.

*Feasibility*

The policies suggested are bound to have an impact on the domestic economies of the industrial countries, on their external trade and payments and on their currencies. This impact should be assessed, especially from the standpoint of compatibility.

DOMESTIC ACTIVITIES

The formidable need for investments in the energy sector, if it is not to be met by domestic inflation, will require a shift in the uses of Gross National Product from private consumption to gross fixed capital investment. Such a shift may be opposed by the population, who have been encouraged to consume more and are asking for better collective equipment.

Assuming the required amount of capital resources can be raised through the usual channels, the allocation of a very large share to the energy sectors may entail restrictions in investments in other sectors such as housing, consumer goods industries, etc., and face governments with difficult economic options. For instance, the export industries may be exposed to a shortage of capital.

Fighting against waste of energy will have positive effects on some industrial costs. On the other hand, the limitation of the production and use of the private car, which is certainly the largest chunk in an energy-saving drive, might cause serious unemployment problems. The part of the labour force employed directly or indirectly in connection with the motorcar is estimated at 20–30 per cent in the United States and 15–20 per cent in Europe[9].

The combination of more investments in capital intensive industries for the acquisition of a highly expensive commodity (energy) and fewer investments in labour intensive industries (consumer goods, motorcars), if not carefully planned, will cause economic disruptions. The reduction in the rate of growth of the economy as a whole is a distinct possibility.

Living in a community with energy rationing will bring considerable change in the work and leisure of the population. Urban and country life will have to be organized on different bases. All activities connected with energy will have to be reconsidered from the point of view of the husbanding of resources. An overall planning of the economy is unavoidable. Social and political structures will be exposed to severe stresses.

### TRADE AND PAYMENTS

The debit side of the trade balance is, of course, dependent on the price-quantity relation of imported oil. Rationing of oil will stabilize or reduce the debit. On the credit side, the volume of exports will depend on effective marketing by the competing industrial countries. Considering the unfavourable terms of trade of the industrial countries for oil (a seller's market) and for manufactured goods (a buyer's market) and the political difficulties of imposing drastic oil consumption limitations, the deficit in the trade balance is bound to increase.

On the debit side of the long-term capital balance, one should list the overseas investments of the industrial countries in oil and natural gas research, production and transportation, the bulk of these investments being located outside the Middle East and North Africa. On the credit side, one should mention the investments in oil or in other activities of the oil-producing countries by the industrial countries in so far as the latter authorize them. Obviously, the debits will surpass the credits.

The best way to prevent an intolerable increase in the overall balance of payments of the industrial countries is to limit the energy consumption.

### CURRENCIES

The industrial countries will be raising a considerable amount of investment capital at the very time when they are exposed to increasing deficits in their basic balance of payments. Such a situation leads to domestic inflation and currency depreciation. It is not compatible with convertibility. Sooner or later, the countries will have to adopt adjustment measures in the form of import restrictions (not only on fuel but on a number of non-essential goods), tariffs and border taxes. They will also have to alter the existing exchange rates in an exchange-control system. With a large share of fuels in the total value of imports, the rate of alteration in the par values might be very high indeed. Devalued currencies will further raise the price of imported oil. The industrial countries are already exposed to a serious monetary crisis. A second oil-induced monetary crisis might bring the destruction of a large portion of the capital they accumulated over more than a century. The dilemma is between a runaway inflation, which would generate massive unemployment, and a curtailment of oil imports, which would involve some sacrifices to the consumer, but much less to the wage earner.

### THE SITUATION BY AREA AND COUNTRY

The industrial countries are not likely to be affected in the same way by the energy crisis. In all respects, the situation of the United States is favourable. The external dependence is smaller percentage-wise than that of Western Europe and Japan. The United States is in the best position in terms of domestic natural resources, technological progress, the capacity to raise capital, the scope of activities of the oil companies, the political and military influence over the oil-producing countries, the launching and the means of implementing a long-term energy policy. The dollar devaluation has improved the competitive position of her exports *vis-à-vis* those of the other industrial countries.

Japan has the greatest external dependence. She has also undertaken a long-term oil policy. She has mastered the technology of nuclear reactors. The very high rate of investment and low rate of consumption in the use of her Gross National Product give her flexibility in the allocation of capital resources. An ambitious environment policy is being started. But the Japanese energy consumption pattern is such that any oil shortage will have a direct impact on industrial activity.

Western Europe is presently less dependent on external sources of energy than Japan in terms of percentage, though more dependent than Japan and the United States in absolute terms. The North Sea oil resources are an asset, the importance of which it is difficult to assess at present. But it is already clear that Norway and Britain will be in a very strong position. West Germany has an efficient nuclear industry. There is no such thing as a common energy policy at this stage. The European Economic Community has not even realized a common market for energy. The member countries are each playing their game single-handedly. As energy is upstream in the economic circuit, it would be contradictory in a time of shortage to practice national energy policies upstream and to endeavour to engage in a community industrial policy downstream.

### THE TIME FACTOR

There is no real substitute for Middle East oil over the next 10–15 years. During that span of time, industrial countries will undergo a structural deficit in energy. They will have to use the present sources of fossil fuels because of the lead time required for finding oil elsewhere and for making serious progress in R & D in the various energy sectors. The nuclear contribution will be very small until 1980–85.

The United States will dispose of Alaskan oil before 1980. She can exploit on a large scale, and in spite of serious land disturbance problems, its open-shaft coal mines and its considerable oil-shale resources – the latter at around $6/bl. She has engaged in a crash $10 billion R & D programme. Through energy saving and rationing she can dispense now with Middle East oil. In ten years' time, she may become a net exporter of energy so that world prices would be tied to the United States' prices. Western Europe will remain dependent on overseas supplies in the 1980s. Though only a fraction of the continental shelf is being explored, it is unlikely that the North Sea will supply her needs for oil. Japan's situation will depend on the possibility of finding fossil fuels in South East Asia.

## *Recommendations*

The correlation between economic activity and energy supply is indisputable. Thus, the industrial countries and especially Western Europe and Japan may soon be exposed either to unbearable balance-of-payments deficits or to unacceptable unemployment. But corrective actions take time, whether geared at exploiting new energy sources or at proceeding to shifts in the use of scarce resources by private investments and government spending. Therefore, action should be taken now. The following broad recommendations should serve as guidelines.

### FACING THE FACTS

The first recommendation is to ask governments to acknowledge publicly the hard facts, i.e.:

1 The industrial countries have to wage an economic war for the supply and fair distribution of energy.

2 This war has to be waged against themselves because of the right of all states, recognized by a 1966 Resolution of the General Assembly of the United Nations, to dispose of their natural resources for the benefit of their own development.

3 Energy has become a scarce resource that domestic and industrial users cannot afford to waste.

4 A limitation in energy consumption is preferable to a runaway inflation.

5 The shortage of energy means the end of affluence and the consumer society and ther return to some sort of austerity.
6 Informing the public at large of the forthcoming state of emergency is a pre-condition to preparing the population for unavoidable economic changes.

### COUPLING ENERGY AND ENVIRONMENT POLICIES

The second recommendation is to couple energy policy with environmental policy. The population will accept sacrifices in the use of the private car if they realize that large public funds are allocated to the improvement in the quality of life. Both policies are complementary. Reducing the use of cars will reduce air and noise pollution. New investments in refineries and power plants will be acceptable if efficient measures are imposed to prevent nuisances.

### INTERNATIONAL COOPERATION

The third recommendation concerns international cooperation (a) between oil-consuming countries themselves, and (b) between oil-consuming countries and oil-producing countries.

On the consumer side, continuous exchange of views to adopt common broad policy lines would be beneficial on a number of subjects: the volume of the allocation of energy supplies in case of emergency, the criteria for rationing energy, the study of the relation between energy consumption and total demand, the ways of financing world-wide oil exploration, the technology and methods for developing alternative energy sources, the setting-up of anti-pollution standards, the criteria for accepting investments from the oil-producing countries in the oil-consuming countries. Some of these questions would, of course, have to be discussed beforehand within the EEC in the framework of a future energy common market.

The elaboration of ground rules by the industrial countries would help to prepare for the continuous negotiations which are bound to take place between buyers and suppliers of oil, and which should aim at developing more solidarity between them. Country-to-country negotiations will substitute for discussions between the international oil companies and the host governments for a variety of reasons such as nationalization, participation, cooperation in industrial vertures, trade agreements linked to the delivery of oil – in short, issues of a political character.

## Notes

1 J. E. Hartshorn, 'Oil Diplomacy: The New Approach', *The World Today*, July 1973, p.283.

2 *Oil, the Present Situation and Future Prospects*, OECD, Paris 1973.

[3] Some American sources consider that in 1980 the United States would import oil up to 25 per cent of her total energy requirements; Cf. his energy outlook, *A Summary Report of the National Petroleum Council*, Washington, December 1972.
[4] *Newsweek*, 21 May 1973.
[5] Arab Funds and International Economic Cooperation, address given by Abdlatif Y. Al Hamad, Director General of the Kuwait Fund for Arab Economic Development at INSEAD, Fontainebleau, on 20 November 1973.
[6] Chase Manhattan Bank, *Capital Investments of the World Petroleum Industry*, 1971.
[7] Compte Rendu du Colloque Franco-Allemand sur l'Energie, Rouen, Mai 1973, *Politique Etrangère*, No. 3, 1973.
[8] Gerald Leach, *The Motor-Car and Natural Resources*, OECD, Paris 1972, pp. 15, 18, 32.
[9] Gerald Leach, op. cit., p. 10.

# Document

## STATEMENT BY MR EMILE VAN LENNEP, SECRETARY–GENERAL OF THE OECD AT THE WASHINGTON ENERGY CONFERENCE ON MONDAY, 11 FEBRUARY 1974

Mr Chairman,

The problems we have met to discuss today involve complex economic and political inter-relationships with world-wide ramifications. As a result of the spectacular rise in the price of imported oil the industrialised countries are going to experience a worsening in both inflation and unemployment. The oil importing developing countries – or more particularly the poorest and most populous among them – are going to have the gravest difficulties in maintaining their painfully achieved and often inadequate economic progress. And the oil producing countries themselves – although they may not fully realise it yet – are going to face serious problems because of their divergent situations, and the need for some of them to invest the major part of their vastly increased wealth productively elsewhere in the world economy. Moreover, these specific problems are bound together in the wider question of the changing economic and political relationship between the so-called third world and the industrialised – or rich – countries.

It would take too long to cover all these questions in any detail. I will concentrate on:

First, the problems of managing the world economy in the period immediately ahead;

Second, the delicate but unavoidable questions of the price and availability of oil in the short and longer run, and,

Third, the position of the non-oil developing countries.

### Problems of economic management

In considering the problems of economic management in the period immediately ahead, it is important to recognise that we were already facing a difficult situation before the rise in oil prices. The strongest and the most synchronised boom the world has seen since the Korean War peaked out around the middle of last year. The prospect was for slower growth and continuing high rates of inflation. There was a hope, but no certainty, that inflation rates would gradually subside. The seriousness of the inflationary situation is illustrated by the fact that in 14 out of the 24 countries of OECD the rise in consumer prices in the twelve months to December exceeded 10 per cent, and in half of those it exceeded 15 per cent. Up to December, moreover, only a very small part of the rise in oil prices had worked its way through to consumers.

It was into this unsatisfactory and worrying situation in the industrialised countries that the rise in oil prices has injected a lethal combination of three unpleasant ingredients: a sharp upward push on prices; a significant contractionary impact on demand and output; and a dramatic deterioration in trade balances. Each of these ingredients is in itself familiar. What is unique is that they should occur in combination, with a suddenness and size sufficient to seriously affect internal and external equilibrium in almost all countries simultaneously.

The reasons for the peculiar nature of the problems now facing us all have already been discussed at the technical level. But I am far from convinced that they are even now fully understood. Essentially, they can all be traced back to the geological and historical oddity that so much of the world's known reserves of oil are to be found under a few countries in the Middle East, with small populations and limited potential for economic development. This probably explains why for a long time the consuming countries were able to obtain large quantities of oil at what now seem excessively low prices. It also explains why once the producing countries got together they could put up their prices so sharply without fear of retaliation. But above all, it is the fact that those few countries which are going to get the lion's share of the increased oil revenues will not be able to spend more than a small fraction on increased imports, which explains the difficulty and unique nature of the problems both we and they now face. This is why the rise in oil price is, paradoxically, both inflationary and deflationary at the same time; and why it involves such a drastic change in the structure of the world's balance of payments. It is worth noting that the magnitude of the rise in food and commodity prices other than oil over the last two years was, in quantitative terms, quite a lot larger than that for oil prices. But the difference was that the extra money received by farmers, forestry workers and mine-workers all over the world was more or less immediately spent on other things. These price rises resulting from sharply increasing demand, and supply shortages, certainly created inflationary problems. But because the extra revenues were spent there was no deflationary impact and only reasonably manageable changes in the structure of world trade and payments.

It was Minister Turner who pointed out in Rome the domestic political difficulties created by this combination of inflation and deflation. Somehow, public opinion has to be convinced of the need for redoubled efforts to reduce domestic inflation, for expansionary action to maintain employment, and for equanimity in the face of a sharp deterioration of the trade balance.

There has been much outside criticism of government for inconsistent and uncooperative action over the last few months. But it is very understandable that governments should be deeply concerned about the immediate impact on their domestic economy. First, of the possibility of a shortage of oil sufficient to create massive unemployment, and now of explosive rates of inflation combined with a slow, or even negative growth of real incomes. Moreover, it is a peculiar feature of the present situation that traditional reactions to each of its ingredients would, in present circumstances, be inappropriate. It would be normal to react to increased inflation by restraining domestic demand. In present circumstances this might only make matters worse. It would be normal to react to a deflationary impulse by expansionary monetary and fiscal policies; but in the existing situation indiscriminate or excessive expansionary action would be foolhardy. It would be normal to react to a deterioration in the trade balance by restrictive policies or measures to stimulate exports and hold back imports; but in present circumstances (and with some qualifications) this would ultimately be self-defeating.

It is quite natural that governments should think first of the economic, social and political problems in their own countries, which in some cases are difficult enough already. But the fact is that a satisfactory evolution of the world economy over the months ahead can only be achieved through joint action.

What is needed is: new and politically difficult action against domestic inflation; expansionary action carefully designed to be consistent with both the conjunctural and structural aspects of the new situation; and a cool and cooperative response to the radical change in the structure of the balance of payments. But no country can embark on such a course unless it has a reasonable assurance that others will follow suit. Now that the initial shock has worn off and the nature of the problem is more clearly understood, the time has come for concerted action.

## The price of oil in the short and longer run

I will turn now to the delicate and controversial question of the price of oil. There are two things which can be said here which should be agreed by all concerned. First, that the price of oil has been too low. Second, that it has risen too much, too fast.

The price of oil to the producers has been too low for geo-political reasons. The consuming countries have been encouraged to become too dependent on imported oil, leading to a concentration of too much economic power in too few hands. But the price of oil has also been too low for more fundamental economic reasons. It was leading to a situation in which the world as a whole was using up ultimately finite supplies of a high quality low cost energy source too quickly.

Because the price of oil has risen so fast from this low level, it has created a situation for the world economy as a whole which will be extremely difficult to handle. I have already discussed the policies needed to mitigate the damage done. But it would be an illusion to believe that these policies can be fully successful. Inflationary pressures and unemployment, we have learned in recent years, are far from being mutually exclusive; and, during the year ahead, we risk having to face what can only be termed an inflationary recession. This will not only be unpleasant for the industrialised countries; it will greatly magnify the problems of the developing countries. It will also, it must be hoped, bring home to the oil producers themselves the need to exercise their new-found power with responsibility and restraint.

Beyond the immediate question of the price of oil in the short run – but closely related to it – is the question of the right price for oil over the longer run. It is a peculiarity of energy economics that there is an enormous jump up from the production costs of oil, particularly Middle East oil, to the production costs of substantial quantities of equally clean and efficient alternative sources of energy. Since oil supplies will eventually run out, it is essential that part of this gap should be closed by price increases or subsidies. Otherwise, there will be insufficient incentive to develop these alternative energy sources against the time when they will be increasingly needed.

The price mechanism must be the essential instrument for bringing about this structural adaptation in the world energy economy. As an example of what a powerful mechanism it can be, let me give some preliminary results from the long-term energy assessment underway in the OECD. These suggest that at present prices the oil imports of the industrialised countries might, already by 1980, be only about a half of what they would otherwise have been at the old prices; that is, they would remain at roughly the 1973 level. This is because, even without special measures by the industrialised countries to conserve energy and encourage indigenous production, the spectacular rise in the price of imported oil will set in motion powerful forces reducing demand and stimulating alternative sources of supply.

The crucial question is how fast this process of adaptation and substitution should go. What is needed for the longer run is a price of oil, which is:

- high enough to discourage waste and to encourage development of alternative sources of energy
- but not so high as to overshoot the mark and lead to over-investment and waste of resources.

This is partly an economic question, which is under intensive study in many places. But it is also a political question, since the right answer depends partly on the nature of the relations which evolve between the consuming countries, and between the consuming and producing countries.

In the first place, the bargaining strength of the consuming nations will be greater the more it is clear that they have the political will to cooperate together to conserve energy and develop alternative sources of supply. It must be hoped, however, that this will lead to a cooperative relationship with the producing countries, since it would be in the interests of both parties concerned for the transition to a new energy structure to come about smoothly through agreement on the right long-term price for oil coupled with the workings of the market mechanisms. This would minimize the risk of serious misdirection of scarce resources and of excessive environmental damage. Moreover, in the event of a continued confrontation between producers and consumers, decisions would have to be taken by the consumers which would become irrevocable with the passage of time.

*Security of supplies*

This brings me to the closely related question of the security of supplies, which is really the other side of the same coin. In any normal economic relationship security of supplies depends on the fact that the consumer wants the goods and the producer needs the money. In this situation, however, what causes such concern to cunsumers is that some of the producers do not need the money – at least until some time in the fairly distant future. It is not surprising, therefore, that each consuming country should be searching for some economic, diplomatic or potential means of strengthening the security of supplies. But it is of the utmost importance to realise that ultimately the security of supplies resides, and can only reside, in the fundamental economic and political interdependence of the nations concerned.

The world's dependence on oil is at present so great that any serious interruption of supplies would have disastrous consequences on output and employment, with incalculable consequences spreading out well beyond the strictly economic sphere. But about one half of the oil imported into the OECD area comes from countries with large populations and considerable potential for economic development, which can only be realised in a favourable economic and political environment. The other half comes from countries with small populations who are going to accumulate immense financial assets in a changing world, much of which is still very poor. They, too, have a strong vested interest in a stable and prosperous world economy.

Security of supplies, like that of prices, can therefore only be assured through a cooperative approach between producers and consumers, in which both sides will not only have to be realistic about each other's legitimate interests, but also fully aware of their joint responsibilities.

What is needed is a long-term policy for diversifying the world energy economy both geographically and by source of energy. This will, however, take a long time to achieve, because of the inevitable lags in developing alternative sources. Moreover, we should realise that it is neither necessary nor indeed meaningful for most countries or groups of countries to seek complete self-sufficiency in their energy supplies.

In so far as it makes economic sense to import oil from OPEC countries, and in so far as they forego the unacceptable practice of selective embargoes and other supply restrictions, then the question would arise of giving them the right incentives to produce the oil needed and in particular:

- technical and financial assistance to speed up their economic development;
- a new range of investment outlets, providing an appropriate degree of security and yield.

### The position of the oil consuming developing countries

This brings me to the serious position which has been created for those developing countries who are not fortunate enough to possess their own supplies of oil.

Here again, I think it is important to remember the context in which the present crisis arose. Over the last two years, the developing countries have been benefiting from the surge in the demand for their exports from the industrialised countries and a rise in the prices of most primary products. But the developing countries are, of course, both exporters and importers of primary products. It has been estimated for example, that the rise in the price of food and fertilisers – prices three times those of two years ago – will alone add as much as $5 billion to the import bill of the non-oil developing countries in 1974. This is half as much as the estimated rise in their import bill for oil.

It follows that the position now facing the non-oil developing countries varies greatly, depending on the pattern of their imports and exports. Those that will be hardest hit are mainly in the Indian Sub-continent, Tropical Africa and the Central American/Caribbean Area. It is important to remember that these countries together contain some 900 million people – nearly half the population of the developing world excluding China. Most of these countries are not only the poorest in the world at present, but also have the most tenuous growth prospects for the future.

Something will have to be done to help these countries. First, however, it is important to establish where the responsibility for giving such assistance lies. If a country benefits from an improvement in its terms of trade, and in so far as this improvement reflects genuine changes in the supply and demand of the products in which it trades, this does not automatically imply an obligation on its part to indemnify those who have suffered from the changes. This would seem to me as true for oil as it is for wheat, for copper or for wool. The obligation to give aid to the poor rests on those countries fortunate enough to be rich, and has nothing to do with why they are rich.

It is, of course, true that some of the oil-producing countries are now going to become rich, although they will also need to save heavily against the day when their oil runs out. And I think there is every reason to expect that they will acknowledge the new responsibilities this imposes on them. But we must also recognise that it will take some time for them to adjust to their new position, and that, like ourselves, they will want to have the major say in the nature and destination of the assistance they give to other developing countries.

In this case, as in so much else, it is up to the countries represented in this room to give an example. First, we must do our best to avoid an economic slow-down in the industrialised countries which would seriously aggravate the problems already faced by the developing world. Second, existing developing assistance programmes must not be slowed down or reduced, and it should be recognised that the change in the structure of the balance of payments of the industrialised countries, radical as it is, does not provide a valid argument for cutting aid. Third, the developing countries that are worst hit will need special help on concessional terms to enable them to adjust their economies and balance of payments to the additional oil burden. Countries in this category account for perhaps $3 billion of the overall increased cost of oil imports. It is to be hoped that some of the oil-producing countries will join in this first-aid operation. Fourth, we should not lose sight of the fact that this new situation presents new opportunities as well as new problems. Because some of the oil producers will only be able to spend a small fraction of their current earnings, there is going to be a substantial rise in world savings. Market forces will tend to attract these savings back to the industrialised countries. But it should not be beyond our ingenuity to find ways by which part of these savings can be mobilised to accelerate economic progress throughout the developing world.

### International cooperation

Mr Chairman, up to this point I have concentrated on the issues facing the international community, rather than the mechanisms of international cooperation. This is because it is only by contributing to a proper understanding of these issues, and by promoting the common political will to handle them, that the existing international organisations can hope to help. Almost all the issues on the agenda of this conference are dealt with in the OECD, and several of them also in other international organisations. Where we have failed to make sufficient progress it is not because of technical difficulties, but more fundamentally because of political differences between the parties concerned. Mr Chairman, we must recognise where the real difficulties lie:

- It is easy to agree on the principle of conserving energy. But it is politically difficult if this involves a change in life styles, and unless all countries are seen to be taking this equally seriously;
- It may seem obvious to agree to develop conventional sources of energy, but very risky to embark on this course without a firm assurance that these high-cost supplies will not be undercut at some later date;
- It is easy to agree in principle to cooperate in research and development, but a very different matter when this in practice means handing over to other countries details of the latest technological advances;
- It is not difficult to work out the technical details of a scheme for sharing oil supplies in an emergency. But, as we have seen, political difficulties can easily prevent such a scheme from being put into operation;
- It is easy to agree that beggar-my-neighbour policies should be avoided. But it is a very different matter when it comes to setting up a practical and effective system of surveillance to prevent it happening;
- It is particularly easy to agree in principle that help should be given to the developing countries. But it is a political matter to persuade public opinion that this is essential, and that each country is accepting a fair share of the burden;
- And finally, when it comes to cooperation between consuming and producing nations, it cannot be ignored that for geographical, historical, as well as economic reasons, there are bound to be divergent interests on both sides.

Mr Chairman, the people sitting around this table have the political responsibilities in countries which together possess the world's main concentration of economic and financial strength, technological know–how, and potential sources of energy, food and other vital commodities. How that power is used will largely determine whether the present difficult situation turns out merely to have been an incident on the road to a wide sharing out of economic prosperity around the world, or develops into a crisis which could easily undo much of what has been achieved over the last 25 years.

That is why, Mr Chairman, as I said this morning, I welcome the calling of this conference, hoping that it will help the international organisations by providing the political impulse needed for them to do the job for which they were created.

# Spotlights on Inflation

**A report on a participating members meeting with an introduction by Louis Camu**

# Introduction

by Louis Camu

We bankers and economists have a very difficult task today. We belong to the happy class of experts. We are professionals who used to know exactly what we were talking about. Recently, however, things have changed, and we have become like the political scientists who freely admit that they are bewildered by what is going on in the world today. We are all afraid of taking the wrong turn in the fog.

The situation today is that nothing constitutes a more dangerous obstacle to a successful future than having had a successful past. As Dr. Kissinger said with nostalgia, we are no longer living in a world where the consequences of our failures are still manageable. We cannot even always believe the opposite of what economists tell us!

Why has the world changed from certitude to doubt, from growth to recession or crisis?

The Western world was guided and pushed ahead by the United States. Its leadership was not in question. Neo-classical economics held sway: we were living in a liberal framework based on the GATT and the IMF, a world of free trade through use of the most favoured nation clause, a world in which the monetary order was centered nominally on gold but in reality on the absolute predominance of the dollar. The system of fixed parities encouraged the development of trade. Balance of payments problems were not insolvable, nationally or internationally, within the free market mechanism. Whatever the protests within Europe, the United States remained the major force: it brought us the Marshall Plan, the OEEC, and thus the basis for more European unity in the Coal and Steel Community and the EEC—and, in their train, economic growth, international free trade, and political and social stability encouraged by improvements in the standard of living. The ensemble was based on respect of international treaties, and protected by the Bretton-Woods "Magna Carta". The international scene as a whole was dominated by the adverse relationship between the USA and the USSR: the strategy of the West, with NATO as the central organization, was one of countervailing power made possible by American nuclear superiority.

There have been changes in this picture! The position of the United States as leader of the Western world has been gravely affected. It is only a comparative reduction of American power, as the economic and financial position of the United States is still extremely strong.

Compared with Western Europe and with Japan, the economic power of the United States has certainly been somewhat reduced. For the first time this century, the United States has had in recent years significant balance of payments problems, and the imbalances in question have led to inflation and a new instability throughout the Western world. This changed situation has resulted in the destruction of the Bretton Woods monetary order, and until now the Western world has failed to conceive or agree upon a system to take its place. This raises the question: "Can the Western economic system function without a natural leader and without a natural centre of power". As professor van der Beugel, in a recent lecture, told us: "Persistent inflation is a menace to the survival of a democratic society. If it goes on for long enough, it will destabilize the political structures of our countries, thus encouraging political excesses, probably the extreme left".

Inflation is a disease that has been with us for several years. A brilliant study made by the OECD in 1970 sounded the alarm and proposed concerted action over a twelve-month period: incomes policies, restraint in budgetary expansion, control of the money supply, coordinated capital market policies. That was when the yearly rate of inflation was at a maximum of 5 per cent.

Today inflation is galloping at between 10 and 25 per cent—except in Germany—and in addition the West is affected by an unprecedented and unforeseen energy crisis.

The energy crisis is not only an example of the re-introduction of power as a visible element in international economic relations, but it also marks a rearrangement of the world power balance. And the shock has not only had its effects on price levels and on international politics, but it has also been prejudicial to social relations within countries, to production and growth, to high consumption and increased standards of living. There is no more a universally accepted law of economic relations.

We are confronted with very serious and basic questions. Inflation, scarcity, *realpolitik* in economic affairs, the protection of the welfare state leading to enormously increased government intervention, are all of these compatible with the neo-classical concept of the free market as well as with the expectation of growth to which the post-war years have accustomed us?

There is a recent example from the monetary field which illustrates this disarray. The last meeting of the IMF, the most brilliant, powerful and perspicacious gathering that the modern financial world can assemble, ended in an atmosphere of anxiety, depression and scepticism, notwithstanding the intelligent and imaginative spadework of the Committee of Twenty. The world monetary system has been allowed to break up, without any serious effort to restructure it in applying the very sensible propositions of that Committee. Earlier President Giscard d'Estaing had said that never have world monetary problems been so completely and skillfully analyzed and resolved: today no government takes account of their work.

Mr. Brezhnev has since spoken of the "profound crisis, without precedent in its force and acuity, which is being experienced by the bourgeois society of the West". He went on to say that irreversible inflation, monetary and financial upheavals, the acute energy crisis, the lowering of industrial production, recession and the growth of unemployment, all of these are the economic symptoms of the sickness of contemporary capitalism. Is it possible that Mr. Brezhnev actually believes what was said at the Fund-Bank meetings in Washington? Is so much gloom justified? But last year scepticism was the key-note.

There is an age when one knows all the questions and all the answers and also an age when one knows only the questions. I don't pretend to know all the answers. It would be too facile for the optimist to forecast the following: a consistent and successful policy in the US which would facilitate consistent policies in the other market economies; the integration and unification of Europe in spite of many disappointments; the strongest possible links between the two shores of the Atlantic Ocean and Japan; a *prise de conscience* by the Western industrial world that no single major problem stands the chance of solution without a deep sense of the interdependence of their economies; the US and the USSR will work together to secure peace and not "go it alone"; and, finally, immense sympathy for imperfections and inexhaustible patience with stupidity. These are the conditions for a return to monetary, political and social order. But the return may be by a long route.

# Controlling Inflation during Recession

by Robert V. Roosa*

The inflation now rampant across the world needs no statistical description to verify its severity. Its menacing impact is by now apparent to virtually everyone everywhere. What we want to know is whether there is something different about this inflation; what are its propelling causes; why does it go on accelerating; where might it lead; what can be done about it?

My own view is that the present worldwide inflation does have unique characteristics, both in nature and in degree, and that its causes paradoxically are at least partly rooted in the most widely heralded achievements of the post-World War II world. Effective demand has spread across the globe so rapidly that matching additional supplies of goods and services could only be wrung out of existing productive capacity at increasing real costs. Moreover, the insistance of that demand made it difficult to defer consumption in order to form more productive capital. And intensified dependence on raw materials obtainable only from controlled sources has added to the inflationary potential inherent in the revolutionary explosion of expectations and demand.

To be sure, other, more traditional and localized cyclical patterns have been superimposed on the underlying force of an inflation generated by the pressures of structural change in the world economy. Inventory cycles, housing cycles, and investment cycles, for example, have been occurring in country after country, often with remarkable parallels among countries. Those parallels, too, are partly a by-product of the great advances made in internationalizing money flows and capital markets since World War II, as the financial markets responded to the need for better servicing of that same spreading of worldwide demand.

The consequence of this present convergence of overlapping inflationary pressures can be, at least for some countries, so extreme as to produce total economic breakdown, or a surrender of democratic government and personal freedom to totalitarian regimes, or perhaps both. The processes at work are not, as I see them, naturally self-correcting; at least not rapidly enough in the modern setting to avert catastrophe. The inflationary forces can be halted, though perhaps not wholly reversed, only through action by many countries; and some of that action must probably be concerted among them.

The introduction of advanced technology will have to be stepped up through increased investment in everything from agriculture to nuclear power. To minimize duplication and waste, some of that capital formation may have to be guided by governments, or through intergovernmental arrangements. Along with

(*) Partner, Brown Brothers Harriman. Former Under Secretary of the United States Treasury.

governmental intrusion on the supply side, there may also have to be some effective form of generalized demand restraint, if not a detailed direction of demand, country by country.

To do what is needed, I now believe that the United States, at least, will have to consider whether it could develop its own "home grown" approach to some form of economic planning—which may only have to mean making more systematic and consistent the many influences which our Government already exerts on the total and the distribution of investment and production as well as on the total and the composition of demand. Whatever we try must, in any event, be designed to protect and perpetuate the conditions of open competition, price flexibility, and private ownership that characterize the market economy—the economic counterpart of democracy and individual freedom as we know them.

That is a huge order. It skirts perilously close to some of the risks of governmental regimentation and loss of freedom that it is designed to avoid. But it is a challenge for the future that the inflation of 1974 is signalling today. At President Ford's recent "Economic Summit," several participants stressed the potentialities for pulling closer together the intended influences of government spending, taxation, and debt management, along with monetary policy and the actions of our host of regulatory agencies, to help limit the present inflation. But little was said about implementation. To make a start in that direction. I want to spin out a few tentative thoughts both on how an overall policy might be evolved, and on how its various elements might be fitted into the present governmental structure. But before starting that, I should step back from these introductory remarks to look just a bit further at the characteristics, the causes, and the possible consequences of the inflation now raging around all of us.

## Characteristics of Worldwide Inflation

For the first time since the middle '30's, the economies of most countries in the world are moving in the same direction together: this time, strong inflation continues alongside weakening real expansion in most countries; then, a prolonged deflationary contraction evolved gradually into reflationary expansion. This time there is a worldwide scarcity of raw materials and general underproduction; then, there was overproduction of raw materials and a general shrinkage of demand. The grave danger is that extremes of either kind ultimately reach the same end—a breakdown in the established channels of intercourse among nations and even in the norms of political systems. That is why it is urgent now, amidst an inflation that has gained worldwide momentum and force, to try to diagnose the process as a whole, even if a spreading recession may temporarily for a few months just ahead, seem more threatening than the disintegrating effects of inflation on the normative conditions of society.

It seems to me that there are seven predominant characteristics of the present inflation. First, is the similarity of patterns among nations—not only in experiencing extreme inflation but also more recently in edging toward recession in current production and employment while prices go on rising.

Second is the almost universal weakening of monetary discipline, partly because of greater concern over the social and human costs of unemployment.

Increases of 10, 20, 30 per cent in a nation's money supply within a year have become almost commonplace, and they create an environment in which it is almost impossible for any single country, with a relatively open economy, to maintain its own independent control over financial expansion. That exposure of individual countries to the monetary weakness of others is, as I shall argue later on, further aggravated when exchange rates are floating freely.

A third distinguishing characteristic is the much more widespread prevalence of commodity speculation, aggravating upswings in prices that originate in natural or manmade limitations on the availability of agricultural or mineral products of all kinds.

The fourth new phenomenon is the enormous increase in international capital flows, not only for fixed investment but also in more liquid forms—aggregating much more now for many countries than their total international receipts and payments for goods and services. The growth of non-national or trans-national financial markets, most notably the Eurodollar markets, has provided a vehicle through which massive anticipatory movements of funds can occur, spreading inflationary impulses from country to country. Much of the traditional analysis of balance of payments adjustement among countries, and many of the criteria ordinarily used in determining, what exchange rate parities ought to be, have been turned upside down by the changed composition of international payments flows and the markets through which they may move. As a consequence, as inflation mounted, established exchange rate parities had to be abandoned. Yet the floating rates that resulted have themselves in turn become at times an engine for transmitting and aggravating inflationary impulses.

Fifth, alongside these other characteristics there has been a revolution of rising expectations across the globe, producing a "growth syndrome" in virtually all countries, large or small, and more or less developed. A wholly new dimension of pressures has built up against the available supplies of food, raw materials, and energy in the world, and against the productive capabilities of existing technology, thereby creating the structural pressure for inflation to which I have already referred.

Sixth, there is now a much stronger and more general political conviction that unemployment must be held to a minimum at all costs, leading to a tolerance for government spending beyond the prudent limits of a full employment budget in the United States and elsewhere, and almost assuring an inflation of "excess demand." At the same time, wages have developed a downside rigidity, so that the option of enlarging employment through explicit limiting of real wages does not even theoretically exist. The one-way flexibility of wages has become another relatively new ingredient of the inflationary situation.

Seventh, superimposed on all of these other factors, at the beginning of 1973, the second formal devaluation of the dollar, coming only fourteen months after the first, created an atmosphere of bewilderment and a corrosion of confidence in the structure of the world payments system. To be sure, the great differences already emerging among countries in their rates of economic change, as well as in their domestic price behavior, made the maintenance of stable parities for exchange rates as a disciplinary check on inflation virtually impossible. But the official recognition of that fact, amidst an apparent state of recurrent crisis, gave further encouragement to a worldwide inflation mentality.

## The Causal Patterns

Interlaced through these predominant characteristics of the world's inflation are a number of strands which need sorting out for attention if there is to be a basis for coping with, or counteracting, the forces that are now so powerfully in motion. To be sure, a number of the aspects of today's inflation are only manifestations, another time around, of the short cycles that rather regularly recur as undulations along the expansionary course of any country's economy and might be considered broadly self-correcting if given enough time to run. What distinguishes the current experience, though, is that corresponding phases of these short cycles are occurring at about the same time in so many countries, and are superimposed upon a strongly rising underlying trend among all of them. My own feeling is that some slackening of price increases may occur within the next few months, at least in some countries, as one or another of the short cycles reaches a downward phase. Such hopeful signs should not, however, obscure the continuing force of an underlying trend that seems to me fundamental.

What has happened, let me repeat, is that the insistence on growth, and rapid growth, has become so widespread as completely to outrun the supply capabilities of the world economy. This is not to accept the "Club of Rome's" discouraged view that the world is nearing the asymptotic limits for growth, but it is to recognize, as the grain of truth in their impressive analysis, that there is a problem of pace. Supply may not have absolute limits, but there does have to be an effective mobilization of capital, and labor and technology—within the constraints of social and environmental requirements—in order to expand the supply of the world's goods and services. And that mobilization has just not been able to keep up with the accelerating pace of worldwide demand. As a result, the economies of all of our countries have moved out along what might be visualized as the U-shaped cost curve for the world economy as a whole, passing beyond the zone of declining costs and well into the increasing cost zone.

The real costs of evoking the supplies of materials and the final mix of products now required by world demand has become, within the present useable applications of technology, increasingly costly. That is not only because the world is running through much of its more accessible supplies of raw materials, so that extractive costs increase in real terms, but also because the increasing incidence and the awareness of environmental hazards lead to increased real costs, alongside the increasing costs of social overhead in a world becoming better attuned to needs for social services of all kinds, including assistance to an ageing population as well as better access to medical care. Moreover, for the more developed economies, a pervasive shift has been underway toward a higher proportion of total activity in the service-oriented sectors. And, as real labor costs have risen, the service-oriented economies tend, by the very nature of that fact, to move into a higher cost zone.

Paralleling these underlying causal factors of inflation on the supply side, there have been comparably profound influences promoting and supporting the demand side, translating aspirations into effective buying power. The private sector has, indeed, been racing far ahead of governments in the multiplying of debt and various forms of liquidity. Financial institutions have been neglecting their traditional role in asset management to begin concentrating their efforts on managing and increasing their liabilities. Their multiplication of supplemental credit instruments has produced a great increase in the velocity of money, faster at times than the expansion of the money supply itself.

This race for growth among financial institutions has been matched by that among many business corporations, and their ingenious and often constructive elaboration of borrowing techniques has converted many of the larger corporations, including most of the multinationals, into the virtual equivalents of liquidity-creating financial institutions. These institutional changes have developed within a cumulative pattern, as each twist of the inflation screw called for larger financing to carry inventory as well as to finance fixed capital requirements.

Alongside the accelerating expansion in the nominal magnitudes of private balance sheets and earnings statements, governments have fallen prey to a revisionist version of the old, once discredited, "needs of trade" justification for deficit financing and money creation. The thesis thus gained wide credence that any increase in the money supply through the banking system, matched by additional credit extension on the part of the banks, was quite appropriate so long as it occurred in line with actual or planned growth in gross national product. The supply of near-money, or liquidity substitutes, need not be taken into account.

With government debt growing in many countries at unprecedented peacetime rates, and with private debt growing several times faster than government indebtedness, these money substitutes have so increased the velocity or rate of use at which any given money supply circulates that inflation became almost inevitable. Perhaps the efficiency of the credit markets has become so great that anything more than a modest increase in the money supply, at least at times, will only feed inflationary demand.

Moreover, alongside the growth of private debt, there has been a relative shrinkage in the equity base underlying the overall debt structure of most countries. Interest rates have ratcheted upward, well above any historically sustainable rates of return, as savers and investors have become more and more concerned with the need for an inflation hedge. They have factored an inflation cost into market interest rates on fixed interest obligations (bonds, mortgages, and savings deposits). The prices of stocks, i.e., of equities, have, partly as a consequence, stagnated. And it appears that the declining proportion of investments flowing into equities (the primary risk-bearing segment of the capital structure of a capitalist economy) is now being paralleled by a decline in the proportion of incomes allocated to saving.

Businesses, in turn, find increasing difficulty in recovering the full costs of rising inventory and even more difficulty in providing adequately through depreciation allowances for the replacement of ageing plants at rapidly rising replacement costs. It is the resulting growth in external cash requirements, outrunning any capability for lasting increases in after-tax profits, which helps to explain the pyramiding of debt. That same pyramiding, at historically high interest rates, in turn also lowers the real return to equity. And that combination not only reduces the attractiveness of further investment, but by building more debt into business capital structures, at shorter and shorter maturities in the inflationary atmosphere, it puts new pressures on the available liquid funds of both business and financial firms. It is that shortage of liquidity which seems to create new justifiable demand for still more money and still more debt.

Some of these manifestations, of course, are part of those aspects of the current inflation which may be considered short run and cyclical in nature. But the accumulation of major changes seems to imply a virtual mutation in the state of the world economy itself. It is these deeper trend-line forces that have generated effective demand on such a scale as to move so many countries up into the increasing cost zone of the output curve for the world economy.

Thus far there has been no mention of the world "oil," although it must be obvious that oil not only symbolizes dramatically many of the problems of causation that have been described but also is the latest and largest among the elements of rising cost for natural resources in the "cost push" pattern. Without digressing into the details of the oil situation itself, however, I do feel impelled to review some of the forbidding consequences that seem to me almost inevitable unless a massive new combination of efforts is mobilized, both in the United States and in other countries, to contain the forces of inflation.

## The Potential Consequences of World Inflation

On the purely economic side, the tendency toward underinvestment and over-indebtedness can become a self-propelling force toward more and more inflation, ending ultimately in utter collapse unless a firm counterforce can be mounted. On the political and social side, continual inflation erodes governmental authority and moral values, and unless arrested contains the threat of total breakdown, followed by a frightening exposure to the risk of totalitarianism from the right or the left.

The only lasting correctives in economic terms must be to improve supply availabilities and costs, while braking the expansion of demand. For supply and costs, that means increased investment and a greater use of new technology—an outward shift in the world's composite production—cost curve. For demand that means restraining the creation of debt and purchasing power, without diverting their distribution away from the less privileged individuals or nations. Short of an approach as simple and drastic as that (which will be further described shortly), inflation in the more developed economies seems now inevitably headed toward a degenerative pattern. Upward price movements are building ever stronger resistance to decline. Within the overheated atmosphere distorsions and imbalances have become more frequent and may become even more extreme. For the allocative function of individual prices, upon which the effective functioning of the market system depends, does require a prevailing acceptance of some norms. And when virtually all prices are raggedly moving upward, under the feverish pressures of speculation and fear, established norms begin to disintegrate and may ultimately disappear.

To make matters even more difficult, today's inflation not only means erratic irregularity among price advances (or even among the occasional declines) within a given country, but also among countries. That is why, as inflation began running out of hand, each country had to abandon the maintenance of a fixed parity for its own currency against other leading currencies. There could be no fixed indicator of comparative purchasing power among currencies when prices were moving in such disparate ways. Nor did floating rates help—except by removing the automatic movement of reserves among central banks, and the related impact of such movement on domestic monetary management.

In a world in which the shift of financial capital among nations can be activated quickly on an enormous scale, the opportunities for quick gain or the understandable need to avoid harsh losses cause pressures upward or downward on individual exchange rates at least as readily under a flexible rate system as under one of fixed rates. But with exchange rates wholly at the whim of those who move into a currency as it appears to strengthen, or out as it begins to weaken, there is even less chance that exchange rates can strike an average among the comparative prices of the goods and services of each country that move across its frontiers in international trade. Indeed the past two years have been replete with examples of countries whose exchange rate changes, aggravated by sensitive flows of highly mobile funds, have actually stimulated domestic inflationary forces. Countries receiving sizeable inflows of short-term funds have had great difficulty checking the resulting swelling of domestic demand, while the same flows tend to push up interest rates and costs in the countries losing funds. While the tool kits of central banking contain traditional methods for offsetting disturbances of either kind, the magnitudes that can now flow have already overwhelmed the capacity of some central banks to resist. This is one reason for the distressingly high rates of monetary expansion in so many countries.

Meanwhile, these same widely fluctuating exchange rates have a distorting effect upon the movements of longer term capital. They make the reasonable calculation of long-term investment opportunities even more than usually hazardous and have already begun to subject the capital intensive sectors of countries with a relatively open economy to fluctuations between excess and dearth.

In time, as the sense of norms is impaired by the continuous erosion of values in the marketplace, there must inescapably be a degenerative influence on the mores of political and social institutions. A premium is developing on sharp trading and legerdemain. This weakening in the accepted standards of orderly conduct in personal, corporate, and political behaviour within nations can spread to the relations among nations, as the scramble for resources, goods and property, and the flight from money, becomes increasingly frantic. The early divisive reactions of various nations to the oil crisis gave a foretaste of what might come if the strains of international inflation should go on cumulating over the years ahead.

The result internationally may be a fragmentation of countries into protective blocs, intensifying the natural conflicts that are continually present below the surface, as countries compete over the division of that major part of the world's resources, that are always relatively scarce, even under conditions of comparative calm and order. Such fragmentation, in turn, would inevitably mean a diminution of the great potentials from that international division of labor which has progressed so remarkably, until recent months, throughout the post-World II period. Moreover, the strong antagonisms that are likely to develop among blocs as they continue their introverted course may lead from fragmentation to outright economic warfare of a frighteningly debilitating kind.

But these are in some ways only the least of the hazards on a continuing path of inflation. For once inflation reaches annual rates of 20 or 30 or 40 per cent, internal turbulence can be expected to lead from a breakdown of political morality to a collapse of democratic political systems. To be sure, there may be a lag. The hyper-inflation of Germany in the early 1920's was first broken by collapse into deep depression, to be followed only a decade later by the final emergence of the Hitler dictatorship in 1933. What may now lie ahead for other countries, including possible dictatorship of the right or the left, is fortunately still some distance away, but the risks are clear.

My overriding fear is that even the deeply ingrained democratic commitment of the American people will be weakened, perhaps ultimately even to the point of impairing our own democratic political system, if inflation should continue and grow from the 10 to 20 to 30 per cent rate during the next decade. It is, in my view, an unconscionable siren song to suggest that indexation, for all forms of payments in the system, can provide an acceptable accommodation—permitting us to live with inflation. For the only generalized indexation that has worked with any semblance of sustained acceptability, has been one imposed by a military government operating with the power of decree, not only in economic matters but in those concerning the civil liberties of the individual.

The United States has a deep responsibility not only in preserving the economic conditions necessary for the liberty of its own people and the survival of its own democratic system, but also in providing the lead and example which most of the western world will depend upon in preserving its own democratic institutions and the economic opportunities of a market system. What then are the paths along which control and correction must begin?

## The short-run problem - inflation and recession

Having recognized the unusual characteristics of the present inflation, having seen a diagnosis of at least some of its causes, and having had a glimpse of the consequences of its continued acceleration, one is tempted to reach out for decisive, fast corrective action. But the inflationary process has already gone too far, and permeated too deeply in too many varied ways into the interstices of the world economy, to be controllable through any single program of drastic, powerful, simple action. So far as the United States is concerned—and we have all along had the capacity to lead in what must be a worldwide effort—the momentum of inflation might have been broken if the freeze of August 1971 had come at the beginning of 1969. Then, a temporary "Phase Two" use of direct controls could have been devised under cover of the freeze, aimed at untangling some of the demand pull, cost push, and supply shortage factors that had been at work since early 1966. But events have moved far beyond the stage for that kind of approach now, and indeed the delay and vacillation in the two sets of freezes and controls, and in the erratic support given them by monetary and fiscal policy, have made today's task even more difficult.

For what must be done now in the United States, to meet the short run problem or a recession within an inflation, requires therapy that could, unless carefully planned, interfere with the surgery needed for the deeper cancer of world inflation. Even though the classical prescriptions of tighter money and budgetary restraint have not been adequate to control our American segment of the world inflation, a decision to turn those prescriptions around in the traditional manner to counteract recession by pumping up demand would be likely, nonetheless, to strengthen the forces of inflation as well. Nor can we just sit back and allow recession to run its course, content in the belief that this is merely one of those fallow periods that must come every so often when the changing parts of the economic machine get out of phase with each other and a slowdown is needed for a short while as market processes restore a balance. Not only have social pressures made such a detached approach to declining output and employment politically unacceptable, but this time the prolonged inflation has created distortions which no recession alone could correct. And even worse, complex price interrelationships as well as the patterns of world payments have been suddenly torn apart by the precipitate quadrupling of prices for oil, the most critical source of the energy that powers the world's economic machine.

Yet through all this discouragement I see surprisingly hopeful prospects—the situation has become so bad that we will simply not be able to delay much longer in developing a wholly fresh approach, instead of merely re-running old slogans. And there are conceivable ways in which anti-recession policy can also be anti-inflation policy, both for the short run and the long. Let me first suggest some of the potentials in terms of overall policy, and then suggest ways of fitting those potentials into the present structure of our economy and of our Government.

To cope with its deepening recession, the United States will have to find jobs for the unemployed and encourage prospects for business, but that does not have to be done by pumping up additional demand through an outright reversal of monetary and credit restraint. Those aims can be met through the Federal budget but selectively, by making room for programs of public service employment already underway; by careful stimulation of urban housing; by allowing for revenue losses resulting from higher standard deductions on personal income taxes and a rise in the investment credit to stimulate capital formation; by re-establishing and enlarging facilities for the stockpiling or raw materials and critical products; and by re-creating under tough leadership a modern version of the old and highly useful Reconstruction Finance Corporation, to inject conditional equity into utilities or other firms made unable by inflation to expand their capitalization and borrowing power and thus to maintain their facilities for service "affected with a public interest." Even all of that need not mean a budget deficit as large as most incurred during the Nixon years; nor need the deficit itself be an additional source of inflationary aggragate demand. It can, in effect, be met out of an unusual form of barred savings. For by a peculiar coincidence, such a deficit may be of the same magnitude as the amount being siphoned out of aggregate demand by the high oil prices—which represent the equivalent of a "tax" on consumption of oil products and a shrinkage of home purchasing power available for other forms of consumption. What this means is that deficit can in effect be financed out of savings, and thus be neutralized in potential inflationary effect, by selling US Government securities to the OPEC countries until the recession danger has passed.

To be sure, neither the savings, offsets nor the production stimuli can be expected to fit into place without some guidance. There will have to be an overview from which to gauge about how much should be done, and when. This is not as simple as the usual anti-recession formula of merely opening the valves for new money, or spending Government funds in huge added amounts. It is a way, however, of beginning to introduce some of the steps needed for an attack on the longer range structural causes of inflation as part of a calculated combination of actions to check and reverse a recession.

It is worth remembering that the Government deficits which spurred the recovery and expansion of 1961 through 1964 were financed over the four years as a whole entirely by savings from outside the banking system, while an accommodative Federal Reserve policy provided money and bank credit that were adequate for the growing needs of the private sector—and prices rose at annual rates of less than 2 per cent. So indeed, recession can be turned around with the help of relatively non-inflationary Government deficits. Those were far simpler times, to be sure, but the conceptual approach is still, I would argue, valid—difficult though it now is to translate that elemental concept into today's environment of short run recession and long run inflation. To do so will, unfortunately but unavoidably, require a closer approximation to conscious economic planning—or perhaps its sounds less alarming to say "the scheduling of priorities"—than has ever been acceptable in the United States, except under conditions of all-out war.

For the longer run inflation problem, the need will not be a recession-oriented effort to find jobs or promote business confidence but to keep our economy within the bounds set by our access to resources. We have to gear ourselves to the conditions of an "economy of scarcity," after many years of thinking in the terms of an "economy of abundance" where any limits were set by our ability to organize for growth, not by any constraints on the availability of physical materials or capacity to produce. An effective fresh approach now is going to have to take three broad lines of action: a more self-conscious and systematic definition of national priorities; the stimulation of technology and investment in accordance with those priorities; and the adaptation of Government programs and the financial system to keep overall demand (and possibly at times particular sectors of demand) related to those same priorities.

There is enough overlap, however, between a carefully designed anti-recession policy and a planned policy to control long run inflation, to permit a prompt start on all of the former and much of the latter.

Monetary policy should not, in my view, be relaxed much further; pronounced ease would create further upward price pressures against the many bottlenecks which pockmark the American economy, while demand stimulus can better be targeted through the budget. Government deficit financing in all its forms should come as fully as possible, directly or indirectly, from OPEC sources, with a minimum net use of the banking system except for initial distribution—in order to avoid the overflow demand effects that feed price and cost inflation.

As for targeting the areas in which demand can most promptly evoke additional output and employment (without spreading generally across the whole economy in an inflationary surge of "demand pull", there are many clear priorities already evident. We do not have to wait until a new government, better attuned to the longer run problem, has worked out a comprehensive scale of priorities. For the present Administration, once focused on the potentials immediately in front of us, has ample scope for assisting investment to help create employment and spur production while the recession lasts. To enlarge the supply of goods available, as a means not only of promoting employment but also of nudging prices downward in the market place, Government can also, for example, suspend many of its remaining restrictions of production or marketing by the extractive industries. It can and should provide an assured stimulus for the exploration and extraction of needed minerals (including oil) through tax relief directly linked to those activities. There will also be scope for enlarging the supply of particular products in the United States by increasing imports—particularly after the current Trade Bill is enacted. That is, in many respects, a better way than through punitive enforcement of the anti-trust laws to invigorate competitive performance in the United States. Such an example by the United States would also help counter the protectionist tendencies that are threatening everywhere as recession deepens and the erratic recycling of oil payments intensifies the efforts of countries to pass a part of their net oil deficits on to others—thereby deepening the contraction of their own economies.

Alongside measures that may serve both ends—that is both to counter recession and to control the long run forces of world inflation—other proposals are being advanced that supposedly will help toward one objective while being neutral toward the other. An incomes policy, reviving the ill-fated earlier controls over wages and prices, is currently being proposed in the United States, for example, as a way of holding down inflation directly, so that the Government can presumably be free to flood out additional demand and thereby raise jobs and output without fear of further price-cost increases. But in the present setting, any such opening of the floodgates would be almost certain to fail again, even if it were not compromised from the top administratively by unsteady hands on the levers (as did happen in the United States though perhaps not altogether intentionally). Our problem, in the late-lamented but discredited phases Two and Four, was that the power of the cost-price spiral had become too strong, in my view, to be held back by specific controls unless there was a reinforcing limitation on the creation of aggregate demand as well. Direct controls simply cannot be a substitute for general controls. Price and wage controls or guidelines can have a place though, from time to time, to break the momentum of a spiral. They cannot be kept too long, however, without providing a false support to all elements of the existing economic structure, and thereby shutting off the kinds of structural adjustment needed in the longer run to remove the underlying sources of inflation. But if a back-stopping similar to what I have suggested for monetary, budget and debt management policies were to emerge over the coming weeks, a reimposition of direct controls for an unspecified period could help limit the escalation process that is still, despite our American recession, creating unsustainable distortions among our wage costs and product prices.

## Controlling long-term inflation by fixing priorities

Turning now to focus more directly on the inflation cancer that is growing underneath the current cyclical recession, it seems to me that our greatest need is to get enough agreement on the causes and characteristics of that inflation for the country to move beyond a "WIN" program, devised for the cyclical inflations of the past, and start on a program for sorting out the critical priorities of the future, within a framework of deliberately limited overall growth targets. Even without that, as I have already noted, the oil crisis itself is fortuitously forcing many of the key questions to the surface, and if they are faced within the next few months, important progress will also have been made in getting at the root causes of persisting inflation. But the better approach would be to develop now a more comprehensive view, and to subject various alternatives to the testing of public debate, will the oil experience serving as a pilot experiment.

The starting point will have to be acceptance of the inescapable fact that neither the United States nor any other developed country can again grow as fast in real terms—with a wide open approach for all sectors of the economy to battle their way forward—as has been taken for granted in the past. In finding our native American version for what the French accomplish under their "indicative planning", we will also have to respect and reflect those conditions of our own economy that are essential to preserving the vitality of the market system. While acepting some limited degree of unifying guidance as to priorities, we must avoid the mistake of 1934, when the United States, having mistakenly cut itself off from many potential trade and financial relations with much of the world by introducing the Smoot-Hawley Tariff of 1932, and by torpedoing the London Monetary Conference of 1933, proceeded to create the National Recovery Administration (the NRA) which, for a few brief months brought our country dangerously close to the forms of a corporate state.

The mistake this time would be to reach for a fullscale plan, complete with detailed schedules and inflexible objectives. All that is needed, instead, is the very rough marking out of boundaries, subject to continuous review and readily adaptable to changing conditions at home or abroad. There should be none of the rigidities that have on occasion characterized the French approach, and certainly not the iron controls that sometimes emerge from the "consensus" of the Keidanren, under the Government of Japan. The choices should be little different in principle, and less complex or exacting, than those which are customarily made (or assumed) in determining the priorities of our Defense Department which, with comparatively little public review, actually contracts for a changing mix of equipment and services that aggregates more than the gross national product of most countries in the world.

Ultimately, most of the primary choices among priorities should undoubtedly be validated through the legislative process, on the basis of executive recommendation. But in our country they will also need the undergirding of extensive public debate and of well supported, intensive research. Somewhere in Government, responsibility will have to be centered for developing an overview of the economy—of the prospective shortages and the basic needs in manpower, materials, productive equipment and services that are likely to lie ahead, and of the major tradeoffs that will have to be worked out not only among them, but also between them and objectives of environmental, social and economic feasibility. In my view, the United States should have a permanent statutory body, comparable to the Council of Economic Advisers, capable of pulling together on a continuing basis the best information available from inside and outside the Government, and of bringing together the best minds to debate and explore alternatives and consequences. Indeed, I believe that was originally contemplated as a major responsibility of the Council when it was first formed—a strategic planning function that has been obscured by the procession of urgent tactical issues appearing from day to day.

To start what I hope will eventually become a critical discussion of all this, I suggest that a unit within the Council, or a comparable new and correlative body located either in the Executive Offices or the Treasury, must be specifically charged with the full-time duty of looking ahead—to appraising long range economic priorities for the country, divorced from the short term exigencies of immediate legislative programs. Yet because the resulting conclusions must be tempered by political experience, and responsibility, there should be Cabinet level review of suggestions and recommendations, leading to a determination of principal longer term priorities. Ultimately, of course, as accepted by the President, these must be reflected in regular reports to the Congress, and will from time to time require enabling legislation. While the members of the Council should be available for consultation with members of the Congress, and with Committees, the primary responsibility for formulation and reformulation of basic priorities over the years must rest with the President, and with whichever Cabinet officier he designates to have primary competence in these matters. In turn, detailed implementation of the various elements of an agreed priority system will necessarily reside in each of the affected departments, and an important part of the Council's continuing duties will consist in monitoring what is being done, to assure that there is communication among agencies involved in overlapping zones of action, and to highlight issues in conflict for resolution at the highest levels.

## Implementing the "scheduled priorities"

Once a start has been made in establishing a long range "priority scheduling" responsibility within the Government, the hard work of developing criteria and priorities can begin. That will require somewhat more competence than I can pretend to command, but perhaps I may suggest some of the broad outlines that might evolve, merely as illustrations to demonstrate the degree of generality (and perhaps of reasonableness) that I have in mind in using the dreaded term "economic planning".

Partly reflecting the new configuration of energy availabilities and real costs, a long range planning council may want to recommend, for example, a major shift in priorities for freight and even passenger transportation. Rails and marine shipping may have to carry more long distance freight, with trucks limited very much to shorter hauls and container deliveries, and air used only for urgent, high speed deliveries. Such decisions will presumably depend partly on forecasts of domestic and of diversified foreign sources of alternative energy supplies, and also on rough projections of patterns of movement by weight and size and location; on whether large exports of grain, or coal, or steel may continue; and on the probable capabilities of various kinds of equipment, including the carrying capacity of the airlines. From such approximations, and the resulting executive decisions on priorities, various implications will also have to be formulated, to be carried out consistently in the relevant actions of all Government departments—ranging from the uses of the Highway Trust Fund to the ruling of the Civil Aeronautics Board. And unforeseen events will sometimes prove that a firm decision, persistently adhered to, was not the right one. But that, I suggest, will prove preferable to wholly unstructured arrangements under which a hit and miss scramble for all materials and products makes perpetual inflation, and intermittent breakdown, inevitable.

Given a finding, for example, that the economy will need another twenty million tons of domestic steelmaking capacity over the next decade, or an approximate doubling of railroad freight—car capacity while the overland truck fleet should be frozen at the present size, or an increase in domestic oil refinery capacity by a magnitude of three to four million barrels a day—the rest would be left to the marketplace although still under the eye of the anti-trust division and the various regulatory bodies or government procurement agencies which have a particular interest in the details.

Once the few "commanding areas" have been given some targets or boundaries within a framework of overall growth objectives for several years ahead, a need will remain, both for the targeted areas and stimulation of technology, investment, and output if the root cause of inflation is to be controlled. And on the demand side, the traditional instruments of monetary and fiscal policy will still be needed. What remains is to implement coherent overall policies effectively, and equitably, within a frame of reference determined by the nation's real potentials, and in terms of the agreed commanding priorities.

Already American industry and the universities, often supported directly by Government funds, are devoting more talent and facilities to research and development than all the rest of the western world combined. What the selection of priorities can do, without disturbing any basic research, is to give particular emphasis to the practical introduction of those elements of applied research which mean most in the priority areas. Indeed this, too, is but an extension of practices already commonplace under programs of the departments of Defense, HEW, and others.

## Domestic financial requirements

The possible missing link is in incentives. Unfortunately the delightful skepticism that is characteristic of personal freedom has led to an avalanching criticism of all American business enterprise, more the large than the small, and "profit" has become a perjurative word. If there is to be any chance of a real turnaround in inflation, that attitude itself will have to change—not the healthy criticism, but the presumption that profits are a guiltridden gain. For the basic answer lies in more investment, which is more highly productive. Such a result cannot be brought about, while preserving all the other attributes of a market economy, unless there is a growing equity base to build upon.

Equity simply cannot be accumulated, or attracted, unless after tax earnings are permitted to rise. Dividends on all listed equities on the New York Stock Exchange have averaged, over the past five years of boom and inflation, less than the prevailing interest on passbook savings accounts in New York City. In turn, dividends have taken about half of all after-tax earnings, with the rest going into the retained capital of the firms. That is surely one reason why the proportion of gross national product going into new business investment has been lower in this country over that period than in any other leading country except Great Britain; and the ratio has not been high anywhere, except in Japan.

To accompany a higher return on equity there also has to be a larger supply of savings available for investment. One source of that has fortuitously, if unwittingly, been created by the sudden quadrupling of the oil price. For few, if any, of the OPEC countries can spend for their own consumption or investment as much as half of the funds they are currently receiving—funds, as already mentioned, that represent a drain from the stream of consumption spending in the oil deficit countries. Several of the OPEC countries may not be able to use all the proceeds at home for many years, if ever. Their objective should, therefore, if properly encouraged, be a ready counterpart to the objectives of the other countries that are greatly in need of capital. For the OPEC "surplus" countries can, and should, exchange the proceeds received from their exhaustible resource, oil, for a source of perpetual future earnings, a capital asset located somewhere outside their own country.

The process may be quite roundabout. Surely it has not gone very far yet. But regardless of which assets of longer term the OPEC countries may eventually decide to own, the proceeds will flow into the capital markets of the more developed countries, through which these funds may, and should, move into the most productive added uses for capital that are available anywhere in the world. I do not mean to imply that I have become a proponent of high oil prices, indeed my hopes are still quite the contrary, but wherever the price may settle, it is still certain to provide most OPEC countries with many more billions of funds than they can use, except in investments abroad. The challenge of the financial intermediaries of the world is to attract those funds into long term assets or equities that prove interesting to the OPEC countries, and then to follow through by moving the proceeds on through a succession of buyers and sellers into the most impelling priority uses for new investment funds.

In the United States and possibly other countries, where the equity share ownership in many firms is already low in relation to their outstanding debt, special arrangements will be needed to help restore the equity base. There may be possibilities for mutual funds to attract OPEC money into special issues of stock shares of companies in priority areas. For the utilities, and possibly other industries, a governmental intermediary, patterned on the old RFC, might help in the prompt rebuilding of equity through borrowing OPEC funds and placing them directly into preferred shares—in the expectation (as proved warranted in the case of the RFC) that such shares would later be retired as earnings improved.

### A linkage among economies through management of exchange rates

There remains one other quite fortuitous by-product of the current experience that can, conceivably, also be turned to good use in limiting the international spreading of inflation. That is the phenomenon of floating exchange rates. For now that nearly all rates are, in some manner, floating, the need has become starkly imperative that the floats be managed, each by its own central bank. But that can only meaningfully be done in cooperation with other central banks which may hold, or occasionally use, a given central bank's currency. There, I suggest, lies the road towards a more effective form of international monetary cooperation than any yet attempted.

As the management of floating develops, each central bank will unavoidably be reflecting two judgments, which it must pair into one general view. First, it must have a view on the broad relationship of its own prices and availabilities for goods and services in trade, to those on average in other countries of importance for its own trade. Second, it must take a position on the likely, and appropriate, flows of capital (long and short) to be expected to move across its own exchanges. In working out acceptable zones for some intervention to help assure a degree of stability of the exchange rate between its currency and others, the central bank will form judgements as to whether the policies of the other countries are consistant with the approach to exchange rates that their central banks wish to take. The other central banks will, in turn, have a similar look at the first central bank, and at the economy it serves. All of this, moreover, will go on under the watchful eye of the International Monetary Fund, to which the Committee of Twenty has just designated additional responsibility of this kind.

The result, I suggest, is likely to be a much more frequent, intimate, and thorough interest (and even involvement) of each leading country in the economic affairs of the others. The effort to introduce some degree of stability in exchange rate fluctuations will, by its nature, lead to a fuller reflection of the requirements for external viability in the policies formed to meet the internal objectives of each government. That means that a route will have to be found for cooperation not only between central banks across the exchanges, but also between the Governments and policies that stand behind the central banks. The common wish to combat inflation through domestic restraint on demand can in these conditions more safely be pursued, country by country, because of the assurance that each is pursuing the same objective, within the conditions of its own economy, and thus the risks of exported or imported inflation can be minimized.

## Conclusion: combatting inflation through an anti-recession program

Indeed, within this new structure, as it evolves, there can be increasing scope for discussion of, and some harmonization among, the longer range objectives of different countries, provided they have some conception of what those objectives ought to be. As various raw material scarcities emerge, the need for some common approaches, under the aegis of the IMF or other international organizations will become more compelling. There will also be renewed opportunity for making more effective use, both in general and in support of key priorities, of the traditional wheelhorses of public economic policy—that is, monetary control and fiscal (tax, spending, and debt management) policy.

All of these prospects are, to be sure, in the main only hopes at the present time. The oil price situation does give a fortuitous impetus to the possible reconciliation of the current need to resist recession with the lasting need to check inflation. To the extent that the forced swings created by the high oil price can be channelled into needed capital formation, jobs will be created for the present and a capital base begun for overcoming in the future the increasing costs that generate inflation. But these potentials will have to be mobilized if there is to be an effective, sustained counterattack on inflation by an aroused and frightened public.

Neither the United States nor any other nation can any longer safely counter recession merely by pumping up the demand, nor can its economic machine be stoked with unlimited cheap resources, leaving its expansion wholly free to run off in all directions. There are limits to growth—not absolute, but elastic limits. Unless that brute fact is to force the world on a self-destructive path of sustained, and eventually explosive, inflation, a way must be found to mobilize all of the existing machinery—which already affects or regulates so much of economic life, into a focused and coherent order for stability. Nations can no longer afford the waste of unplanned use of their resources—that is the message that inflation is sending all of us.

The challenge is to find ways to approximate a systematizing of priorities, while preserving the essence of a market economy rooted in the motivations of private owner-ship. The alternative, as I see it, is an inexorable destruction of the market system under the crushing force of inflation. The way out may, at least on superficial appearance, seem to veer dangerously close to an abrogation of that market system in the effort to preserve it; but the risk must be taken.

# The situation as seen from Europe

by Jürgen Ponto*

Surely inflation or deflation, inflation or recession, are questions for our continent, too. If there should be a particular European answer, it will certainly not be brought forward by just one voice—this is our particular European handicap. We are confronted with bewildering contrasts: wages and prices are rising more rapidly than ever before, with—for the time being—Germany being the only exception. On the other hand, the current money value of practically every type of property, ranging from shares over real estate to commodities, is suffering enormous declines compared with price levels of only half a year ago.

Are we, in the midst of deflation or inflation? We are confronted with a dramatic turn of the economic and monetary climate all over the world, and in my opinion this change is governed at least by three identifiable influences: firstly, credit restrictions at last produce their effects on our economies; secondly, accelerating inflation absorbs more money and credit: greater amounts of money and credit are necessary to support a given volume of goods and services; and thirdly, on top of these two contractive influences, the fourfold increase of oil prices. Initial forecasts made a year ago concerning the size of the problem look like being confirmed; allowing for imports, the combined surplus of the OPEC countries should reach about $60 billion this year. To put this figure in perspective, this is 2/3 of the book-value of total existing US direct investments abroad; and more than the total value of German shares as quoted at our stock exchanges.

So it can easily be agreed, the combination of inflation, growing recession and oil confronts us with an unusual and explosive mixture of problems which no country is spared, except, for the time being, the oil exporters. And we are familiar, with the claim of a massive transfer of purchasing power to these countries, resulting in a marked shift in the pattern of world income, of world savings and of world payments. We now know the model, but do we accept it? Is Europe, in particular, prepared to realize the wide divergencies and the degree to which countries are affected? While, for example the oil input bill of the European Community as a whole rises within just one year, from $32 billion to $48 billion. The additional costs to the US amount to not much more than just $10 billion.

(*) Chairman, Dresdner Bank.

Trying to assess the European economic situation in the worldwide context, one has to state in the first place the obvious: What is bad for world economy and what is bad for trade and free access to free markets, is even worse for the European economy, for trade within the community, and that is even worse for the balance among the free European countries. The European continent depends much more than others on the outcome of the crisis, this transformation of basic conditions of life, this farewell to standards, preferences and pretensions, and once more we have to realize extreme divergencies from country to country, measured by inflation, measured by balances-of-payments, and measured by economic activity and domestic demand. To give you a brief sketch of the inflationary picture, Germany, as is well known and was stated here this morning, stands out as a country with the lowest rate of inflation—about 7 per cent, a group of smaller countries, like Switzerland, Austria, Belgium and the Netherlands has broken to about 10 per cent, well above some countries like France, Britain and Italy with inflation rates ranging from 16 per cent to 20 per cent and more. Inflation is most rampant in the whole residual group of lesser developed countries, on the outer circle of Europe starting from Finland over Turkey, Greece, Yugoslavia, Spain and Portugal. Here inflation is at its highest, now between 20 per cent and 40 per cent.

With inflation so divergent, it is also clear that balance of payments positions differ extremely. Oil now comes for various countries on top of high existing deficits, Germany and the Netherlands together will record this year a current surplus of around $10 billion which squeezes other countries in addition. Among the industrial countries the bulk of the deficit falls on a few in Europe, the UK and Italy with about $10 billion each, and France with about $7 billion. To understand the meaning of these figures it may be worthwhile mentioning that in the case of Britain and Italy they account for about 6 per cent of the GNP; by contrast, in the height of the dollar crisis of 1969-70, the current account deficit of the US did not surpass an equivalent of just 1 per cent of the GNP.

These differences in inflationary pressure correspond to differences in demand pressure between European countries. In all major countries of the community except Germany, economic activity gained momentum and accelerated sharply in the first part of 1973, in particular industrial and housing investment. Inventory formation was generally extremely strong, and this coincided with strong demand from the US and the Third World. Overall, the dollar value of exports and imports of the European Community grew by about 40 per cent, the corresponding volume increases being both around 13 per cent—a clear indication of what inflation really means.

The majority of one year of higher oil prices now lies behind us; though payments on the basis of these prices did not start before April, the impact is already of staggering proportions. During the first half of this year, OECD countries as a whole have registered a deficit of their current account amounting to $19 billion, compared to a balanced current account in the first half of last year. Of these $19 billion, roughly 60 per cent or $11 billion were covered by capital imports, the remaining $8 billion by drawing on reserves. Again these figures hide wide divergencies between countries; three in Europe—Britain, Italy and France—together managed capital imports, whilst Germany had a capital outflow. These figures explain a lot about the movements of exchange rates during the last months.

Contrary to earlier expectations, Europe has to recognize that up to now the oil exporting countries obviously preferred to invest in the US market—largely in government papers, partly with banks—instead of lending in a straight line to European oil consuming countries. In spite of all the dire warnings of impending trouble, the international financial machinery, has worked satisfactorily up to now, and the private markets have done their work quite smoothly. In all fairness, it should be stated that the American banks have played the major role in the immediate aftermath of the oil price increases following the removal of capital restrictions on the balance of payments of late January. They very actively embarked on massive international lending amounting to no less than $14 billion during the first seven months of 1974 which exceeded the simultaneous inflow of oil money. All the existing financial arrangements have responded reasonably well to the strains of the present situation, and it is to be hoped that they will continue to do so. We have to realize that the situation could and will change, for many countries. Banks still have to follow prudent banking practices, and they are unable to lend indefinitely to countries whose international solvency is already or soon will be in doubt. Among these will be European countries, and what is now urgently needed is careful preparation and probing analysis on the adequacy of existing mechanisms and proposals for a new supplementary arrangement, for what we may call "secondary recycling", because the primary will not work.

To return to the question of the present economic situation in Europe and possible future developments. By now all countries have strongly reinforced their counter-inflationary policies. However, both inflation rates and external deficits have remained stubbornly high—but the repercussions of the measures taken to restrain inflation are clearly to be seen in a general weakening of demand. What is most significant here: the western European current cycle downswing is close to what seems to be evolving in the US—not only in its origin, but in its time-phasing. The slowdown began at the turn of the year, and as in the US and was relatively moderate through midsummer 1974, the latest date for which sufficient information is available. In outstanding harmony with the US residential construction, automobile production and financial institutions, share markets and bond markets have been hardest hit. One of the reasons behind this disquieting phenomenon is that all countries are deflating concurrently, so the US, and so Germany. The question really is who deflated most. In this respect it is possible that Germany continues to be at the head of the league, the result being the rise of export surpluses, which continues unabated. Due to slower domestic demand, exports are slowing down, too, but imports are declining even faster. During the first eight months German trade surplus with the rest of the European Community has more than tripled against last year. In figures: from $1.5 billion to nearly $5 billion. 75 per cent of this increase has fallen on Italy, France and the UK.

In trying to assess German policy and future development it is unlikely, that there will be a really worthwhile relaxation of monetary policy before the end of this year. Taking account of the usual time lag between measures taken, and their effect on the economic activity, it is difficult to conceive an upswing of domestic demand before the middle of next year, provided that expansionary policy will be successful in time. In order to avoid misunderstanding here are a few figures on German performance: unemployment has risen over the year, seasonally adjusted from 1.6 per cent to 3.7 per cent, the exact figure is under political dispute: is it 600,000, 700,000, 800,000? It might be one million—but it's in full compliance with the fact that we have more unemployed people all over Europe today than ever after World War II. Capacity utilization in Germany has come down in a very short time from 92 per cent to 80 per cent. The Centres of weakness are business investment and building, and gross investment into plant and equipment has fallen by about 25 per cent.

Trying to make some comparisons about national anti-inflation policies in Europe, it seems that Germany and Switzerland certainly were the forerunners in monetary policy setting the tune for very tight money. In most countries national authorities increasingly turned to direct action in the incomes field with a view to bringing wage-price inflation under better control. These initiatives for which the UK and France were notable, stem from the fear that too much reliance on demand restraint policy would inevitably produce heavy unemployment. Generally the control of wages was combined with corresponding controls and guidelines for prices. The results of these efforts have been mixed, if not outright disappointing, not least because a cardinal prerequisite of their success—containment of demand pressure—has been lacking. On the other hand, in Germany monetary policy with all its stringency, utterly failed to retard wages—it was effective on prices, but it never reached wages. In point of fact, relative to the upward movement of consumer prices, wage inflation was among the worst in Germany, considering that wage contracts for 1974 exceeded 12 per cent, whilst inflation rates stopped at 7 per cent. In other countries wages moved up roughly in line with the consumer prices. So from experience, we should be warned that monetary restrictions have too long proved quite ineffective at the wage front, the result now being a rapid escalation in unemployment.

Recently OECD has given us figures about wages in the main countries which give some food for thought. Making figures comparable we have further to take into consideration different gains in productivity as well as changes in exchange rates. On this basis the OECD comes, for Germany, to an increase of unit labour costs on a dollar basis of 64 per cent for 1970-1974; UK 30 per cent, France 42 per cent, Italy 55 per cent, Japan 62 per cent, compased with 11 per cent for the US. Needless to say that in all countries with production and productivity down, wages however run readily upward; the wage cost push is uncomfortably escalating. During the last months all European countries have intensified their anti-inflationary policy relying mainly on monetary weapons. However, it is impossible to make a judgment about existing differences in degree with interest rates at new peaks, nor can it be predicted when the various countries would ease up—in particular those with very high balance of payments deficits may find it difficult to do so. It is likely that Germany should and will move in the near future; indeed it is the one country in Europe than can best afford it whether we look at the balance-of-payments or the inflation rate. No doubt, monetary relaxation in Germany would tend to give great relief to other European countries which might be even more important.

One of the most puzzling features of general economic and financial scenes today is the erosion of wealth, caused by steep declines of market values of all kinds of capital assets, bonds, shares, real estate, or companies. Taking share markets, a dismal picture has unfolded in Europe, in some countries even worse than in the US. French shares have fallen from their last peak by almost 50 per cent, Swiss by 47 per cent, Dutch and Italian shares by 43 per cent, the German ones by 38 per cent, the Belgian by 35 per cent, compared to an average decline in American shares of 35 per cent.

One fact of central importance must be kept in mind: market values of real as well as of financial assets are always determined by transactions of minimal and marginal volume relative to the total of the existing assets. Nonetheless these prices at the margin, serve as the yardstick for the evaluation of similar assets as a whole. We all invest on the basis of these marginal market prices, hoping for the next round of higher prices; prices which become more and more insensitive to the relation between current profits and current interest rates and costs. In time however, speculation gets out of touch with real markets. Market values of all assets favoured by speculation are thrown out of balance with the general price level and out of balance with the current return on these investments simply becoming over-priced. As long as owners hoped for sizeable capital gains, compared with which the interest burdens seemed light, they did not mind low current yields; now however, with tight money and credit, there suddenly are more sellers than buyers. Even if there is no wave of selling, the crucial thing is that the fringe of the market has gone into reverse gear. Monetary influences which were very expansive during the last years are contractive everywhere, in particular in Europe now. And money is no longer in favour of the markets, it is against them. Marginal changes from buyers to sellers are enough to turn a bull market into a bear market. As capital gains expectations disappear suddenly markets quickly become much more sensitive to higher interest rates.

So it is an obvious fact now that we are in the grip of quite contrary pressures. We must give priority to the international dimension, both of inflation and the threat of recession. It has been truly said that no country with a highly developed social and economic structure has ever had an inflation rate over 20 per cent and continued with a democratic government. It is sobering and alarming to see social and political unrest escalate in more and more countries of this continent. With economies shaking we all will be confronted one day, maybe soon, with growing international and domestic pressure to resort to unilateral "beggar thy neighbour" actions- competitive devaluations, dumping, import and exchange controls. Though inflation remains our public enemy number one we must pay greater attention than hitherto to the danger of a world-wide slump.

After disintegration by inflation, we should be very clear about the risk of disintegration by unemployment, disintegration by something which might turn out to be European and inter-European economic warfare.

Where is, in the face of this ocean of problems, we ask ourselves, where is Europe now? For many years our efforts to create the European Community were favoured by steady economic growth—even then we suffered painful set-backs. Trouble is not new to us, but we always, somehow, kept moving on. However, let us not fool ourselves today: our present problems are unprecedented in proportion. We have unprecedented inflation, unprecedented threats in potential recession, and unprecedented external imbalances. All this is putting and will increasingly put enormous strain on the European community, considering in particular the extreme differences in the domestic and external positions of the member countries. Looking thus at the European currency situation reaching the throes of the agricultural market, it is easy to become pessimistic about Europe. When the oil crisis broke out, at first any community spirit seemed to have gone to the winds, for some months "sauve qui peut" became the order of the day. Later the Turkish-Greek war painfully demonstrated what we knew before: the political weakness or should it be said, the political non-existence of Europe. Political unity seems so far beyond our present horizon that we have practically stopped speaking or even thinking about it.

At the same time, even economic union seems on the retreat. On the other hand, with the vital importance, with the urgency and the huge dimensions of the energy problem one could imagine that over time this might well give a new stimulus to concerted action on a European basis. There is ample historical evidence that weakness, when such a process is going on, might turn out to be a compelling force to concentrate on solutions and to unify existing energies. Europe today is shaped by a common desire to be stronger, financially, economically, politically. And some rays of hope begin to emerge. When main countries adopted flexible exchange rates we all felt that we would finally move apart, last but not least because flexibility in itself includes all elements of disintegration. While the system has worked well in some respects, experience has meanwhile given the lesson that the possibility of countries to pursue their independent monetary and fiscal policies has been wildly overrated; and the need to coordinate policies is finally being realized as being hardly less pressing than under a system of fixed rates, which governments are again making the basis of their decisions.

In the recent French-German pledge to coordinate anti-inflation targets, the sense of interdependence seems to be returning when you witness for example the planned venture of a joint European loan issue in favour of those countries who have no access to the market. There is certainly always some scepticism about the meetings of the heads of governments and the conferences on ministerial levels, which produce so little in the way of concrete measures. Nevertheless one must appreciate what has been achieved: we have achieved a better understanding, certainly, of the leading politicians of this continent, and though the trends and efforts cannot give rise to euphoria they seem at least to justify a moderate optimism. For some time to come, however, it will be necessary to live with flexible rates on the one hand and the little snake on the other. As to the snake, hopefully the monetary nucleus of Europe will keep together, as the positions and the policies of these countries are not so much apart.

It is to be hoped that inflation is being detected as the illness of the West, the illness of the free markets, and that this illness is definitely nothing but the fair result of unfair play, playing against the rules of balance between the different partners of free markets. Inflation finally is nothing but a reflex on a misuse of power. We know the addresses; and we all hope that our governments will realize that the pilosophy of more pay for less work is at the end of its tether, and that there is no escape from disaster just by building and buying flats for those who can afford it.

It is to be hoped that monetary policy, and even indexation being detected as an excuse that we do not have the courage to fight for a better social machinery, a machinery that can do better than produce just once a year a wage increase, and in consequence a price increase, and which can give once the only reliable answer to social welfare by linking again productivity and distribution of wealth.

There is really no problem in Europe which can be solved by just one country. The partnership which we started to try has to go on, and it will go ahead if we continue to work on joint actions, and one day for something which may be called a joint Europe.

# Japan's Inflation during 1972-74

by Hisao Kanamori*

The wholesale price in Japan showed no noticeable upswing since 1952. In fact, a downward trend since the beginning of 1970 was registered. Then, in August 1972, the price began to rise. At that time few people predicted that this was the start of a grave inflation which would prevail for more than two years. On the contrary, it was even welcomed as a sign indicating recovery from depression. The price rise tempo, however, was so sharp that, by August 1974, a 56 per cent increase had been marked. On the other hand, the consumer price rose by about five per cent annually from 1960 on and then accelerated its tempo at the beginning of 1973, totalling about 40 per cent during the period from August 1972 to August 1974.

The period of price-rise which was especially grave during the past two years can be divided into three subperiods, that is pre-oil-crisis (August 1972 - September 1973), oil-crisis (October 1973 - February 1974), and post-oil-crisis (March 1974 - September 1974).

## The pre-oil-crisis period

There were two factors responsible for the price-rise during the pre-oil-crisis period (August 1972 - September 1973); these were the sharp rise in import prices and the rapid expansion in demand. To cope with the depression which dated from the summer of 1970, the Japanese government embarked upon a demand expansion policy increasing fiscal expenditures and lowering the official interest rate. During the summer of 1972, demand began to expand, coinciding with the rise in international prices. The result was the serious price-rise which proved to be so sharp that no comparable one can be found in the developed world.

That the increase in import prices was an important factor for the inflation is shown by the fact that the rise in wholesale prices and in import prices coincided in time. The sharp climb in the price of corn, wool, natural rubber,

(*) Chairman, Japan Economic Research Center.

lumber, copper ore, copper ingot, etc., naturally led to the rise in the domestic prices in Japan which depend greatly on imports of food, feed, industrial raw materials, etc. The jump in import prices during this period was about 25 per cent; it was particularly sharp for textiles (68%), lumber (47%) and food (37%).

The expansion of domestic demand began to be noticeable around April-June 1972. Its chief contributors at the initial stage were increased fiscal expenditures and the recovery in inventory investment. Equipment investment also began to recover toward the end of that year. During the July-September quarter of 1972, the rate of increase of the GNP, computed on a yearly basis, was as high as 20 per cent at current prices and 13 per cent at constant prices. Several factors in the demand expansion of this period differed from the past:

— the higher rate of creation of money (MI) supply, making Marshall's "k" higher; this increase in money was a result of the big favorable balance in the balance of payments which took place under the system of fixed exchange rates;

— the policy for increasing fiscal expenditures and for lowering interest rate; the bank rate hit a post-war low of 4.25 per cent when it was lowered by 0.5 per cent in June 1972;

— the bottle-neck in the supply capacity, which appeared somewhat earlier, causing real economic growth rate to slow down and the rising trend in price to be stepped up; one of the factors responsible for this situation is found in environmental problems which prevented equipment in electric power and in the iron and steel industry from being increased as scheduled;

— large speculative inventory investment based on three factors: the movement in the overseas market was interpreted as the sign of subsequent rises in the price of lumber, grain, etc.: there were abundant funds on hand, and the money market was slack;

— a steeper rate of wage increases after 1973; in the spring of 1973 the record of 20 per cent was reached again. This resulted from the general labor-shortage and from the brisk rise in consumer prices. Due to the sharp increase in labor productivity, the rise in labor costs was not so steep for the manufacturing industry but increased wages became a key factor for the price-rise in the service industries, *et cetera.*

Due to the coincidence in time of these factors, the jump in nominal demand was so much higher than in the past that it surpassed the supply capacity. Acocrding to an estimate by the Bank of Japan, about 40 per cent of the price-rise during the one year from the third quarter of 1972 to the third quarter of 1973 was accounted for by the rise in the import prices, while about 60 per cent was accounted for by domestic factors.

As a consequence, in January 1973, the Bank of Japan enforced the following measures: increased deposit reserves, stricter window guidance, control on credits to be extended to trading firms, etc. The official interest rate was raised from 4.25 percent to 5 per cent in May, again in June and July, and then upped to 7 per cent in September. Again, the Ministry of Finance postponed the fiscal outlay. Thus, the inventory investment calmed down in July-September, 1973, and the demand expanding pace slowed somewhat. The price-rising trend, however, did not slacken in the meantime, due probably to the further rise in import prices.

## The oil-crisis period

It was at the time when this stringent policy began to show its effect that the oil-crisis broke out (the period, October 1973 - February 1974) causing Japan's price index to climb as sharply as the increase in the wholesale price. The rise was 37 per cent as compared with the same period in the previous year. The oil-crisis accelerated the price-rise in two ways; that is, it led to the view that the oil shortage would decrease production and result in insufficient supply, and that the sharp upswing in oil price would raise production costs. During this period, the first factor was far stronger than the second and, after November 1973, apprehension about a future supply-shortage was manifested in lower sales and in speculative buying. The result was a price-rise which was reflected simultaneously for such commodities as petroleum and coal products, textiles, wooden products, iron and steel, electrical household machines, automobiles, etc. The rise in the wholesale price, compared with the previous quarter, reached 8.7 per cent for the October-December quarter of 1973 and 14.6 per cent for the January-March quarter of 1974. According to the Bank of Japan's survey, the international factor is estimated to account for 66 per cent of the price-rise in January-March.

Measures taken to counter the rising indices included raising the official interest rate from 7 per cent to 9 per cent in December, tightening window control by the Bank and constricting the size of the General Account Budget. Further actions to cope with this situation were also taken. A Law of Emergency Measures for the Stabilization of National Living was enacted in December with the result that the price of kerosene for household use and LPG was frozen. The price of key commodities, living-related commodities, etc., was curbed (price-rise is liable to report in advance). The price-rise of living-related commodities which are sold in department stores, supermarkets, etc., was curbed in part by freezing the price of 148 commodities.

## Post oil-crisis period

The price-rise continued even after March 1974 due chiefly to the rise in costs. Thus, the character of inflation swiftly changed from a demand inflation to a cost inflation.

The decrease in the supply of crude oil was not as serious as had been predicted. General over-supply began to occur as a consequence of speculative investment and led to a sharp increase in the inventory of finished products after March 1974. The reason why prices kept climbing even under these circumstances lay in the increase of the production costs due to higher wages and to the rise in petroleum prices.

The annual rate of wage increases was 15 per cent for 1970-1972, and about 20 per cent in 1973. It then increased by 33 per cent in 1974, a record-breaking jump accounted for partly by the sharp rise in consumer prices (27 per cent in February 1974). Soaring consumer prices made large wage settlements popular with the public although, in fact, labor productivity declined in 1974 as compared with the previous year. The big wage hike which was accorded meant an increase in the per-product-unit labor cost of about 30 per cent. It seemed as if a vicious cycle were underway in which the higher prices led to higher wages, then these increased wages caused the prices to mount even further.

Production costs were also up, affecting pricing. The steep rise in petroleum prices resulted in a price hike for electric power of 57 per cent, for LP gas of 39 per cent, and for petroleum products of 62 per cent.

The strict tight-money policy observed by both financial and banking circles up to the fall of 1974 made it gradually more difficult to attempt to shift the higher costs onto the price of products. The money supply had increased by 27 per cent over the same period in the previous year by September 1973. The increase then slowed down to 13 percent by July 1974. The consequent stringency in fund demand-supply compelled much equipment investment to be postponed and the construction and inventory investment to be restrained. Although wages were up substantially, prices kept rising sharply, with a resultant lag in consumer purchases. The rate of nominal consumption slowed and personal savings rose. The combination of these results brought forth a phase of over-supply beginning in the spring of 1974 for quite a few commodities, including textiles, automobiles, construction materials, durable consumer goods, etc. It was expected that this phase would become gradually more severe towards the year's end and would affect the whole economy. These changes slowed down the tempo in whole-sale prices (notwithstanding the sharp rise in cost). That rate, as compared with the same month of the previous year, was 37 per cent in September. The government is attempting to decrease this rate to 12 per cent before March 1975; and such an attempt seems not to be out of reach.

It was feared that the inflation and the higher oil prices would place Japan's balance of international payments in serious difficulty but, on the contrary, it improved and showed a favorable current receipt-payment balance in August 1974. Increased overseas demand for iron and steel, chemical fertilizers, etc., was largely responsible as exports rose. Imports slackened given Japan's business recession. In sum, inflation had no serious repercussion on Japan's balance of payments. The most serious effect occurred in the form of the lowered, real economic activity. Since the strong pressure of cost inflation was countered by a tight fiscal and banking policy, production began to decrease after peaking in November 1973. It registered a decrease of 7.2 per cent in September 1974 (as compared with the same month of previous year). Economic growth rate for fiscal 1974 is therefore estimated to be zero. This represents a new situation of serious stagnation for Japan's economy which has enjoyed increases of 15 per cent in the mining-manufacturing production and of 10 per cent (annually) in the real economic growth over the past 15 years. Japan's economy faced serious stagflation for the first time.

## How to deal with inflation

*Reflections:*

At the start of Japan's inflation, the over-supply of money had a great impact. Analysis suggests that the inflationary spiral could have been made more moderate by absorbing the excessive favorable balance in the international balance of payments through adoption of a floating exchange rate and by curbing the over-supply of money through market operations by the Bank of Japan. These measures might have reduced speculation and thereby have reduced the rate of wage-hikes which had been encouraged by speculative price-rises.

The stimulus of the demand-expanding policy, which was taken in the latter half of 1972 by both fiscal and banking circles, was too strong. The difficulty in estimating the time-lag of the policy's effect seems to have led to some misjudgment. Upon reflection, it would appear that business recession could have been rendered more moderate had positive measures aimed at stimulating business activity been taken as early as the beginning of 1971. The delay in enforcing effective policy permitted a more severe depression, with the result that the speed of business recovery later was too rapid.

An important imbalance between supply capacity and demand resulted since the business recession had continued too long with equipment investment excessively curbed. Similarly, productive investment faced strong criticism due to environmental problems. A third source for the imbalance was the growing demand for larger public investment and for more adequate social security. We should be well aware that the improvement in social security must be supported by growth in production.

At the time of oil-crisis, prices should have been frozen earlier with a view to halting the speculative price rises. The direct price curbing measures of March 1974 were enforced so belatedly that they only consecrated the interim climb in prices. Those higher prices then caused a sharp business profit in the March 1974 account settlement which weakened the capacity to refuse a strong pay raise even though a 10 percent surtax was imposed on excessive profit earned by business.

Without the stabilization of international prices, no nation can resist imported inflation. About half of the rise in Japan's prices was accounted for by increased costs for imported food, raw materials, energy, etc. Such rising prices, obviously, cannot be resisted by Japan alone. Notwithstanding this fact, the problems of inflation were the basis of criticism about political misjudgements and against business irresponsibility. Such criticism hindered the enforcement of effective measures.

*Future directions:*

The current policy of curbing demand, which has been undertaken since early 1974, is too strong. Since the present inflation is a cost-inflation in nature, the rise in prices cannot successfully be controlled by curtailing demand. In any event, such measures provoke secondary reactions. While demand should be limited to some extent, the avoidance of lowered real economic activity should also be seen as an important task to be undertaken simultaneously. Japan's economic stagnation not only hampers the improvement of domestic social welfare, but also has an ill effect on the world economy. Tight fiscal and banking policies should be mitigated so as to be capable of expanding the demand while harmonizing it with latent supply capacity.

As to the measures for coping with inflation, the government should publish any appropriate guidelines for permissible pay raises, for instance, labor productivity plus the permissible rate of increase in consumer prices. In doing so, the government should request the cooperation of the labor unions. In exchange for such cooperation, the government would enforce such measures as improved social security, softened conditions on home loans, tax cuts for low income brackets, etc. (Japan's trade union system makes enforcement of the guidelines policy easier than in most other countries). Social inequities due to inflation can be tackled through such measures as the introduction of a sliding system for old-age pensions, raising the interest rates for deposits, etc. (Since 1974, pensions are to rise proportionate to increases in consumer prices when these go beyond 5 per cent a year.)

The present inflation resulted from the complicated mixture of the increases in oil prices and in the wage costs. It is unlikely that this sort of inflation can be arrested effectively in a short time without serious secondary reactions such as business failure, unemployment, etc. Today, our task is to moderate wage hikes and to curb increased costs by raising the labor productivity. By so doing, we should deliberately undertake to stabilize the economy as a whole.

# International Politico-Economic Aspects of Inflation

by Nathaniel Samuels*

The underlying assumption of my remarks this afternoon is that the struggle against inflation is essentially a political rather than an economic problem. Obviously, it has all the economic elements we have been discussing today, but grappling with the problem is essentially political in nature because political decisions are required in each of our countries to adopt economic programs and to achieve the necessary international cooperation. If this is so, then the industrialized countries of the world, and I stress industrialized, have before them a set of problems that is different both in content and dimension from anything they have hitherto faced as a group. They are going to have to close ranks as industrialized countries to a degree that they have not previously been prepared to accept. However great the elements of international cooperation have been in the post-war period, I do not think it is going to be possible for the industrialized countries to play the role they will have to play in these coming years, both to sustain themselves as a group and to assist the developing world on a broad front, unless they take the necessary steps to integrate their cooperation at the political level, beyond the international institutional framework now in place.

The amount of international tension that is almost certain to grow as the industrialized world finds itself subjected to new strains can be very great. In addition to the internal problems that we each have in our respective countries we will have increasing tensions among the industrialized countries. Are we, for example, in a continuing inflationary trend or are we entering a deflationary period? Or how do we deal with a combination of both of these trends, when the economic situations diverge in different countries? There is certainly no unanimity, and the different situations prevailing in the different countries make the necessary harmonization more and more difficult. Apart from our internal problems and those among the industrialized countries, the difficulties between the developing world and the industrialized countries will, in

(*) Former U S Undersecretary of State for Economic Affairs. Chairman, Louis Dreyfus Corporation.

my opinion, grow greater, not less. I believe that the gap between us, whatever our intentions and motives, is growing deeper rather than narrowing. It was striking at the International Monetary Fund meetings in Washington a few weeks ago to listen to one Minister after another among the developing countries, and particularly the Ministers of the least fortunate countries, discuss international problems, the impact of the oil increase and the impact of the deficits on their individual situations, without a word of criticism about the actions of the oil-producing countries in increasing their prices so sharply to the detriment of so much of the developing world. Criticism was directed only at the industrialized countries, without taking into account the new problems they will face in continuing and increasing assistance to the least fortunate countries. The outlook between the two worlds is so different, the perceptions of the problems so different, that I think we have a seriously growing fissure in the international structure.

Speaking in broad and simplistic terms, we have built the institutions of the post-war world and pursued a combination of post-war policies aimed at one essential target, namely, that the terrible catastrophe of the 1930s, mass unemployment and all it signified, should not happen again. The problems we now face in the 1970s are, I think, an outgrowth of the policies we adopted in pursuit of this central aim—and one should be grateful that we did manage to avoid a repetition in the quarter of a century that has followed World War II. Part and parcel of this economic objective was a political commitment to economic growth. The consequence of almost a quarter of a century of the pursuit of ever-increasing growth has been the infusion of a strong inflationary bias into all our economies. For the rest of the 1970s, therefore, perhaps longer, a major problem will be inflation. We shall probably have an extended period during which we shall have to wrestle with the consequences of our post-war economic success.

I think it is true to say that not a very great deal of attention has hitherto been given to the international aspects of the inflationary phenomenon, how it is transferred from one country to another, what are the elements that produce it and the impact of one national policy on that of another. What we do know is that the inflationary problem today is worldwide and that national policies have a serious impact on the whole international structure. The confusion in our minds as to how to deal with the problem in its present dimension and intensity is enhanced by our awareness of modern interdependence but our limited knowledge of how the interdependence process really works in all its manifestations.

As I indicated at the outset, the industrialized world as an entity has a very special problem. It is going to have to deal with a number of contemporary issues affecting its own health while, at the same time, fulfilling responsibilities toward the developing world, particularly the least endowed nations of the developing world. I think it will have to deal with these issues in an institutional framework separate from but parallel to the all-embracing international institutions of the post-war period, without in any way diminishing its role in the existing international organization. Everyone can have his own prescription for how to do that, but I believe that the time has come when we ought to reconstitute something akin to what the Group-of-Ten finance ministers was in the recent period, but on a more comprehensive, consciously political decision-making basis. I don't mean the Group-of-Ten finance ministers as such; I use that description because it is well-known and simply to indicate what I have in mind. I think that we can no longer deal with our common economic problems in the narrow framework of finance ministers, but something much more broad than that, operating at the Ministerial level on an informal, ad hoc basis, outside of the existing international institutions, although utilizing them to the fullest extent possible. I think our problems are so strongly political that they can only be dealt with politically, and we need the flexibility to function parallel with, but procedurally outside, the structured international system for certain of our affairs. By the Group-of-Ten, I don't mean ten or twelve countries or whatever particular number, but essentially the major industrialized countries, not just five or six of them. The recent tendency to limit financial discussions to five entails useless frictions inside the European Community without corresponding advantages, and there are signs that we are gradually returning to a wider framework inside the industrial world.

We are going to have to deal with a series of problems—inflation, recession, monetary flows, energy supply, commodity supply and terms of trade problems, and others as these emerge and as they keep changing their aspects and their impact, and that can be done only by cooperation and decision at the political level. The Group of industrialized countries should consist essentially of Foreign Ministers, Finance and Economic Ministers, and such others as required for specific matters, but ready to be called almost into session frequently and without long periods of preparation. The existing institutions, such as the OECD, and the universal institutions such as the IMF and the World Bank, do magnificent work and can be the sources for providing the underlying work. In the OECD the policy discussions, and the efforts to harmonize them that take place in the Economic Policy Committee and Working Party Three, for example, are of a very high order and have been invaluable. But the task is to get beyond that to a much closer political coordination.

What would such a group do that is not now being done? The mere organization of such a group is by itself of no importance, although the need to have it is so great that it becomes more than just form and becomes a matter of substance.

We talked earlier today about the harmonization of growth policies, or whether growth policies should have a lesser emphasis during the next year or two. This might mean, in more specific terms, a better coordination of deficit financing policies in various countries, perhaps setting out parameters on budget financing for a year or two at a time to which governments might be prepared to adhere. This would be vital, since budget policies affect so sharply the supply of money and credit and thus levels of inflation or deflation in our countries. The impact of money and credit supply on growth over a number of years has surely been one of the most fundamental factors affecting the world-wide inflation we have been suffering. This has gone on inexorably in country after country, without coordination. The analyses of what may be the right courses to pursue may be financial and economic, but the necessary international cooperation requires a conscious act of political coordination. It is, of course, unrealistic to expect governments to surrender authority over the supply of money and credit in their respective countries; this goes to the heart of sovereignty, but it should be helpful to any individual Minister, in dealing with his own parliament on such matters to speak on the basis of international policy consensus.

To take another matter—the balance of payments deficits that are going to become increasingly cumulative if the present oil prices remain. This problem may turn out to be even more troublesome for us than the inflationary problem. Despite Bob Roosa's optimism this morning on how we might perhaps utilize these funds, their scale, by any estimate, will impose great burdens of debt, of debt service, of monetary stability, or of real resource transfers, and burdens on political tempers. The uneven impact of this debt and recycling problem on different countries will be great. In all probability, the US will ultimately be the recipient of a very large proportion of these oil earning funds as the years go on, since it has the only economy and the only capital market capable of absorbing these funds on the necessary scale. In the US there exist differences of opinion about the banking role we would have to undertake. To what extent do we want these funds? To what extent can we absorb them? The task of funneling these funds out into the rest of the world may be a difficult and serious one. Who takes the risk of short-term money to be lent out at long-term? Unless we find some kind of mechanism whereby the world as a whole, whether it be through the IMF or whatever international institutions that may be set up, to diffuse this risk, I think you will find in the US government, as constituted today, a reluctance to take this risk and to act as the world's banker again, as the US did immediately after World War II. The mechanism for dealing with these problems as financial and economic problems are at hand or not difficult to envisage, but political decisions are required to make the mechanisms work effectively. For example, what will ultimately be the attitude of the industrialized countries if the new surplus countries seek to put increasing amounts of their earnings into direct equity ownership of key industries. The psychological and emotional reactions to one or two situations which we have already witnessed are perhaps a portent of political problems to come.

As far as the energy coordinating problem is concerned, very substantial international progress has been made toward an institutional framework of cooperation. The talks in Brussels on sharing in cases of need have been most constructive, and the International Energy Agency may be the nucleus of a new international institution designed to respond to new international problems. If you look at the draft protocol with its voting arrangements set out, you will see an encouraging example of agreement on formulas designed to make international cooperation work when the need for it is felt. Although there has been much discussion in recent years, in academic terms, of restructuring and remodeling our international institutional framework, events are bringing forth their own responses. This is probably sounder than theoretical reforms.

Increases in agricultural and raw material supplies generally has become an urgent problem with strong political overtones. Maintenance and management of reserve supplies, long-term supply and access arrangements, the terms of trade and related questions will require political cooperation and decision-making. We have long shied away from commodity agreements, and in a few cases where we have done something along these lines the results generally have not turned out to be very salutary. However, I think that the problems of assured access to markets, adequate supplies of raw materials, not just oil, may lead us to examine the usefulness of long-term contracts, perhaps with floor and ceiling prices, and with governments involved in a contingent role to give these arrangements long-term credibility. I think this requires a whole new area of examination and open-mindedness of a kind that in the past we have tended to exclude from political consideration.

On the food side, let me mention one political element I think so important between the US and Europe. I know of no issue that has irritated relations between the US and Europe in recent years more than the question of European Community agricultural policy. The fact is that as we look at the food situation today it looks quite different from what we in the U.S. considered it to be and perhaps quite differennt from what Europe considered it to be until recently; perhaps we both misread the nature of the problem. Today, the problem is not essentially how do we get American exports of grain into Europe against the protectionism of the Common Agricultural Policy, but should we aim over time toward a global agricultural policy in which Europe should largely take care of itself while the surplus producers, such as the United States, Canada, Australia and the Argentine supply the growing needs of the rest of the world? The European effort at self-sufficiency is at great cost to itself and one can argue against it on economic grounds, but at least there may be ground, under an emerging picture of growing world grain requirements, for a harmonization of policies between Europe and the countries with large grain export availabilities that was not possible when perceptions of the world food situation were somewhat different from what they are now. This requires an act of political cooperation. For the first time in a number of years there is the possibility of constructive action arising out of a previously divisive environment. What needs to be added is a strong political hand to fashion the new structure.

The same goes for that other element of divisiveness of the last few years, namely the preferential areas problem between Europe and her former colonial areas, where perhaps we can begin to talk about collaboration to help increase suppiles of raw materials from these countries on lines mutually advantageous to them and to the industrialized world. Previously, it seems to me, Europe has maintained a politically unsustainable conception of this problem, while the United States has not sufficiently understood the political importance of the relationships with the former colonial areas. Now we might begin to look at this problem in its wider context of economic and political relationships between the industrialized and developing worlds.

I think it is likely that in the next few years we shall have an emergence of trade problems that will divert our attention from the GATT negotiations, even if we get a trade bill in the U S. * As the industrialized countries see their balance of payments deficits piling up, and recession threatening important economic sectors, with every country seeking to minimize the impact on itself, one or another country is almost certain to turn to trade restrictionism despite its pledges of good conduct. The pressures to protect one or another vested economic interest in each of our countries will be severe, sometimes on the import side and sometimes on the export side, depending on the situation in each country and whether it turns out to be recession or inflation that we are fighting. These problems, if they eventuate, will have to be dealt with as they emerge, and not left to become cumulative. I think we run the risk of having a cascade of restrictions if the inflation continues at its present level and particularly if the recession gets deeper. In my opinion, only ad hoc political cooperation at the Ministerial level is capable of dealing decisively to prevent or to mitigate such trade restrictionism, if and as it arises.

Let me just say one word on labour, which was touched on this morning. I don't think anyone can minimize the problem of dealing with labour in all of this. The widespread attacks on multinational corporations are less a rational criticism of their conduct and role than a manifestation of disenchantment with the economic system. The gulf in perceptions that makes communication between labour and business so garbled and so confusing is very frustrating indeed. One of the more difficult issues is productivity. We can't ignore this topic in a world of inflationary pressures where productivity gains, such as they are, are almost consistently expressed in higher wages and costs rather than price decreases. Perhaps we have to think along different lines from those we have been accustomed to in the past. Perhaps we have to think more about relating productivity gains (or lack of them) to tax benefits. We have to find some method of direct and visible benefit to the whole of the population arising from increases in productivity and perhaps tax rebates can be tied to an overall productivity index. It should be done on a universal, not on a sectoral basis, because increased productivity is a deep moral and psychological problem, involving civic mindedness and civic spirit in the whole population, labour and management alike, industrial workers and service workers alike. It is not only a question of more investment, more sophisticated machines and harder work, but a shared spirit and ethic. The productivity problem has aspects in the industrialized world which are different from the productivity problem in many developing countries, and should be dealt with by us in the context of industrialized world harmonization policies.

In sum, our need to close ranks in an industrialized world under stress requires the industrialized countries to pursue policies that are relevant to their

* The Trade Bill has since been enacted.

own peculiar situations and intended to provide mutual support to each other in a new situation of danger to them. It is only by so doing that they will be able to maintain their balance and their health. And it is only by greatly enhanced cooperation on a political level and expressed in an effective political format that they will be able to do this and also be in a position effectively and willingly to supplement the universal international institutions, such as the IMF, the World Bank and others.

# Summary of Discussions

A German economist opened the discussion with—what he called—a "subjective" view. He identified four problems of the world economy: inflation, unempolyment, the international adjustment problem and the risks accompanying the shortening of the term structure of the international capital market.

Inflation has been with us since the end of the second world war. Although much of the inflation that is going on is due to the deficit in the American balance of payments and the supply of dollars, it is the short term view of solving the unemployment problem which has brought current high rates of inflation. Thus, the two problems are interconnected as a result of what could be called the Keynesian thinking of our time.

The Keynesian thinking has been carried to its extreme in terms of what the economists have been calling the Phillips curve. That means that there is a constant relationship between the level of employment and the rate of inflation. To put it in terms of one politician, it is better to have 5 per cent inflation than 5 per cent unemployment, as if the connexion were stable. Inflation can raise the level of employment above a normal level, but it's only unanticipated inflation which does the trick. As soon as inflation is anticipated you don't get a quantitative effect and when monetary demand is increased one gets only the price effect. This medicine of increasing the total aggregate demand for raising the level of employment above the normal level has been used about thirty years, and now the patient has become resistant to that kind of medicine. He has become accustomed to it and is anticipating it. So the medicine is not working anymore with the same force as it did immediately after the war, or immediately after the great depression. Thus we now have inflation and unemployment at the same time, and we are going to have both inflation and unemployment in the immediate and distant future unless we substitute for this Phillips curve thinking a different approach, namely an answer to the question: what is determining employment in the long run?

The answer to this question is that the level of employment—in the long run—is determined by the relationship between real wages and productivity. This is made clear by a typical structure of Europe. When we look at the various regions in Europe, we see that unemployment is rising in every direction from the centre to the periphery: in England, from the south to the north of England, Scotland and Northern Ireland; in Italy, from the north to the south; and from northwest to southeast Europe including Yugoslavia. Yugoslavia presents the particular situation that workers participate in the running of companies, so they tend to maximize profits not per unit of capital but per head of employed; the peculiar result is that those who are in have no interest in expanding the demand for labour, hence in having others come in and participate in the profits; thus there is a high level of structural unemployment in Yugoslavia, a socialist country, which supplies the industrial reserve army for the capitalist Federal Republic of Germany and other countries.

The explanation for the long-run rise in unemployment when one moves from the centre to the periphery of Europe is that labour productivity also declines. This is quite clear in Italy. Now it would not matter if real wages fell in the same way as productivity declined: profit rates would be the same everywhere, and capital would move to the periphery instead of being invested in the centre and attracting labour *from* the periphery. So the structural unemployment at the periphery is an indication of *why* you have unemployment. You have unemployment when profits are too low, because real wages are too high in relation to productivity. This can of course also be seen in the business cycle and in the present situation.

The present situation is characterized in a number of countries by fighting inflation through curtailing demand—this will lead to a squeeze in profits, and the squeeze in profits has as a consequence an increase in unemployment. Now if the diagnosis is correct, i.e. that what is needed is an improvement in the relationship between real wages and profits for the benefit of investment, then of course the solution would be a kind of incomes policy as has been mentioned several times here. With high wages and low productivity in marginal firms the only answer is to dismiss workers. So if an incomes policy is to succeed both to fight inflation and unemployment, then the trade unions and the public will have to be told that this is the way to raise the level of employment. If real wage claims could be kept at moderate levels this would help provide the kind of profits which are necessary for business to invest more than in the present recession. This would open the possibility of higher real wages in the future. If business firms do not invest now the increase in productivity in the future will be lower than it could be. So a kind of wage pause is required if our economy is to become more healthy.

One might say that the present difficult situation is a result of an adverse attitude towards profits for a long period of time, an adverse attitude towards the market economy, and towards entrepreneurial guidance of it. However, it is clear that without profits there will not be risk takers who are prepared to enter into new ventures. This is particularly true, in a period where investment opportunities, as they arise from technological progress, are not very visible.

The steel industry is still experiencing a boom partly as a result of the fact that since 1962 there hasn't been much investment in steel in the US because prices have always been under attack within some form of incomes policy. Therefore steel suffers from a lack of capacity. The chemical industry is booming but the major industries which have in the past been responsible for upswing and growth: the car industry, the electronics industry, seem to have exhausted their innovative potential. In the future innovations will have to be much more widespread. One cannot presently identify any particular industry in the world which could be the leading industry for the decade of two to come. So what that means is that our economies have to rely more on entrepreneurial spirit on a wide front, and this cannot happen with a profit squeeze or a definite strategy to redistribute income at the expense of risk-taking capital.

The third point is the international adjustment problem. This closely resembles the German reparations problem of the inter-war period, and this resemblance may lead to a pessimistic view. There is to be a transfer of real resources from the oil consuming countries to the oil producing countries, just as there would have been a transfer of real resources from the German Reich to the US and other allies if reparation payments had had to be made in kind. In the inter-war period the US and other countries did not want to absorb the real resources from the German Reich and therefore the German Reich was forced into a recession and a depression.

At present, we have the difficulty that the Arab countries cannot absorb the real resources which the deficit countries would be prepared to deliver them. Even if oil importing countries moved into a deep recession, the oil producing countries could not absorb the goods and services which the former would be able to supply. Now the German reparations problem of the inter-war period was solved by short term credits and this was disastrous as a small loss of confidence led to the international spread of the bank failures and a number of other disastrous events which finally led to the world-wide depression.

The present problem is called the "recycling problem". If this problem is short term, it means that one must bridge the gap between the present and the future when the oil producing countries will be able to absorb the real resources. If short term credits are used to do this, for example by using the Eurodollar market as the main intermediary, then a slight shake in confidence in banks may lead to the collapse of the international credit system.

What is required in order to bridge the gap in a solid manner are long term loans. But the market is not yet prepared to offer long term loans. Why is the market not prepared to do so? The explanation seems to be that under periods of inflation the expectation of future price trends is very different among debtors and creditors. No one can predict how high the rate of inflation will be in 5 or 10 years. So five-year loans, rather than ten-year loans are floated because there is this uncertainty about inflation.

Now there is also the uncertainty about the exchange rates. This uncertainty has been partly coped with by the market with some fantasy and imagination by issuing the "cocktail loans". But the cocktail loans are not a hedge against inflation, so what one has to invent are new instruments for the international capital market which are a hedge against inflation. That means instruments which neutralize the inflationary impact. What is needed is a kind of value guarantee for the loan, so that those who give credit know what they'll get back in real terms. The rate of interest for such loans could be of course very low, at the present moment the real rate of interest (and we will have to talk in real terms in this respect) might even be negative, but this is due to the recession. In the long run the real rate of interest will be much lower than it was in the immediate post-war period, but will be even lower than in the recent past (in the last 6 or 7 years) maybe close to zero. It is hard to know how an economy can work with a real rate of interest close to zero or even negative.

However, by inventing new instruments which would help to get rid of the inflationary problem, the national capital market could revive.

Countries which are in surplus like Germany have to expand in real terms, in order to increase absorption of imports. The expansion can be brought about by subsidizing investment, and by public infra-structure investment complementary to private investment. That's the course which has to be taken, but it should of course be done in a non-inflationary way. That means it has to be done through the capital market and in particular national capital markets in surplus countries will have to be revived.

A German banker pointed out that the genuine German balance of payments surplus from 1 January 1970 until the end of 1973 was only $ 2.4 billion. The exchange and central bank reserves increased from 26 billion DM to 92 billion DM but 60 per cent of this increase was derived from borrowing abroad: about 1/4 short, 3/4 medium term and very little long term. So today 60 per cent of the German reserves is borrowed money which is due for repayment sooner or later.

Now, interest rates must go down, but how is this to be accomplished? If one fights inflation by a restrictive credit policy, high interest rates at home are reflected in international borrowing and capital market transactions. It is true that the oil producing countries have given some of the money, bought interest bearing treasury bonds, made some long term investments, but most of their lending is short term. The interest rate in the Euro currency markets is somewhere near 10 per cent. Thus, the accumulating surplus of oil producing countries may be in two or two and half years more than the total oil bill of 1972.

There are some countries where even the best debtor cannot borrow directly from the oil producing countries. Therefore they demand the intermediary of some well-known international credit institution, but there are only a very few left—probably fewer than ten—who are being asked to step in and guarantee loans. Now the question is whether it is possible to see a development of lower interest rates payable to those countries who have a tremendous surplus in their balance of payments, and at the same time continue a restrictive credit policy at home with high interest rates.

On account of recession and unemployment, it is very difficult to convince the trade unions not to demand high wage increases. One needs a very strong government to step in and to start by curtailing wages of state functionaries.

In the general German situation, the dependence of the German economy on exports is becoming excessive. There are some sections of industry where exports take anywhere between 36 per cent and 60 per cent of production. Volkswagen exports 70 per cent. Exports will go down because some importing countries will not be in a position to allow such a high level of import from Germany. How can France go on having a deficit in its balance of trade with the FRG of 500 million francs a month and at the same time carry a huge overall deficit on account of the heavy oil bill? How can we expect to finance a continuation of exports to Italy whereas Italy can only be on its feet if it reduces its dependency on imports?

Germany has issued long term capital market bonds denominated in DM amounting to 32 billion DM and that are exclusively in foreign hands. If the holders of these bonds ever lose hope for further revaluations, they will sell in the German capital market which has already deteriorated. The main capital borrower is the federal government, the Länder and the municipalities plus very little by industry. On account of the profit squeeze there is too little investment. Because of the tremendous export success of Germany (the inflation in other countries is much more advanced) and in spite of various revaluations German goods are still considered as cheap compared with some of our trading partners. But that cannot go on.

Chancellor Helmut Schmidt said the other day "There should be more profits in the economy and the industry, because the profits of today will be the investments of tomorrow, and employment the day after tomorrow".

After the Second World War, Western Germany faced the great problem of the reconstruction and rehabilitation. There was a very low level of output of coal or energy and many other things. One of the trade union leaders—Buckler—insisted that Germany had to rehabilitate its structure before one could consider an increase in real wages.

Our nations must reduce the consumption of oil while avoiding a deflationary policy. How can this be done? If oil consumption could be decreased by 20 per cent to 30 per cent it would have an effect on the overall oil situation. There is need to invest in order to find substitute sources of energy. Nuclear energy power plants will have to be built in spite of problems of environment and hesitation by many people, and in spite of the fact that it takes 8-10 years before such plants can produce energy.

There is also the need to increase coal production which takes much time and tremendous capital. In the Western part of Germany there is much brown coal which, by an investment of 5 billion DM could produce for 50 years at 60 million tons per year. Our countries must consume less and invest more. How this can be done is a political issue of utmost importance. If our political leaders do *not* find a way to consume less and to invest more we will not solve the problem.

A French professor stated that our countries have learned much about economics, about various types of inflation, and are nonetheless applying the the wrong diagnoses and the wrong policies. Among the papers that have been distributed to this audience there is one by James Tobin. He is a great economist and his paper is extraordinarly clear—he says there are three types of inflation: the increased cost of imported materials, the wage-price or the price-price spiral and the excess demand. Our countries are not fighting the two first ones but an excess demand just at the time when there is a recession.

Why don't we analyse the situation as it really is? In this report a few months ago the OECD had rightly recalled that an increase in oil prices or imported commodity prices, while inflationary in a sense because it pushed up prices—and particularly in the structures of our economies where everybody adds a percentage margin to the prices of his purchases, in another sense was deflationary; it acts like an indirect tax, it increases the value of resources in relation to income, it pumps up incomes. How can we use classical means when we are in a non-classical situation? Let us address ourselves to the real rigidities, that is how prices are administered, not only by large corporations, but even by small shop-keepers, who practice an implicit cartel by applying the same uniform markup, and how the trade unions push for increased money wages and disregard the conditions of an increase in real wages.

The gist of what Robert Roosa tells us, is that we are in a period when a reconversion of our economies is both necessary and desirable. It is necessary because we cannot assume that raw materials and energy are going to be available on demand in unlimited quantities. It is also desirable because we know of the pollution of the environment and of all the dissatisfaction which has gone along with that type of unbridled growth which cares more for the GNP than really for the poorer sections either of *our* communities or of the world. So this could be a very welcome occasion, but this is contrary to what is being done. What the governments are applying is just a kind of extrapolation of their previous budgets, maybe with a certain reduction of public investment just at a time when more public investment is necessary, and credit squeezes with the very unfortunate consequence that this affects construction much more than any other form of production. Construction relates to an unsatisfied need almost everywhere, and is relatively one of the least energy-consuming activities. Why should we reduce employment where it's not really a cause of increased energy consumption, and when it corresponds to a very obvious need?

The net effect of our restrictive policies will be to slow down the creation of capacities to meet future needs and thus lay down the conditions for a further and fiercer inflation ahead. They have very little impact on our internal prices, but, by reducing the rate of growth of industry, they bring down the prices of raw materials: this will deeply affect some of the poorer countries and their ability to import from us.

Another point which has been mentioned is the structural nature of some of our deficits—let's take the case of France. We always mention the increase in the price of oil, but the truth is that there is also a very serious French deficit on all industrial products vis-à-vis all other industrialized countries and this is certainly due to a faulty industrial policy. So this is a moment, and it is significant that all our speakers have stressed this, where we need more investment, not less, more investment to either create additional basic resources or else develop new techniques to *conserve* them. Both are costly. Another direction which has frequently been mentioned is the need for an incomes poilcy. Up to now it has not been very successful. Perhaps it came at the wrong moment but mostly it was just a wage freeze in thin disguise without covering the entire range of incomes. One has to be more imaginative and to combine the short term aspects *and* the longer term aspects. To a large extent an incomes policy means reducing structural inequalities which come from very different productivities in different industries, in different firms and also in different areas.

There is also an essential need for a very active regional policy. We now have our more or less uniform wages with different productivities in various regions from the centre to the periphery, and unless we are able to develop those areas, this discrepancy is going to be: *one,* a major factor in inequalities and *two,* a major factor in inflation.

Another point which I think emerges from the papers is the need to have longer term borrowing, and a restructuring of the financial market which is in a very shaky position if all this oil money is only lent on very a short term basis. The problem of how to avoid the erosion of the purchasing power of lent money will emerge. In France, indexing was used before 1958. It was eliminated as a sign of mistrust in the currency. A financial reform was supposed to suppress inflation for all time. Today indexing is more difficult to reestablish than it would have been to maintain.

One of the consequences is that the only way bonds at fixed and high interest can be placed in the public is by the government putting a ceiling of 25 per cent on the taxation of bond interest. This has two consequences: one is that in a sense the government is paying, by this kind of fiscal expenditure, in lieu of the firms (this is a fantastic transfer); and secondly, this ceiling on the taxes is much more advantageous for high incomes in the high tax brackets than for lower incomes. If the only alternatives are indexing or this kind of government subsidy to industry and to the rich, then there would be a good argument for indexing.

An American professor stated that, to the accusation by Mr. Samuels to the economics profession of not having learned enough, and not having taught enough about the international inflation transmission mechanism, the answer could only be a mea culpa. His comments would bear on the relationship between global inflation and floating exchange rates.

There has been a lack of commentary on the connection between global inflation and the current monetary regime of floating rates. On the subject of the connection between global inflation and exchange rates, and on the subject of the transmission of international inflation, through the exchange rate regime, economists have tended to suffer from somewhat of a perceptual or a cultural lag. For many years economists had the idea that fixed exchange rates were a barrier to the international transmission of inflation. They were a barrier to inflation because of the danger of loss of reserves which an inflationary policy would create and consequently they would be a way of forcing governments to avoid inflation. But this could be so only so long as all countries were forced to finance deficits in their balance of payments with assets, with reserves, rather than with liabilities and of course this was no longer true in the post war period in the United States. When the United States after 1964 followed a rather inflationary policy, the system of fixed exchange rates transmitted inflation to the rest of the world through the obligation that other governments had a buy dollars in the foreign exchange market, expanding their own reserve base.

So the world, after February 1973, came to a system of floating rates, where they were adopted in part because they were seen as a barrier against importing inflation from the United States: they were seen as a way of getting out of that obligation to buy the surplus dollars that the United States was using to finance its deficit. Once inflation has become international, floating rates in fact become a reinforcing mechanism rather than a barrier to the further transmission of inflation.

Floating rates have traditionally been regarded by economists as an insulating device, an insulator against disturbances arising from abroad: floating rates can then be a barrier to the international transmission of inflation but only if two conditions are satisfied. One is that there be symmetrical reactions in surplus and deficit countries, and the other that there be no lags in the system or alternatively that all lags be of the same duration. The problem is that in the modern world neither of these is true. Reactions in surplus and deficit countries are not symmetrical, because we have price and wage flexibility in one direction only, we have prices and wages which move up but they rarely in aggregate, move down. The principal reason for this has to do with the kinds of phenomena which have already been discussed. The building in of inflationary anticipations in all sectors of the economy i.e. the labour market, goods and services markets, has created a situation where money illusion is absent or virtually absent, so is exchange rate illusion (a depreciation of the exchange rate leads very quickly to a cost-push type of wage and price inflation). So, one does not have symmetrical reactions. In a country where the currency is revalued, a downward push of wages and prices does not occur. On the other hand, there is an upward push in those countries whose exchange rates depreciate.

In addition, the lags are of unequal duration. Whereas the post-push reaction to a depreciation of the exchange rate comes about very quickly, the reaction of the balance of payments to a depreciation of the exchange rate comes about only with a considerable lag, due to the complexity of the markets. This results in a situation where the balance of payments may not begin to improve as a result of a depreciation for 12 to 18 months, the famous J effect that economists refer to. The result of these two facts, the lack of symmetry and the unequal duration of lags, creates a situation in which, if a country experiences a negative impulse on its balance of payments there will be a depreciation of the exchange rate which will result fairly quickly in a cost-push inflation.

There is also a tendency for monetary policies to validate such cost push inflation—this gets built into the economy fairly quickly. As the impact on the balance of payments takes longer, by the time the balance of payments has begun to react to the change of the exchange rate, there has already been a building in of inflation into the economy. The result is that in the country which experiences the deficit and the downward presure on its exchange rate, by the time its exchange rate begins to reverse itself, inflation has been built in and one now has a second country in that position of having a depreciation of its exchange rate. It will experience the same process and a series of fluctuations will occur where country after country will experience a ratchetting up of the rate of inflation through these fluctuations of exchange rates. There is a kind of perpetual motion inflation machine, which is a serious matter.

Floating rates under current conditions can turn out to be a transmitter and reinforcer of global inflation rather than something which prevents its international transmission. How does one deal with this? It seems to me that there are only a few possibilities: one of course would be to move back toward a pegged or fixed exchange rate regime, but for many reasons that would be unfortunate—if for no other reason but that the oil price increases have necessitated massive adjustments within the industrial world and it would be very difficult to accomplish them within the OECD world, in the absence of exchange rate changes. Another possibility would be to move in the direction of more effective incomes policies as was advocated at these meetings by several people. Incomes policies which would reduce inflationary anticipations and which would be able to forestall the kind of very rapid cost push reaction to exchange rate depreciation, would help considerably: this would involve not just a suppression of wage demands but a suppression of inflationary demands by all sectors of the economy as well.

Incomes policies are unlikely, for political reasons, to be pursued very vigourously, and a return to fixed exchange rates seems undesirable. What is needed is a country which can perform the function of shall we call it "an inflation sink": there must be at least one country in the system which, when its exchange rate depreciates as a result of what happens elsewhere, does not experience rapid cost push inflation, a country which does not perpetuate this process and transmit to some other country the inflation, but which itself absorbs the impact of the exchange depreciation which generates a continuing balance of payments surplus. This requires a country with a foreign trade sector so small relative to its economy that money and exchange rate illusion will continue in that economy. There seems to be only one industrial country which can fulfill this role and that is the United States. If floating rates continue and incomes policies are not pursued vigourously, then to halt the international transmission of inflation we are going to have the United States performing the function of "inflation sink"—that is to say the function of absorbing into its own economy the inflationary impulses transmitted through the floating rate mechanism.

A British industrialist wished to underline what Mr. Samuels said. All of the speakers have recognized that the four-fold increase in oil prices is at the root of our problem, but most of them, particularly this morning, went on to discuss it as though it was a domestic concern. As though this was some outside factor which was given and which was not likely to vary, at least was not likely to vary in an upwards direction and indeed as though we could rely on the existing quantities of fuel being available to our industries at present prices, which is by no means a certainty.

The idea of prices falling is pure wishful thinking. The classical economic argument that the high prices lead to reduced consumption is true and there is a surplus of capacity today. But what this approach leaves out of account is that all oil producing countries are receiving far more income than they can possibly spend at home or abroad, and this will remain true at least for the next five years even for countries with large populations and heavy development programs like Iran and Nigeria as well as for the desert countries. It is easy enough of course to talk about price reductions by OPEC or anyone else, they can reduce he posted price, as it is reported today that some of them are proposing to do, provided that they alter the formula by taking Y per cent of the new price instead X per cent of the old one, the governments take remains the same or even higher. There is a great need to start a dialogue and this might well start with the problem of recycling, but technical solutions are not going to get at the root of the problem. The root of the problem is the price and it is not wise for the consuming governments to go into the discussion unless they know what they want.

The second doubling of the price last January (which is what really caused the trouble) was in large part brought upon us by our own governments in their failure to take any notice at all of the warnings which had been given to them at least a year previously namely, that the price situation was getting out of control of the industry and was one which only consuming governments, if they got together, could do anything about. That is still true today, and the recent agreement for the establishment of an energy-coordinating group is a very important development. However, it remains to be seen whether that body is going to have any teeth—there are some important absentees—and it remains to be seen whether the essential cooperation between the governments and the energy industries is going to be achieved or whether domestic shibboleths like the US anti-trust laws are going to be used as a pretext for everybody going his own way. Some have been talking about this point in public and in private for over two years now, and saying that unless the governments of the industrialized countries hang together they will hang separately. That still seems to be the message.

An American banker and former high official underscored and emphasized the importance of attempting through political leadership in the major industrialized countries to achieve a *modus operandi* and to effect a greater coordination of national economic policies between these industrialized countries, on a scale and at a depth during the years of the Marshall Plan. The single most important cause of the global inflation is that the industrialized countries have pursued fiscal and monetary policies which simultaneously, if unwittingly, have been excessively expansionary, particularly if one takes into account the accompanying inadequacies in the efforts to expand supply in key material and product sectors. Both macro- and micro-economic policies have been out of phase with reality.

The resulting excess global demand that was referred to by Mr. Roosa and by Mr. Kanamore has pushed up prices both of industrial products and services and of numerous raw materials. Of course wage increases, substantially in excess of productivity, in many countries have added a general inflationary thrust. Special factors coming on the heels of these others, demand pull and cost push, such as poor harvests in some parts of the world in 1972, contributed to a steep rise in food prices—and then the oil price explosion in late 1973, and echoing forward movements in many other commodity prices, have added to the situation. Now given this kind of a world economy, which is the fruit of success (that increasing interdependence of which we are all very proud) all would agree that a substantial proportion of the inflation each country suffers from, is *imported* inflation. Diseased fruits and vegetables can be stopped at the customs borders, but neither inflation nor recession can, in the kind of international economy that we have developed. And given this kind of world economy several points of view emerge: one, that it can only be arrested, even though it is *international,* by national policies—this school of thought argues that the responsibility for arresting inflation rests with the larger countries, such as the US, taking the lead. Another point of view is that restraining demand in one country—even in the huge US economy—would not reverse the total world imbalance between supply and demand, and cause prices to stabilize. Therefore there is a point of view that holds that, an excessive unilateral action by the US could throw the world into a severe recession, and that point of view is one that has probably prevailed here in Western Europe in recent months. There is a fear accompanying this, by those concerned, that the principal governments may, just as they have unwittingly acted to fuel the fires of inflation, unwittingly be acting in an unduly restrictive manner simultaneously, eventually provoking a collapse in total demand.

Against this background one proposition could be offered: that these various points of view can only be reconciled by the major democratic industrialized countries acting through their governments to take concerted action; first to achieve a coordinated level of real economic growth in the international economy, that will not threaten to exceed available resources and give rise once again to demand pull inflation, whatever the pattern of recovery from the present stagnation, which will take shape as a result of public policies in these countries.

Secondly, to set in motion in some coordinated fashion, along the lines Mr. Roosa was indicating today, those expansions in the supply or conservation in use of the particular materials that are contributing in a major way to world commodity inflation. We need at least to *dramatize* the importance of this economic coordination which may require some form of international summit to hammer out a program of common action designed to bring this international economy into some acceptable norm of price stability and to keep it there.

No single meeting or series of meetings will provide the solution, miracles do not happen at international conferences! Such meetings can only serve as symbols of a common desire and common national wills to achieve objectives that can lay the base for day today, week to week, month to month acts of consultation and cooperation that precede and follow the summit. Now what is gravely needed, in dealing with these twin problems, is in the words of Chancellor Helmut Schmidt in an interview reported last August in the *New York Times,* "The closest personal and almost daily contact between the acting people, between the dramatis personnae in the US and Germany, Britain and France and Japan. A concerted and coordinated program to deal with world inflation, adhered to by the leaders of the major countries, based upon jointly developed recommendations of their ministers of finance, central bankers and economic advisers, would carry great weight will the legislative assemblies and the public".

The key weakness in any proposal of this sort is that the implementation lies within national state policies to be agreed on an international level. Electorates are becoming very weary of and disaffected with the increasing inflation and its distortions, its social injustices and its resulting fragmentation; and they are becoming increasingly fearful of a resumption of the boom and bust cycle that marked the breakdown of international cooperation in the 30's, when the economies of the world were much less closely interrelated than they are today. Therefore, the maximum chance that any national leader would have of implementing these necessarily disciplined policies on the various separate, and sometimes antagonistic, special interests, would be if those policies seemed to stem from some kind of international concord that indicated that the good of everyone would be served by a common practice toward a common objective. Therefore, there is a grave need for a giant step in the coordination of national economic policies. This will involve some simultaneous, although not identical, effort to hold down excessive demand, increase supplies of vital materials, assure equitable distribution of materials on reasonable terms and avoid a competitive deflation that would cause a risk of world depression. Without this international coordination on a scale and to a degree that we have not hitherto envisaged, it seems to me that the whole free-world economy, including that of the US, will fall on increasingly evil days.

# Inflation in Brazil: The Principles of Monetary Correction

by Roberto Campos*

In the late 'sixties and early 'seventies, together with an unprecedented industrial boom and expansion of international trade, signs of tension and disruption began to emerge in the market economies of the Western World and Japan: firstly the inflationary upsurge, then the breakdown of the international monetary system culminating in the dollar devaluation of August 15th, 1971, then the food crisis of 1972-73 and the increasing tensions within the European Economic Community. The recent energy crisis was a rude jolt that aggravated all of those problems and added a touch of political frustration: raw material producers, traditionally price-takers, suddenly became "price-makers" in the world market arena.

Many people who had regarded the euphoria of the late 'sixties and early 'seventies as a *deuxième belle époque* now bemoan the onset of a strange disease, "the sinistrosis," perhaps a recurrent and more vicious manifestation of the *malaise de fin de siècle* which at times afflicted the history of Western civilisation.

Inflation, undoubtedly a major component of this "malaise," is now too wide-spread and too unwieldy to conventional treatment to be dismissed as a tropical disease or as a sign of moral laxity. It is likely in fact to become a permanent companion rather than an obnoxious visitor.

## The new faces of inflation

We have to reconcile ourselves to four facts of life, unpleasant as they may be. *Firstly,* money has lost some of its conventional functions. It is still a means of payment, but inflation has eroded its reliability as a store of value and unit of account. *Secondly,* present inflation is not only quantitatively more violent and geographically more wide-spread than before, but it is also qualitatively different, deeply embedded as it is in modern social structures, because of

(*) Former Planning Minister, Brazil.

sundry factors: the rise of the service economy; the unidirectional flexibility (in the upward sense) of wages and administered prices; the claims of the welfare state; the political intolerance to unemployment and the societal commitment to economic growth. This commitment may result either from exercises of "*gapmanship*" in developing countries, that is, the desire to emulate the achievements of wealthier nations, or from "*consumerism,*" that is, the continuous dilation of the consumers' horizon in developed countries. The theory of a "zero-growth" economy that might alleviate inflationary pressures and protect the environment is an interesting intellectual exercise but certainly not yet practical politics.

The third fact of life is that more and more, due to costs and price rigidities, rebellious to the conventional medicine of monetary and fiscal policies, except at the cost of temporary unemployment, inflation is more and more associated in many countries with stagnation, generating, stagflation or slumpflation.

The fourth fact of life—and indeed a novel one—is the threat that inflation is posing for the fabric of Western democracies. Even well-established democratic systems are beginning to feel the onslaught of two-digit inflations. The political discomfort derives from two phenomena attending the anti-inflationary battle: the lag and the asymmetry. The lag is composed of three intervals: the technical delay in identifying the root causes of inflation; the administrative delay in enacting the appropriate monetary, fiscal and income policies; and the operational lag—that is, the time lapse before meaningful results are harvested. This period of waiting is fertile in doubts, anxiety and political bickering. The asymmetry derives from the peculiar fact that, though inflation is unpopular, the measures to combat it don't enhance the political acceptability of governments. The pains of inflation are diffuse, while the specific corrective measures hurt directly some of the most vocal sectors of the community: labour unions, which fret about wage controls; business, which resents credit restrictions and price curbs; and politicians, who dislike constraints on public spending for their constituencies.

Under those circumstances, frequent electoral consultations characteristic of the democratic system are likely to prove disappointing; they may result at best in "stop-go" policies, through an ineffectual alternation of austerity and relaxation; at worst, they generate excessive political instability. In weaker societies, and that is the case of the developing countries, tensions are likely to be stronger, for those countries cannot afford to postpone growth—pressed as they are by poverty and unemployment; a desperate search for authoritarian solutions to arbitrate conflicting claims may ensue, an outcome which, though certainly not commendable, is at least understandable.

If there are any favourable by-products of the present inflationary travail of industrial societies, I would list two: firstly, a welcome degree of humility of their politicians and economists, who no longer claim mastery over recipes of social discipline and economic viability; and a greater tolerance in relation to the plurality of political systems, in recognition of the impossibility of uniform solutions for the delicate and vital "trade-off" between liberty and social discipline, welfare and capital accumulation, price stability and economic growth.

## Cohabitation versus eradication

If this analysis is correct, if modern inflation is a much more intractable beast than it used to be—it is time that the frustrating pursuit of policies of eradication be tempered with the study of techniques of cohabitation. In this chapter, the Brazilian experience of indexation becomes a relevant subject of enquiry. It is certainly not a novel technique. Indeed, it has an honourable place in Anglo-Saxon economic literature. As noted by Professor Milton Friedman, the idea was broached as far back as 1707 by William Fleetwood, a Cambridge don; John Whitley pursued it in 1807; Joseph Lowe in 1822; while Jevons in 1875 explicitly proposed the creation of a "Tabular standard of value." And no lesser a person than the great Alfred Marshall in 1885 made a spirited defence of the "Unit of constant purchasing power." Irving Fisher in the United States, around 1911-1912, defended the idea of the "Commodity standard." Lord Keynes, belabouring on Marshall's earlier idea, suggested the creation of an index-linked Government bond in 1924. In the practical world, limited pioneer experiences in indexation have been staged, with indifferent success, by France, between 1951 and 1968, and somewhat more boldly by Finland between 1946 and 1958.

## Preconditions of the Brazilian experience

But if the Brazilians have not the merit of inventing indexation, they discovered the need for cohabitation with inflation and acted rather boldly to generalise its application, in an effort to convert sin into virtue. Historical, structural and political reasons, which may not be present elsewhere, combined to render the experiment both possible and reasonably successful. Historically, there was a tradition of chronic inflation. In the immediate post-war period inflation hovered around 11 per cent per year, rising to 17 per cent between 1958 and 1968, galloping into a pace of over 30 per cent between 1959 and 1963, escalating to more than 80 per cent in 1963 and exploding into a rate of over 100 per cent in the first quarter of 1964. Structurally, the existence of a dualistic economy with surplus labour, in either overt or disguised unemployment, particularly in the north-east, facilitated the implantation of wage restraints. Also the trade unions did not trace their creation to social battles in the market place, but originated rather from paternalistic prodding by the Government, thus lacking some of the political combativeness and revindicatory vigour of trade union movements elsewhere. Politically, the near chaos into which the country was plunged in 1963 and early 1964 created a yearning for social discipline, and rendered acceptable some temporary constraints on two of the traditional revindicatory coalitions—Congress and the trade unions—which, indispensable as they are in modern societies, do tend either to inflate the Governmental spending budget or to push wages beyond the limits that can be accommodated by productivity increases, or yielded by a reasonable manipulation of income policies.

## The mechanics of the system

Let us now consider the methodology of the Brazilian experiment and the components of the system before trying to assess its results.

The experiment started from the realisation that, since a shock-treatment for inflation was unfeasible, gradualism was inevitable. Given the psychological vices arising from chronic inflation and the deformation wrought into the asset structure of the firms, a shock-treatment involved the risk of a wholesale destruction of the entrepreneurial class followed by heavy unemployment, without in itself correcting distortions in relative prices, some of which had remained pegged, in a desultory effort to conceal the symptoms rather than extirpate the roots of inflation. An ensuing political backlash might result, forcing a relaxation of anti-inflationary policies and inaugurating a vicious "stop-go" pattern of behaviour.

The effort then concentrated on analysing the textbook "evils of inflation," with a view to minimising them, in order to give us time for attempting to reconcile gradual disinflation with a resumption and, if possible, acceleration of growth.

Those textbook evils attributable to inflation can thus be catalogued:

1. Erosion of the savings instinct and distortions in the credit mechanism, brought about by the prevalence of negative interest rates. These either discouraged savings or channelled them into undesirable directions, such as property or foreign currency hoards. As a consequence of the dwindling supply of savings, medium- and long-term credit, including mortgage credit, tend to disappear, while the allocative function of the interest rate as between more or less productive uses is also impaired.

2. Instability and disorderliness in the wage structure. Labour groups vie with each other in frantic and increasingly short-spaced wage claims, rewards going not to the most productive but to the politically most strident labour sectors.

3. Balance of payments disequilibrium, as excess demand, often coupled with inflexible exchange rates, stimulates imports and inhibits exports.

4. Disincentive to investment in the economic infrastructure—utilities, transport and heavy industry—both as a result of the shrinkage of long-term savings and of the almost irresistible temptation of freezing certain strategic prices and tariffs of basic services and goods.

5. Distortions in the tax system. As book values cease to reflect the real value of capital assets, income taxation begins to bite into illusory profits, working capital is depleted and depreciation allowances become inadequate. There is abnormal incentive to evade or postpone tax payments. Finally, unintended tax progression at the wrong place may occur, as lower income groups start being taxed simply because of a rise in nominal income even though there may have been no real welfare gain.

A number of devices were engineered and gradually implanted between 1964 and 1967 to neutralise the main evils of inflation. The essential components of the Brazilian formula were:

a) *Generalised indexation for all forms of saving.* Government bonds, housing bonds, medium- and long-term banking deposits, medium- and long-term acceptance papers. As a counterpart, medium- and long-term loans were also indexed. These measures had a healthy effect in preventing bottlenecks in the financial market and created a strong market for Government bonds, enabling the Government to raise non-inflationary revenues for developmental projects.

b) *The wage formula.* This formula, enacted by law, disposes that wage readjustments be spaced out at intervals of one year, on the basis of the following elements: recomposition of the average real wage of the preceding 24 months (modified now to a 12-month period), plus a productivity coefficient estimated by the Government to represent the average increase in the productivity of the economy, and, finally, a coefficient representing the inflationary residual—that is, half of the expected rate of inflation in the ensuing 12-month period.

The wage formula is certainly the most difficult and the least exportable component of our indexation system. It certainly was fundamental to permit Brazil in the last four years to reconcile declining inflation with high growth. It had the advantage of eliminating the bitter competitiveness of wage disputes and avoiding the "wage-push" as an autonomous factor of inflation. It also divorced wage readjustments from the coercive power of politically prestigious labour unions, which otherwise might get more than their fair share. Despite that, or perhaps because of that, its implantation proved difficult and is likely to be even less palatable in other countries. Fair and rational as it is, the wage formula does not make the individual worker psychologically happy because he is, as everybody else, subject to the money illusion: large nominal wages, even though rapidly eroded by inflation, are psychologically more exciting than moderate, though more sustainable, wage boosts. From the viewpoint of the trade union leaders, the objections stem from the "power play": they derive their political power from the conflictive process and bargaining victories rather than from other paternalistic concessions or statistically determined wage upgrading. It must be noted however that the wage policy is only one of the components of our labour incomes policy. Great emphasis has been given to non-wage benefits such as fiscally financed housing and sanitation works which further employment; and to educational programmes which upgrade the human capital. There are also non-contributory funds financed by employers, which can be drawn by the workers only in special circumstances, but which represent employees' assets, protected by indexation and available as capital for housing programmes and industrial expansion.

c) *Tax reform.* The tax system was converted to a real base, which in turn compelled enterprises to adopt real accounting methods; taxes, profits and depreciation allowances are computed on capital assets revalued each according to official indices of monetary correction. The same principle applies to the tax exemption threshold of low-income groups. The indexation of fiscal debt rendered tax dodging dangerous and payment delays unattractive.

d) *The mini-devaluation system* (*the "crawling peg"*). Parallel to the internal monetary correction there is a periodical devaluation of exchange rates, at uncertain intervals and in mini-steps, so as to avoid speculation in foreign currency. The rate of devaluation is based on the rise of the internal wholesale price level, after deduction of a certain percentage representing an estimated average of the rate of inflation in our main trading partners: the steps are always kept below the current market interest rate, so as to discourage borrowing for speculation in foreign currency; and the periodicity is variable depending largely on the export behaviour and reserve position.

e) *The saving-bias*. Both for anti-inflationary and developmental purposes, the system is biased in the direction of stimulating savings. Thus sight deposits and short-term financed papers are not indexed, while savings benefit from adjustment at intervals shorter than wages.

## Results and exportability of the system

What are now the results of the Brazilian experiment? On the face of it, quite impressive. The rate of inflation abated gradually from 100 per cent in early 1964 to around 40 per cent in 1965-1966, hovered about the 20 to 25 per cent level from 1967 to 1969, and fell within the range of 15 to 20 per cent in 1972 and 1973. There was the recurrence of a severe inflationary bout in the first half of 1974, as a result of both the inflation of import costs, including oil, and the liberation of certain prices repressed during 1973, but in the last few months inflationary pressures abated substantially. The real success however lies not so much in the deceleration of inflation—for it remains at levels still considered unacceptable in Western societies—but in reconciling it with a very high high rate of growth—over 10.3 per cent in real terms for the last five years, and a hefty 11.4 per cent in 1973. The per capita income in the last five years increased by some 40 per cent in real terms. Exports quadrupled in the period 1964-1973, rising from a level of about $1.5 millions to $6 billions, and in 1974 are likely to reach $7.5 billions. Foreign exchange reserves, which were negative, reached $6.4 billions by the end of 1973 and although declining somewhat under the impact of the oil crisis are still almost $5.5 billions. The investment rates increased from some 14 per cent as a percentage of GNP to some 22 per cent, of which 20 per cent was locally financed and 2 per cent through the inflow of capital. Budget deficits, which in 1963 were about 5 per cent of GNP, declined to negligible proportions in 1972-1973 and were replaced, so far this year, by a budget surplus. On several different tests—deceleration of inflation, budgetary discipline, acceleration of real growth, export expansion and reserve accumulation—the economic performance was quite satisfactory.

The remaining questions are then to what extent the Brazilian experiment is exportable and what has been the role of indexation in the economic performance.

The conditions in Brazil which made generalised indexation both possible and desirable were: *a*) Chronic inflation, which created deeply ingrained expectations that prices would continue to rise; indexation was a way to discipline those expectations and avoid disorderly impact on different sectors of the economy. *b*) The political viability of introducing some shock absorbers that prevented inflation from becoming explosive. Those shock absorbers were (i) the *wage formula,* which prevented an autonomous wage cost push; (ii) the *expenditure constraint,* implemented through a constitutional provision, which forbade Congress from increasing budget expenditures, thus permitting the achievement of a balanced budget; the establishment of minimum periods for adjustment of wages, rentals and other income items, so as to avoid excessive multiplicity and frequency of shocks.

Whether other countries can meet these preconditions, it is not for me to say. But to judge from the resistance of inflationary pressures in Western Europe and Japan to conventional treatment, and considering the danger of lapse into a frustrating alternation of restrictive and permissive policies, it is high time that the search of the elusive goal of eradication of inflation be tempered with a humble search for techniques for minimising its negative effects on savings, investment and income distribution.

But not more should be claimed for indexation than it can deliver. It is certainly not a cure for inflation; at best it can facilitate its control; at worst it can prevent it from causing major distortions. Basically the fight against inflation presupposes a skilful orchestration of monetary and fiscal policies to regulate demand, and incomes policy to minimise autonomous cost impulses and equitably apportion restraints as between wages, profits and prices.

If indexation does not cure inflation, it does not cause it either; just as the thermometer that registers the fever does not play a causal role in it. By institutionalising protection against inflation it may in fact discourage claims for excessive wage and price increases in anticipation of inflation.

Indexation, again, is no formula for economic growth; the Brazilian development boom has required several coordinated pieces of policy to increase savings, rationalise management, render the economy more extroverted and competitive through the promotion of exports and the absorption of foreign capital and technology. But indexation can help in preventing bottlenecks, either in the financial sphere by preserving the supply of savings, or in physical output by preserving the capability of the public sector to invest in basic infra-structural services essential for overall economic expansion.

Certainly, price stability is still better than indexation, for the latter involves both technical complexities and social costs. But if price stability proves, as it has been the case in the recent experience of Western Europe and Japan, an almost unreachable goal, indexation may be helpful in avoiding a number of unpleasant outcomes:

"Stop-go" policies that neither cure inflation nor contribute to minimise its distortions; and/or price stability through shock-treatment, at the price of stagnation and with the risk of reversal, because of the political backlash of unemployment.

Any of those denouements would be melancholy indeed for the anti-inflationary travail of our modern societies. Indexation need not infirm the ideological fervour required to fight inflation, while it keeps free the option of co-habitation, if the battle proves long and uncertain and the political will may be subject to dismay.

# Toward a new international economic order

JACK N. BEHRMAN

# Preface

The fact that the postwar economic order has disintegrated has been discernible for some time, the keystone of United States leadership having been removed and the success of its postwar policies having produced greater strength in other countries. The need to construct a new basis for international economic relations has become evident to many observers. This essay is an attempt to further the dialogue by drawing attention to some critical aspects, that generally fall outside the economic/technical discussion of solutions proposed.

The ideas have been gestating in my mind for some years and have been strongly influenced by research done on the co-operative projects under NATO, on problems of Latin American integration, on new approaches to international industrialization, and on the role of private foreign direct investment and the multinational enterprise. To fit the means available to the needs and demands of different countries seems to require new approaches.

I wish to thank Jack Tuthill for encouraging me to continue my thinking along these lines, Curt Gasteyger for editorial guidance, and Pierre Uri for extensive and intensive criticism through several readings, which has forced me to delete irrelevancies, to sharpen my ideas, and to explain them more precisely and understandably. Any imprecision or inadequacy remaining is my own responsibility.

Jack N. Behrman

Chapel Hill, N. C., June 1974.

# List of Abbreviations

| | |
|---|---|
| AID | Agency for International Development |
| ASEAN | Association of South East Asian States |
| CIPEC | International Copper Development Council |
| CIDEC | Intergovernmental Council of Copper Exporting Countries |
| COMECOM | Council for Mutual Economic Assistance |
| COMSTAT | Communications Satellite Corporation |
| ECOSOC | (United Nations) Economic and Social Council |
| ELDO | European Space Vehicle Launcher Development |
| ESRO | European Space Research Organization |
| GARIOA | Government and Relief in Occupied Areas (Post World War II) |
| GATT | General Agreement on Tariffs and Trade |
| GNP | Gross National Product |
| IATA | International Air Transport Association |
| IDA | International Development Association |
| IFC | International Finance Corporation |
| IMF | International Monetary Fund |
| INTELSAT | International Telecommunications Satellite Consortium |
| IRS | Internal Revenue Service |
| ITO | International Trade Organization |
| LAFTA | Latin American Free Trade Association |
| LDCS | Less-Developed Countries |
| ME | Multinational Enterprise |
| MRCA | Multi-Role Combat Aircraft |
| NATO | North Atlantic Treaty Organization |
| OPEC | Organization of the Petroleum Exporting Countries |
| R & D | Research and Development |
| SATCOM | Satellite Communications Agency (United States Army) |
| SDRS | Special Drawing Rights |
| UN | United Nations |
| UNCTAD | United Nations Conference on Trade and Development |
| UNRRA | United Nations Relief and Rehabilitation Administration |
| UNRWAPRNE | United Nations Relief and Works Agency for Palestine Refugees in the Near East |
| US | United States |

# Introduction

One of the slogans of World War II was that the war was being fought in order to achieve a just and durable peace. But as some of the pundits said at the time, we have rather created 'a just endurable peace.' A major reason for that failure is the absence of acceptable concepts of justice in the international economic system. Justice in the society of nations is not a matter of inviolate borders or national independence, and peace in this world will not be guaranteed merely by the absence of armed conflict. A durable peace is a matter of economic justice—an economy that answers, in a manner that is ethically acceptable, the critical questions of who *owns* what, who *does* what, who *decides* what, who *uses* what, who *serves* whom, and who *receives* what.

Answers to these questions imply answers to the specific policy issues of the location of economic activities over the world, the markets that are to be served, the distribution of income (and governmental revenue) received from the production and distribution of goods and services, the fairness of prices charged, the locus of decision making, the location of the centres of creativity and respect for the rights of the individual and associative groups. These are the critical policy areas in which acceptable solutions need to be found—those of trade and exchange rates can come later.

The present international economic order assumes that acceptable answers for these problems fall out of playing by the rules of the game—therefore, the system is 'just.' But the rules employed in the postwar period 1945-70 apply only within a highly constrained system, one known as "neo-classical," and one which has not been practiced *fully* at any time and seldom outside of the Western world. With increasing power and influence in the hands of non-Western states, and with many of these not having practiced the neo-classical rules, we can expect a demand that the rules of the game be changed significantly.

Rules themselves, of course, do not achieve justice. They do guide the decisions and how they are implemented. The rules do not guarantee that the answers sought will, in fact, be achieved—anyone can cheat. If enough do cheat on the rules, the system is readily seen as flouted and will break down. Or, if enough players simply demand new rules, the past system is rejected. Both situations are occurring today. And the policy of the United States is lagging behind because it still assumes that the *rules* provide justice, whereas justice arises out of the conditions behind or prior to the application of the rule.

The self-regulating market of the neo-classical economy was, in fact, never permitted to work fully because of the quickly perceived injustices of poverty, ignorance, disease, and squalor that resulted from unemployment, and because of the perceived ability of some individuals to gain more for themselves by violating the rules. Under such conditions, the game played was no longer the game described by the rules.

A market is no more than a mechanism and, like a computer, cannot itself make decisions; it can only reflect what flows in and out of it. To say, therefore, 'let the market decide' is to avoid the recognition that it will merely perpetuate the injustices which exist already; it cannot of itself produce justice. But a just system can employ market rules of implementation quite effectively.

Any attempt to define justice or equity is likely to get bogged down in a host of specifics and disagreements stemming from philosophical and value differences. Since situations differ and conditions change, we can say only that 'equity' consists of an acceptable sharing of the costs and benefits, without duress in any form. What will be accepted (even if not seen as 'equitable') does, of course, reflect power relationships; since these are also changing, we can expect substantial shifts in negotiating positions and pressures for 'more equitable' solutions. Whether these changes will merely reflect shifting power positions or move us toward a more just society is a question that should be kept before the eyes of policy makers.

However, it is probably not possible to obtain even conceptual agreement on the nature of a 'just society'. Plato, in his search for a definition of justice, wrote *The Republic,* encompassing the social, economic, and political life of the community. Equity cannot be achieved finally without creating an entirely just society, however described. Its basic characteristic of the absence of tyranny in any form is caught in the last written words of Thomas Jefferson, penned on 26 June 1825: 'All eyes are open, or opening, to the rights of man. The general spread of the light of science has already laid open to every view the palpable truth that the mass of mankind has not been born with saddles on their backs, nor a favoured few booted and spurred, ready to ride them legitimately by the grace of God' [1].

But, if we cannot agree on perfect justice, we probably can agree on what constitutes injustice. By what criterion of justice does the United States consume nearly one third of the resources of the world and over one third of its industrial production, with a population less than seven per cent of the total? In the disparate consumption of food and the repeated famines in large parts of the world, [2] where is the justice in the continued skewed distribution of income both among and within countries, including the less-developed countries (LDCs)? In systems that degrade the individual by rejecting his talents and disregarding the 'need to be needed'? Where is the justice in economic growth that does not improve the lot of the poor? (Note the perceptive observation of General

Medici, President of Brazil, that 'the economy may be doing well, but the majority of the people are still doing poorly' [3].) In a system under which the centres of decision making are concentrated in a few metropolises? In the faster growth in world industrial centres compared to slower growth in the periphery? In the instability in income of basic commodity producers compared to stability in incomes of industrial manufacturers? In 'equal access' to energy materials based on incomes? [4]

Increasingly, rationales for inequalities are difficult to explain and accept, but there is little likelihood that we can remove inequalities sweepingly. The best we can do is to nibble at them marginally or piece by piece. But we will still need to know where we are trying to go. To achieve that requires first a recognition that the past system cannot take us there.

Justice, if achieved, will not be through the market but in the overall economic system within which it operates. *All* economic systems employ markets—none of them is wholly self-regulating, nor are all systems equally just. Nor is there a direct correlation between degrees of freedom in a market and economic justice; a free market may merely mean that existing power and injustices are perpetuated. A free market can sustain justice only if there are a number of other institutions and conditions surrounding it that cause it to operate justly. These institutions have to do with the motivations of individuals, the ownership of property and the extent to which its use is constrained by concepts of stewardship, the opportunity for the propertyless to provide for themselves, the degree and extent of knowledge and information provided in the system to guide decisions, the extent of control or power in the system and its structure and use, the role of the government in providing public goods and services, etc. Without a full description of these institutions, one cannot judge whether the market is operating justly.

Like the market, the monetary system is only a mechanism, for money has no value of its own (apart from commodity money). Being a mechanism, it should either be used effectively to achieve specific objectives, or should not be permitted to interfere in the *real* economic structure or decisions made by the members of the society. It should, therefore, either be a completely intangible asset managed in such a way as to achieve agreed goals *or* be an automatic lubricant for the system facilitating the operation of the economy.

Money has quite specific functions as a medium of exchange, a standard of value, a bearer of options, and a store of value (for the future). Existing monetary systems create injustices by warping decisions and by altering inequitably the relative positions of individuals and groups vis-à-vis one another. Inflation, therefore, is an injustice in itself which could be offset only by a number of other policies aimed at rectifying *each* of the injustices imposed—a task much better achieved by adopting policies of monetary rectitude.

Since both the market and monetary systems are mere mechanisms, both the United States' and the Atlantic Community's international economic policies have been focused on the *rules* and not on what exists behind the rules! In this approach, 'fairness' is defined as playing by the rules, and not designing the game so that it is a contest among relatively equal participants [5]. But freer trade and stable (or flexible) exchange rates do not produce equity or justice, even if the rules of the game are followed, and they will not be if the system itself is not equitable, which it has not been. So far, the keystones of American foreign economic policy are, therefore, either inadequate or irrelevant, or both; and, consequently, so is the international economic system that the United States Government has been trying to build.

This is not to argue that there is *no* place for free trade or for stable (or flexible) exchange rates, but only that their acceptability rests on the creation of a just and equitable economic system *within* which they are to operate. Refinements of trade rules or technical monetary mechanisms will, therefore, not meet the problem [6]. Being mere mechanisms, they cannot do more than reflect the justice in the system, and if injustice exists, they are likely to accentuate the inequities. Consequently, nations and individuals are constantly trying to remedy the injustices, through interferences in the market and the monetary mechanisms rather than by addressing the underlying problems [7].

The focus on mechanisms and technical solutions has precluded consideration of the system as a whole and the extent to which it is unjust or inequitable. Instead, considerations of a more just and equitable distribution of economic activity over the world have been relegated to the mercies of the market (operating under the 'law of comparative advantage'); considerations of an equitable distribution of incomes have been left to market determination (operating under the theory of marginal productivity?); considerations of 'fair price' have been abandoned to the market mechanism (operating under the theory of monopolistic competition?); and considerations of individual freedom, opportunity, and self-respect (gained through an employment that is seen as needed and useful to society) have been left to the tender mercies of an 'impersonal and objective' market—forgetting that the system should be designed for men and not men for the system!

Peace (economic or otherwise) waits on justice, and justice is significantly an economic matter, but also political. It is economic, since the costs and benefits are worked out in the economy; it is political, since the acceptability of the system is decided in the policy. To try to avoid seeing this unity is to keep our heads buried in the sand.

Once it is recognized that politics cannot be divorced from economics, we will not pose questions such as how to obtain agreement on the principle of 'equal access to raw materials' without also raising the question of whether that principle will operate justly. Such a rule will result in quite different patterns of resource use, depending on the structure of economic wealth and power over the world. Its proposal assumes that those holding the resources are willing to reject use of political power to alter the economic rewards—an unrealistic assumption and one based on a particular concept of justice that perpetuates existing power and wealth relationships, or even magnifies them.

Economic power will be used for political purposes (as shown in the United States' ties with Taiwan and South Korea and those of the Soviet Union to COMECON) and political power for economic purposes (as shown by agricultural policies over the world). No set of rules can avoid this mixture of economics and politics *unless* a politically and ethically acceptable economic system is created first—then the rules are mere conduits for the play of the entire game.

This essay attempts to raise the questions that must be asked, and to examine the criteria that must be pursued, if a just economic system is to be erected internationally within the existing conditions of nationalism [8]. No effort is made to design the entire system but, rather, to demonstrate that repeated attempts have been made through various international agreements and institutions to find a more just solution to specific problems. It should be possible to build on these experiences to create a more just and equitable system for all international economic activities. But it cannot be done unless the question is posed, which is not being done at present by American or European officials.

Since the time of the preparation of the postwar economic plans in 1944, conditions throughout the world have changed significantly, making nations dissatisfied with postwar institutions and solutions, as discussed in the following section. Added to this, economic conditions and the power positions of nations have shifted, altering the setting within which the creation of a new order must take place.

# Dissatisfaction with the postwar system

The post-World War II system was built, largely at the insistence of the United States, on a series of assumptions as to what was the most desirable international order. These assumptions related to both the political and economic realms and require at least a brief enumeration for an understanding of the shifts that are taking place and the dissatisfaction that has arisen.

## Postwar assumptions

The most basic of the various assumptions was that concerning 'international democracy' and 'one worldism.' The American view that the world should be ordered under a concept of equality of all nations rather than that of regional blocs (under which the weak and small were protected by the strong) carried the day in both the political and economic realms. International political institutions were to be based on the principle of 'one nation, one vote,' and international economic affairs were to be built on the assumption that 'equal treatment' would bring an acceptable distribution of economic welfare among nations. Policies were to abstract from the problems of size or dominance (although exceptions were built into the United Nations, the World Bank and the International Monetary Fund [IMF]). All nations were to be treated equally, in the world market, the benefits of which would be distributed according to the contributions of each nation to the welfare of all [9].

To bring all nations to this level of equality, relief and reconstruction programmes were established—UNRRA, GARIOA, UNRWAPRNE—for reconstruction and relief of refugees in allied, enemy, and the Near-Eastern countries *. After a few years of such aid, these countries were supposed to be able to join the others in the move toward international democracy.

The world economy would be constructed under the principles of 'free market' behaviour, the rights of private property, and 'rule of law'. The last meant that governments would exercise the Acts of State Doctrine only in the most extreme cases and, when used against private (corporate) property, would

* The failure of the UN to follow through on the problem of the Palestine refugees must be one of the more mistakes within postwar policies; the world has been and will be paying for that error for many years.

provide 'prompt, effective, and adequate compensation' or submit disputes to international tribunals.

The world's basic economic problems were assumed to be solvable by sufficient increases in GNP, under the further assumption that material advance was more desired than other objectives or that any other goals could be gained through economic growth. Further, economic growth was assumed to be obtainable through infusions of capital (under the implicit assumption that all the institutional framework existed to make such an infusion successful). Therefore, domestic capital formation and international capital transfers would be a nearly adequate means of achieving growth in LDCs. With this stimulus to growth, the 'gap' between the advanced and the poorer countries would be closed in the foreseeable future, removing another obstacle to 'true international democracy.'

Among the industrialized countries, full employment was accepted as the prime economic objective, which was seen as achievable through a mixture of monetary and fiscal policies. It was further assumed that such policies would not themselves lead to disequilibria in international payments and that nations would be willing to make the adjustments necessary to prevent disequilibria, or to regain equilibrium when lost. Consequently, international growth would be maximized and the benefits would be distributed equitably, through the market, with some adjustments through foreign aid.

To provide for easy adjustment to payments disequilibria, the IMF was created with resources to throw into the breach temporarily. If a fundamental disequilibrium arose in the payments position of any nation, it would so evidently be in the interest of all to rectify it that a change in the par value of its exchange rate would be accepted. In the event of insufficient liquidity in the entire system, the price of gold could be raised. Otherwise, stable exchange rates would provide for maximum growth through expanded international trade and investment.

Capital flows were presumed to follow market criteria of return on investment and would, therefore, if left free, contribute appropriately to the maximization of international economic welfare. However, since trade was seen as a more significant contributor to economic growth, *if* capital flows de-stabilized the exchanges or forced countries into disequilibria in payments, such flows should be controlled. When capital did not move as appropriate, because of continued political instability or 'risk illusions,' incentives were seen as appropriate to stimulate a more acceptable flow. Since private capital sources were not seen as likely to be adequate even under stimulus, international lending institutions were provided, first in the World Bank and then through its associates International Finance Corporation (IFC) and International Development Association (IDA), and later through regional banks such as the Inter-American Development Bank and the Asian Bank.

Trade, however, was seen as the primary long-term means of increasing world welfare among those in the international economic realm. In any case, factor movements were considered unlikely to occur (following trade theory) and as an imperfect substitute for trade. Freeing of trade was considered the paramount international economic objective, benefiting all national participants. To achieve free trade required the removal of barriers—tariff and quantitative—and the establishment of a competitive world market as proposed under the International Trade Organization (ITO) and the General Agreement on Tariffs and Trade (GATT). The expansion of free trade would be supported by stable exchange rates.

Therefore, the primary international economic policies were aimed at liberating trade, stabilizing exchange rates, and expanding the flow of capital to developing countries. Once the LDCs became advanced, they would join the other countries in enjoying the fruits of a system of stable exchanges and expanding international trade, becoming full partners in international democracy.

## Inapplicability of assumptions for the 1970s

The problems of the 1970s (and maybe even 1960s) demonstrate that the post-war assumptions are no longer valid. The American Government has successfully de-throned the dollar as the key currency of the world and nothing has been put in its place. Governments have repeatedly employed bilateral negotiations to rectify trade and payments problems despite the prior agreement on multilateral arrangements. American labour has reversed its stand in favour of freer trade. Multinational corporations have come upon the scene and are indicted for currency speculation on the one hand and for political and economic subversion on the other. International production has superseded international trade as the major economic activity among countries. And the centres of economic power have been and are shifting, first, away from the United States toward Europe and Japan, with the developing countries beginning to show their muscle through increasing importance as markets and their control of primary commodities needed by the industrialized countries, and, more recently, back toward the United States as a result of relative weakness in Europe and Japan—with the result that no country or group seems both able and willing to assume the leadership role.

The breakdown of the post-World War II international economic system is a result of the change in underlying conditions and the increasing disparity between reality and the assumption of *laissez-faire*. The changing conditions have altered the operation of the system, and the unreality of the assumptions has become much too apparent to be disregarded. In fact, the unreality of the assumptions can be seen by an examination of the basic principles and their lack of acceptance in critical policies.

The post-World War II system of *laissez-faire* called for 'non-intervention' in international trade and capital movements. It applied the secondary principle of 'multilateral, non-discriminatory trade and payments' when interferences were found necessary. Governments agreed to a set of international rules, constraining their power to interfere in international markets, as reflected in the Fund, the Bank, the GATT, and various regional associations. Economic and commercial decisions were supposed to be made in a self-regulating market system, which was assumed to provide not only the most efficient use of the world's resources but also a just and equitable distribution of the benefits of economic growth.

Efficiency is supposedly achieved by 'clearing the market at an equilibrium price' and justice and equity are achieved by the fact that those served in the market are those that *should be served,* as reflected in their having purchasing power. That is, demand arises from those who work in the system for income, and only income earners *should be served* by the market. The market system has never been *fully* employed by any nation because of the evident inequity of its results, which is a reflection of widespread understanding that the assumptions underlying it are not wholly acceptable or relevant.

Two basic characteristics describe the free-market or 'free-trade' system: an 'undistorted equilibrium price,' which clears the market, and a distribution of income (benefits), which is equitable. For these characteristics to exist requires non-intervention by *any* interest group or government which would 'distort' the price and allocation, and requires that all participants and non-participants (willing or unwilling) *accept* the result as equitable. Further conditions are necessary for these to exist: one is that the participants in the market do not have overriding interests outside the market (e.g., there are no 'natural enemies' to be fought through the market of by constraining its operation); the second is that all *relevant* information is available to all buyers and sellers; the third, all relevant costs are included in the supply price; and the fourth is that all those willing and able to work are employed.

*None* of these conditions has existed in the postwar period. We have not built a competitive system: witness the extent of oligopoly and monopoly ranging from the large corporations to the local shopkeeper, each of which retains a share of profit which would not be available in competitive markets. Nor has the distribution of income within and between countries reflected that which would occur under a competitive model. The more advanced countries have been able to tie the less advanced to the dominant economies through investment and trade in ways which did not always reflect an income distribution that would have occurred in a more competitive society. And these effects have tended to be cumulative: the absence of basic infrastructures for internal development (as opposed to those used to serve the metropolitan countries) meant that foreign investment for national economic growth was not attracted. The only mitigating policies were those adopted by the advanced countries after World War II in the transfer of public loans and grants to developing countries—but this was a recognition that the competitive system had not functioned as supposed and was an attempt to reduce the 'weight of the past' on countries which had been made dependent through colonialism. The LDCs that have so far shown an ability to advance significantly and rapidly are those which were not so tightly tied to a metropolitan economy free trade—reducing barriers to trade and payments and eliminating all discrimination in whatever barriers remained. So long as its economy and the dollar remained dominant, the United States could impose the necessary rules, offering the inducement of opening up its own large and growing market and providing supplies of the key currency for both transactions and reserve functions. Having backed away from performing the role of a key currency, it cannot now impose the rules. Few countries in the rest of the world believe in the efficacy or equity of the postwar system and none is able to replace the United States as the leader [10].

Without a leader, the contradictions of the system are more evident, for there is no one to absorb the imperfections and to pay the costs of making it work. Pressures from both changed and underlying conditions have increased, introducing more non-market factors into decisions and eventually into the system itself. It is now evident to the developing countries, at least, that the system has not been equitable in the distribution of the benefits of growth and that they can alter that distribution more in their favour—not simply through claims for more aid but through the power of markets and raw materials supply. It is increasingly evident in the activities of major trading companies and the multinational investors that not all relevant market information is available and that decisions as to the use of the world's resources are not made by market criteria of efficiency but according to company criteria of efficiency. The existence of oligopolistic markets introduces a power component in the market in the hands of the companies. And the increasing polarization of economic groups within regional groups or around major economies introduces power factors from the governmental (and political) direction. Finally, the increasing concern for the quality of life—for environmental protection, social cohesion, and humanism—emphasizes the absence of all socially relevant costs in supply prices in the market.

With a recognition that the existing system produces neither efficiency nor equity, the fundamental questions of *how* to organize the use of the world's resources and *how* and to *whom* to distribute them are raised anew. Within these must be answered the question of fairness—a question which is critically evident when 'absolute scarcities' exist, as during the Korean War and recently in the petroleum embargo. These questions can be answered either by a redesign of the system or by *ad hoc* solutions to specific problems, but either route requires an adequate system of representation of all the interests involved.

Presently, international institutions are not structured so as to provide those involved with an acceptable representation at the negotiating table. Therefore, many countries are seeking new associations to strengthen their positions. Many prior colonies are seeking nation status to strengthen the voice of previously divided peoples. Some nations are forming regional blocs to negotiate from strength with neighbours or other large groups. And some blocs are tying themselves to one or more advanced countries to gain still stronger representation. In addition, special-interest groups, such as labour, agriculture, and business (management), have formed international associations to strengthen their voices at international conferences. As has been the case historically, the one interest left aside—and *for* which the neo-classical system was supposed to work—is the consumer. But aside from this, there is an imperfect representation of various interests at the local, national, regional, and international levels, meaning that efforts to set new rules or to find *ad hoc* solutions are likely also to be imperfect and subject to further change as the power balances shift. It appears highly unlikely that any 'return' to the free-market assumptions of the postwar world can be achieved, despite the pleading of neo-classical economists, who see in the present situation only a proliferation of second-best solutions.

In efforts to meet some of the present problems, the advanced countries have attempted to dissociate themselves from the developing countries, implying that there are some major problems which can be resolved without participation of the LDCs. Though there are specific problems that concern predominantly one group or the other, and although particular solutions may be found for one that are inappropriate for the other, all major problems affect both groups and will require accommodation between them. Even if a solution is found, for example, for patent problems among the advanced countries, patent policies will remain a problem for the developing countries; and an arrangement between the two groups of countries will have to be worked out to satisfy mutual interests if foreign investment is to play a significant role. The same can be said for a variety of other problems, including sectoral trade arrangements which can be separated off for a group of countries and treated on a less-than-multilateral basis [11].

Regardless of whether specific problems are handled on a bilateral, sectoral, regional, or multilateral basis, these solutions must be accommodated to wider international economic arrangements. For example, interregional or interbloc agreements will be necessary to form the international economic system, since economic blocs seem likely to proliferate. Whatever the building blocks, an international system of one sort or another will exist. The questions remain as to in what form and under what criteria of acceptability.

It is the purpose of the present essay to show that, though the breakdown of the postwar system is largely a result not only of changed conditions, the ensuing chaos and delay in re-structuring a new order result from the absence of agreed criteria. Examination of several of the segments of the international economic order shows that the lack of agreement in each results from an effort to employ *technical* solutions that do not reflect the basic national interests of governments. These interests are wider and more complex than efficiency, and market efficiency is an unacceptable measure of even that criterion.

A new international economic order will be reached, if at all, only when new principles of co-operation are developed and agreed upon—principles reflecting the complex criteria of social and political life rather than merely the economic criterion of efficiency. All the postwar agreements had both social and political impacts, which were subverted for the goal of efficiency as a result of the dominance of the United States economy and its willingness to pay the costs of the postwar system—in terms of maintaining the key currency, opening its markets, and extending aid. It is now unwilling to do any one of these to the extent necessary to maintain the prior system; and no other country is able or willing to take up the burden, though several could do so in concert.

The absence of agreed criteria of burden sharing is the crux of the inability to come to further agreements along the lines of the postwar system and to embark in any new direction. Until that problem is resolved, the international economy will face *ad hoc* technical solutions, each breaking down under the strains of disagreement over the sharing of burdens and benefits. Economic theory has been of little help in providing models for such sharing, assuming that equity flowed from the market mechanism and the underlying conditions of supply and demand—which was, of course, not the case.

The problem of burden sharing extends not just into military expenditures and foreign aid, where the discussions have been held primarily, but also into every other economic arrangement. Whether or not specifically incorporated in the agreements, each international institution or arrangement has an implicit pattern of distribution of both benefits and burdens: the International Air Transport Agreement (IATA), all commodity agreements, regional associations, etc. In fact, the recent problems in the re-negotiation of the IATA were principally those of disagreement over the distribution of flights and earning capacity resulting from the limitation on rates under the agreement. Commodity agreements are essentially a means of distributing income between producers and consumers differently from the pattern that would exist under free-market sales. And the European Community has recently run into considerable difficulty over the formation of a common policy toward Mid-East petroleum embargos strictly on the question of the distribution of the burdens, with France particularly not wanting to suffer any inconvenience to assist others in the Community [12].

For successful agreements in the future, the criterion of equity must be placed alongside that of efficiency. This fact has often been espoused in phrases asserting the need for 'an effectively functioning and reasonably equitable international economic system,' but it has been given little more than lip service when the solutions have been brought forward [13].

The following three sections review the changes in the underlying conditions that require a re-assessment of the structure of the international economic order, examine the reasons why governments will try to prevent the undesirable impacts of 'technical economic solutions' to foreign economic problems, and offer some tentative steps toward a new international economic order based on more complex criteria of acceptability.

# New international setting

During the past decade, the international economy has undergone some critical changes which make futile an effort to continue negotiations or trade and payments under past principles. At least eight new elements have entered this picture: one is the tie between international trade and foreign direct investment which has produced a kind of industrial integration known as 'international production;' second is the control exercised by the multinational enterprise over the location of industrial activity and the resulting trade and payments; third is the rising priority given by governments to industrial development in the long term, often sustained at high short-term costs, and altering the international division of labour away from 'comparative advantage;' fourth is the expanding role of the LDCs, which have acquired economic (and political) power through an expansion of their markets and a critically increased demand for some of the materials which they supply; fifth is the East-West detente, which introduces new economic opportunities that can be seized only by adaptations of the rules of the game; sixth is the shifting economic power among the advanced countries; seventh is the growing concern for non-market costs of economic growth, represented in the moves to protect the environment, to inject social costs of development, and to foster self-respect of individuals, races, and nations; and eighth is the introduction of a 'new nationalism' in advanced countries, which reinforces an old-style nationalism in the LDCs. None of these factors supports initiatives towards greater freedom in trade and payments either as a means of achieving adjustment in the system or as a means of achieving the ideal economic order. Not only is the concept of the 'ideal' different in the views of different groups, but also there is disagreement on the means of achieving the ideal. One can even agree with Preeg that 'the most enlightened way to achieve the greatest good for the greatest number would be for all nations to refrain from exercising the leverage of national power and, instead, to follow mutually agreed rules and procedures, adjudicated by some form of supranational body [14].' However, disagreement remains on how to create or get to a supranational body. Some would turn over the task to the multinational enterprises; others would seek to create it by fiat, and still others would build slowly on the nation state and then on regional associations. Many would argue, however, that supranationalism is likely to be stultifying and would be undesirable from many points of view.

International production consists of the sales of companies owned by foreigners. It is often guided by considerations not wholly related to the national market of the host country, but rather related to demands in the world market or other national markets. The volume of international production—covering extractive industries, manufacturing, and a variety of service activities including banking— is conservatively estimated at between $400 and $500 billion, or nearly 20 per cent of the GNPs of the countries of the free world. Nearly $100 billion of total world exports come out of these sales, leaving some $200 billion of exports to arise outside of international production. Counting both international production and independent exports, over $600 billion, or some 25 per cent of the free world's GNPs, passes through the hands of international business.

The fact that decisions as to the volume of production, the location of sales, direction of exports, prices, and qualities are made on the basis of inter-company relationships, and under a variety of governmental interventions, means that the flow of trade and payments is increasingly influenced by non-market forces. The significance of this fact for national policy is shown by the report of the British Department of Trade and Industry that over 80 per cent of British exports are in the hands of international companies; of this, one quarter is held by affiliates of United States companies, and over half of this quarter by other affiliates of the same companies. Therefore, the British deficit is *potentially* a matter of inter-affiliate trade of foreign companies. The United States Department of Commerce calculates that over 50 per cent of American exports are by 298 international companies, with just under half of this being to and through foreign affiliates. These companies and their 5,237 majority-owned foreign affiliates generated 51 per cent of total American exports and 34 per cent of total imports during 1970. During the years 1966-70, the trade surplus of these companies increased, while the overall American trade balance declined. Within these companies, those in manufacturing (as distinct from extraction and services) accounted for all of the trade surplus of the group. The greatest increase in exports was to affiliated companies as compared to independent companies abroad, but the balance of trade with affiliates remained smaller because of the large number of imports from Canadian automobile affiliates. The expansion of trade during the four-year period covered was faster in industrialized countries than in LDCs, and exports of these companies rose 55 per cent compared to 43 per cent for the total. If all American international companies are aggregated, the Department estimated that some 63 per cent of total exports came from them in 1966, rising to nearly 70 per cent in 1970. They accounted for 45 per cent of all imports in 1966, rising to some 50 per cent in 1970 [15].

Given this institutional tie between the international companies' investments and total exports and imports, it is not unrealistic to stress that over half of the free world's GNP is at some point under processing, by companies directly involved in international investment and exports. The 298 companies in the

Department of Commerce survey had consolidated sales (United States and world, with intercompany sales eliminated) of $390 billion in 1970 (probably $450 billion in 1972 and over $500 billion by 1974). Other American international companies probably had another $150 billion of consolidated sales, and international companies based in Europe and Japan easily had over $350 billion. Consequently, the international companies of Europe, Japan, and North America accounted for $900 billion of sales in the free world GNP in 1970, though this sum is larger, of course, than the value added by their activities. To this should be added another $200 billion of exports by independent sellers of materials and agricultural products, aggregating $1100 billion over which they held control at some time—a sum nearly half of the total GNPs of the free world in that year.

The size of the companies, the relationships between investment, trade, and licensing, and the integrated strategy of the international companies means that decisions are taken within the institution over a wider range than for smaller or less integrated companies.

## The international enterprise

The multinational enterprise (ME) is more a concept than an institutional reality. However, the concept is important in terms of international economic policies, for the decision criteria employed under it alter economic and social conditions. The ME concept is that total operations of the international company should be integrated so as to achieve least-cost production and distribution in serving the world market [16]. This means that the parent company and its affiliates will be dovetailed and the affiliates will specialize in components or subassemblies, integrating operations with each other to serve the various national markets most economically. It is to be contrasted, conceptually and operationally, with an international company whose affiliates produce and sell wholly within a single national market.

The ME, by nature, centralizes policy decisions so as to enforce the degree of integration desired, including product lines, the technology employed, marketing areas, selling efforts, pricing, financial flows, etc.; Research and development activities are usually concentrated in the parent. These decisions directly affect the balance-of-payments positions of the countries involved, for good or ill; they are hardly made under free-market criteria. Many of the decisions are intercompany decisions within the ME. Obviously, they are ultimately affected by market criteria in the sense that final sales are made to customers. But there are many markets (governmental, institutional, industrial, etc.) in which the forces at work are not free; even if they were, their effect would be altered by being sieved through the decision layers of the multinational enterprise. Given its capabilities and its existence in many national economies, the ME has abilities to soften, reinforce, or negate adjustment pressures brought by other forces or by governmental decisions. For example, the impacts of the recent devaluations on MEs, that had funds in many national currencies were different from those on purely national companies. In addition, the ME has the power to reinforce or avoid policy decisions in industrial development, trade, or integration.

### Industrial capacity

The new background for economic policy is further coloured by the fact that the longer-run goal of all governments is development of industrial capacity in key sectors. The European Community has the consideration of a regional industrial policy on its agenda, related to the selection and location of industries to be developed and the means of facilitating their growth, especially in the high-technology sector. The pressure on the British computer company International Computers Limited (ICL) to join a new merger of the German, French and Dutch companies (Siemens, CII and Philips) is the strongest example of this attitude, but the aircraft mergers also reflect it. Japan is already embarked on a government-industry policy of shifting emphasis to the high-and-new technology industries such as those in the de-pollution, rapid-transit, and communication fields. Many LDCs, such as those in the Andean Group, are stressing means to determine the best industries to develop and how to relate them to the international division of industrial activity. These long-run policies will alter significantly the international division of labour as compared to what would have occurred under 'free markets,' for the latter would have continued to favour creation of new industries in those countries already highly advanced.

Among the short-term goals is maintenance of employment and utilization of capacity in existing industrial sectors, even if high costs are incurred. For example, the Japanese have been increasing their bids for logs exported from the United States in order to assure supplies for their sawmills, which would shut down in the absence of United States exports. The consequence for the United States was price rises of 20 to 50 per cent for lumber and plywood within one year. The trade-off in this sector is between the American construction industry and its sales and the Japanese lumber industry; neither, obviously, desires to bear the burden of adjustment, and both will call for governmental support and interference.

### The role of the LDCs

The role of the less-developed countries is changing significantly from what it was 25 years ago. They are separating into at least three different levels of advancement; they have quite different capabilities to interfere with the prior international order, and they are forming into regional blocs to enhance their power.

The power of the LDCs is increasing through the fact of success in economic development, as seen especially among the most advanced ones. These countries now have markets which are attractive to international companies for both export and investment opportunities. Rather than merely permit their markets to be exploited in ways beneficial to the international companies, these countries are taking steps to attract the particular investments they desire and prevent others—viz., Taiwan, Mexico, Brazil, Singapore, South Korea, Nigeria. Even those in the middle range of development—such as Ivory Coast, Kenya, Peru, Ecuador, Thailand, and Algeria—are stressing industrialization for local development rather than merely opening their markets to imports, and are being selective as to those companies that are allowed to enter. Only the least developed are unable to entice such industrial investment, being able mainly to attract investment in raw materials and agricultural activities, out of which they can pay for needed imports. However, even those with raw materials hold significant power: Zambia and Zaire with copper, Jamaica and Guyana with bauxite, and Bolivia and Malaya with tin, to say nothing of many with petroleum (which are not poor but still relatively undeveloped).

The LDCs do not adhere to the postwar system and have never accepted its rules as applicable; they see it as having been developed by 'imperialistic' governments for the benefit of industrialized countries. The UNCTAD, of course, is a reflection of the rejection of the GATT and IMF rules. There are, in effect, *no rules* by which the LDCs feel they are bound in the reception of foreign investment, the gestation of international trade, and the formation of materials policy. To emphazise this fact, they have created state enterprises in both the development and sale of materials; in the processing of some resources prior to export; and in key industrial sectors to seek their national interests in whatever way is found desirable at the time. Not even the contractual obligations of a government, present or past, are considered inviolate if it is found undesirable to adhere to them.

If new rules are to be formulated, the LDCs must find that it is desirable to do so and then must participate in their formulation. One avenue by which this attitude is likely to be developed is the formation of regional blocs among the LDCs themselves. To form them will require acceptance of rules of behaviour and their fulfillment; otherwise, the arrangements will be voided. The failure of the East African Community is a case in point, as is that of the Central American Common Market. The Andean Pact countries appear to have learned this lesson; at least, they have so far avoided openly breaking the rules in ways such as to rupture the Pact. The rules which they will formulate for themselves are unlikely to duplicate those among the advanced countries, such as 'equal access' to goods and materials or to investment opportunities in the region. Even if they are similar, the same rules are not likely to apply to outsiders. Thus, the plea of the advanced countries for 'equal access' will go unheeded [17].

For the United States to respond that it will develop self-sufficiency in energy or other critical materials is a proclamation that international economic interdependence is unacceptable, and is a reversion to economic isolationism—far from the principle of equal access and still further from that of international economic co-operation under principles of efficiency and equity [18].

### East-West relations

Another change is that the East-West detente has opened up both trade and investment opportunities that did not exist before; more so for the United States than for European companies, which have not refrained from sizable trade with the Soviet bloc over the past decade. Even if the volume of trade and co-production arrangements does not reach the optimistic levels predicted by over-eager governmental and business officials, the impact of new arrangements will be felt in the formation of new rules for East-West relations and also in other areas, magnifying their effect.

The alteration of the postwar rules is likely to be in favour of doing business the Soviet way. An unresolved controversy in the debate on the aborted International Trade Organization (ITO) was how to incorporate trade with state-trading countries under 'commercial' or 'laissez-faire' rules. The recent eagerness of the Western companies to trade and combine with state trading enterprises has meant the adoption of state trading procedures and rules more than of Western 'commercial' practices [19].

American and European companies have lined up to do business with the Soviet Union and China on the latters' terms, giving up majority ownership to join with state enterprises, accepting long-term contracts and bilateral trade and payments agreements involving barter of components and final products. These acts have opened the eyes of many LDC governments and businessmen who now see that the 'inviolate' principles of the free market and of wholly-owned foreign investment are readily broken down when sufficient power is exercised (and the market is sufficiently attractive).

It is likely that they will be encouraged to make similar impositions in favour of their state enterprises, where they exist. They will see less of an obstacle to their socialist economic policies in the fact that the international companies are eager to play by socialist rules when profit is to be gained (and even sometimes when it is not, as in the case of Fiat). Once again, then, the rules of the game with LDCs will be re-formulated.

### Withdrawal of the United States

Bolstering the increasing strength of the LDCs and the power of the Socialist countries is the fact that the United States has chosen to withdraw from the centre of the stage in international economic policy—in favour of domestic economic goals. Despite the fact that the United States market, the American dollar, and foreign aid were keystones to the postwar system, the American Government decided in the early 1960s that it could not bear the burdens of the international system at the expense of domestic unemployment or instability, and began to eliminate the key currency (reserve) role of the dollar. Subsequent administrations made the same trade-off, progressively devaluing the dollar through restrictions and, finally, in the exchange market itself. This act alone finally fractured the keystone to the postwar system, and it has not been replaced.

But the decline in foreign aid, relative to the growing needs and the abilities of the donors (the United States and others) also showed a withdrawal from the key role played by the United States for 20 years after World War II. More recently, events within the camp of labour and in the trade field have shown a preference for domestic policies over foreign commitments, as will be detailed in the following section.

This conscious United States withdrawal coupled with the growing strength of other nations in trade and investment has loosened if not removed the leadership baton from the hands of American officials, at least in economic affairs. And any relative shift back towards the United States is not likely to induce it to pick up the baton again—at least, not in favour of a change in the rules of trade and investment. Therefore, any new rules will probably be set in accord with the interests of others as much (or more) than with those officially supported by the United States.

## Inclusion of non-market costs

The free-market system will be altered or undercut still further by the growing insistence on inclusion of non-market costs of development in the calculations as to the best use of the world's resources. The concern for the quality of life as well as the quantity of material goods means that new cost concepts will have to be developed. As argued earlier, if *all* relevant costs can be determined and are included in the market, a self-regulating market *might* work acceptably. This means that social, cultural, environmental, educational, and even familial and ecclesiastical costs would have to be included.

Environmental costs will be difficult to calculate if for no other reason than that we do not have adequate means to calculate damage to various elements in the environment, nor do we know how long it will take to rectify damage nor whether it is important to do so, given the possibility that man will himself adapt to changes in the environment over the long run or new elements be discovered. These problems arise *over* an indeterminant time; time itself must be costed if the calculation is to be precise, which we do not know how to do.

Social costs would include the impacts of mobility on communities, which lose the talents of capable people who are moved about for the purposes of business and government, without regard to the costs imposed on the community or family involved. These external costs are not even calculated by those responsible since they are borne by the family or community, which also does not calculate the costs. The loss of social cohesion and a sense of community is reflected in the disorientation of many in the younger generations, who seek often long and fruitlessly to find out 'who they are, where they are, and why they are there.' Little effort is bent to determining the advantages of a dispersion of activities so that smaller communities may be maintained rather than agglomerated in large urban centres, where social welfare costs add to the losses in outlying areas from the exercise of both voluntary and forced mobility.

Cultural costs are imposed through the loss of 'place' and of self-respect when an individual is uprooted from the land or from his community, separated from family ties, and made a commodity in the market or a cog in the industrial wheel without being given a 'place' that is an adequate substitute for that which is lost. This loss is seen in a lack of pride of workmanship and a drop in opportunities for creativity, which are the basis for self-respect—that is, the knowledge that one *can* contribute and that this contribution is *needed*.

Finally, the ecclesiastical costs must be counted in the substitution of material values for ethical or spiritual values—a primacy of materialism over spiritualism, or of things over people (if one wishes to avoid any religious connotation). As de Tocqueville reputedly said: 'The officials of the world seem to be committed to making things great. I wish they would be more concerned to make men great. That is, that they be more concerned with workmen than with work.' If man will turn to spiritual aspects of his being only after he has reached a high material plateau *or* only if he rejects materialism itself, it is conceivable that we are approaching such a period. If so, the rules are likely to become much more imbued with concepts of 'fair price,' 'fair incomes,' etc., as a reflection of the fact that highly relevant costs cannot be included in the supply price and that equity in distribution is important.

Destruction of the currency, as is occurring in repeated inflations over the world, and arguments that growth must be slowed if the world is to survive, will only intensify the demands for 'justice' in the market—in prices, incomes, and access to goods and services—both at national and at international levels.

## A new nationalism

Finally, the 'new nationalism' will alter the nature of the rules of the new international economic order, returning it toward the mercantilist concepts of maintenance of employment and provision of necessary goods. The new nationalism is characterized by an increasing (and seemingly unceasing) demand on the part of citizens for governmental assumption of responsibility for much of economic and social life. The list of governmental policies appears exponential, increasing rapidly in the postwar period compared even to the expansion during the Great Depression. Governmental responsibilities during the pre-World War I period included protection of life (police and armed forces), education, judicial services, antitrust legislation, and some incentives to creation of infrastructure; in the 1930s, they added a number of welfare, agricultural, employment, and labour policies; in post-World War II, the list grew to include housing, transportation, basic industries, increased social welfare, medical and health services, stimulus to depressed areas, manpower training, productivity programmes, incomes policies, maintenance of currency values in domestic and international markets, balance-of-payments equilibrium, the level of employment and GNP and the rate of growth of each, regulations on business activities, and prevention of discrimination among races in a wide range of activities. (The list is undoubtedly longer.)

The impact of these new responsibilities on the subject of this essay is that they will cause changes in the international rules of the game because they make governments wary of disturbances to the economy; foreign disturbances are especially upsetting because they cannot be corrected at the source. Rather, they force adjustments in the domestic policies, showing the populace that the government cannot protect their interests as it should—since it does have responsibility!

Consequently, the government will attempt to reduce the influence of foreign economic activities and, when it cannot, will seek to make certain that the adverse impact is minimal and that any burden is seen as equitable in the eyes of its citizens. If it cannot do these things, it will be seen as incompetent or incapable and rejected by the voters. Strong pressure, therefore, will arise to control and guide international economic activities so as to force them to fit into the domestic requirements. This orientation can be seen in the policy areas discussed in the succeeding section.

The thrust of these eight changes in the international scene is to require new initiatives to reform the rules and thereby create a new international economic order. These rules, whether general or made for specific problem areas, will have to recognize that many international activities are interdependent—e.g., investment directly determines much of the trade volumes and patterns and consequently the benefits from industrial activity for the countries involved.

Such an approach would begin with a recognition of increasing interdependence not only of economic factors but also of political, social, and even cultural and spiritual aspects around the world. Given this interdependence, *significant* adjustments are not likely to come from changes 'at the margin,' though such changes will occur. Significant advances can come only through modifications of attitudes which give rise to new institutions (patterns of behaviour). Since such institutions tend to be rigid and to resist change, they require large pressures to force adaptation. Such changes affect sizable and important sectors, raise social and political issues, and involve substantial non-economic costs. Because of these multiple effects, governments interfere to protect national interests and slow the adjustments, reducing costs to vital sectors or to critical institutions. The result is a rigidity in the adjustment mechanisms; whether this is 'bad' or 'good' depends on the underlying values, the goals sought, and the weight attached to rapid or slower change. The revolutionist will argue the necessity to 'break eggs to make an omelette,' while the evolutionist will seek not to 'throw the baby out with the bath water.' Value differences remain at the root of the opposing positions.

# Interferences in the market

An understanding of the changes in the postwar situation provides the basis for a further understanding of the difficulties nations have had in accepting and implementing the postwar rules of the game and therefore their insistence on exceptions.

Numerous interferences have been injected into the system—some aimed at making an imperfect market work more perfectly, but most at preventing the market from operating because of the undesirable adjustments it would require. The former interferences are exemplified by antitrust regulations and the latter by those supporting agricultural policies. Both of these existed prior to World War II. Although a major effort in the postwar period was directed at establishing 'free-market' rules under IMF and GATT, significant interventions have been made for the purpose of providing equity where free competition has been seen as inequitable. The goal of equity was reflected in the 'escape clause' and in the GATT provision, permitting American export subsidies and import quotas on wheat to buttress and prevent frustration of its domestic price support programme.

## The gamut of interferences

Beyond the GATT, exceptions to market determinations have proliferated for the purpose of creating a more equitable system in specific problem areas. They include the 'voluntary quotas' imposed by exporters of products ranging from textiles, iron and steel to mushrooms; the United States-Canadian auto agreement; the International Air Transport Agreement; maritime rate conferences; various commodity agreements on coffee, wheat, cocoa, and tin; export controls for short-supply purposes on items such as walnut logs, soybeans, and logs to Japan; the Organization of Petroleum Exporting Countries (OPEC); and the division of tax revenue; the nascent agreement among the copper exporting countries (CIBEC); co-production arrangements for military systems under NATO, for the European Airbus, for the Concorde, COMSAT, and the Multi-Role Combat Aircraft (MRCA); the complementation agreements under the Latin American Free Trade Association (LAFTA) and Andean Pact; and the private compensation agreements for allocation of production among companies in both selling and purchasing countries. The major set of interventions, however, has been in preventing adjustments in the balance of payments among countries. Not only have the LDCs continued to reject the rules of the IMF but advanced countries have progressively voided them, on the grounds that it would 'hurt too much' to apply them, that is, that the results would be inequitable in their view.

## Protection of the textile industry

During the 1950s, the American textile industry began to feel the pressure of imports from LDCs as a result of the latter's efforts to industrialize. Imports rose to such levels in specific items that United States companies claimed they would be forced out of business by the volumes and low prices; they sought relief from their Government through import duties or quotas. Imposition of duties would permit the countries harmed to claim damages under the GATT and to raise their own duties against American goods—a result not desired since the United States was seeking additional rounds of tariff reductions under the GATT. Import quotas were prohibited under the GATT rules.

President Kennedy was induced during his campaign to promise to 'do something for textiles' in order to garner the votes of the South. The textile companies had asserted that 'if the Government wants us to die a little, just say so, and we'll find some way to do it; but let us know the rules of the game.' The political consequences of letting textiles 'die a little' were considered too great, and an imposition of 'voluntary export quotas' was sought on the part of the exporting countries.

Imposition of overall quotas per country was first sought, but it became necessary to specify types of goods, and the ability to shift from one category to another (not so stringently restricted) proliferated the quotas. Continuing efforts were made to prevent harm to individual segments of the industry.

Underlying the debate was the question of justice and equity: who should make the adjustments to the industrialization of LDCs, and what should be the pace of that adjustment? Only the subsequent prosperity of the industry as a result of the Vietnamese war and general growth in GNP eased the import pressures sufficiently to prevent even harsher quotas and more acrimonious negotiations.

Similar but less excruciating negotiations occurred with reference to iron and steel, stainless-steel flatware, and mushrooms. In each the question was whether or not adjustments should be imposed on particular industries in the United States simply because of the success abroad in achieving economic growth. In the case of mushrooms, South Korea had developed this activity at the suggestion and with the assistance of AID, which also proposed export to the American markets. Should not American producers have also been aided, or at least not harmed by the programme? Or should they bear the burden of successful AID efforts abroad?

These questions underlay frequent attempts by congressmen to amend the AID legislation to prevent use of its funds to promote activities abroad which would encourage imports into the United States of items already adequately supplied by local producers. (Apparently it was all right to shift the source of imports, putting some burden on other foreign suppliers.) All such efforts were rejected in final votes—as were the repeated efforts by the shoe industry to obtain voluntary agreements similar to those in textiles.

## The Canadian auto agreement

The Canadian auto agreement arose out of a complaint by the Canadian Government that the balance of trade in autos and parts continued to run at a deficit of some $200 million during the early 1960s and that this was the result of company decisions rather than free-market forces. Canadian officials proposed to the companies that they export more components and autos from Canada to the United States and, as an inducement, offered a rebate of the import duty on an equivalent amount of American auto exports to Canada.

The United States Government considered this a violation of the GATT rules against a subsidy for exports and threatened imposition of a countervailing duty if the Canadian Government persisted. Negotiations ensued; in the hopes of moving toward a situation of freer trade, an agreement was concluded permitting duty-free trade in automobiles and original parts and accessories (but not replacement parts) *. The American companies were also asked to give guarantees that they would increase their investments in production in Canada so as to provide a basis for exports, reduce import dependence, or at least balance trade volumes.

The pattern of investment and trade that developed brought a substantial reversal in the trade deficit, with the United States facing a bilateral deficit in autos and parts with Canada by the early 1970s. At this point, the State Deparment argued for a re-negotiation of the agreement, with Canada dragging its feet.

Canada's seeking a more 'equitable' solution was met with an agreement for the expansion of trade and a re-direction of investment, which later produced an inequitable situation in the view of the United States Government, despite the fact that it had earlier considered that the freeing of trade would produce a highly acceptable result. But trade followed investment, which changed the 'comparative advantages' and the basis for trade. Both investment and trade were determined by governmental and company objectives—not by market criteria.

* This preferential arrangement violated the GATT and required special dispensation from its members.

## The IATA agreement

The International Air Transport Agreement (IATA) was formed for the purpose of preventing the destructive impacts of free competition, of subsidized competition, or that among governmental airlines. Given the fact that, at the time of the agreement, the United States was the only country capable of placing planes on all important routes, the agreement was essentially a means of reserving equitable participation for other countries in anticipation of their being able to enter the field. Each new nation insisted on participation with its own or a sponsored airline.

Although landing rights and schedules frequency remained regulated by each national government, the tariffs and services were placed under IATA. The fact that non-scheduled carriers were not covered meant that periods of heavy demand were often met by substantial increases in 'charter' flights with cut-rate fares. Some of the scheduled carriers decided to break the agreement in order to meet this competition, and re-negotiation ensued. But it was again agreed that cut-throat, unrestrained, or free competition would be unreasonable and inequitable.

This experience indicates that where the interests of important customers (countries) are involved they can constrain the suppliers and enter the game under rules different from those of the market. And, where it is clear that open competition would damage the interests of many if not all suppliers, combinations in restraint of competition are readily agreed upon. The division of the benefits is, however, not made in the IATA directly, since the frequency of schedules and landing rights are not within its control. Despite this, the members consider that greater equity is obtained with the IATA than would exist without it, and that the higher cost to the customer is acceptable. (Of course, when governments own the airlines, such an agreement takes on the form of a tax or 'fee for services rendered' without a direct relation between the service and the fee.)

The Maritime Rate Conferences are similar in effect to the IATA. Their purpose was to prevent destructive competition among the shipping companies and to provide a means of dividing the benefits of the higher income resulting from controlled rates. The rate structure also favoured certain types of shipping and commodities and therefore certain countries more than others.

Whether or not equity considerations were to the fore in the early agreements—and one would imagine that they were more monopolistic in intent than equitable—the impact of the agreements has equity implications. Many countries have seen 'inequities' in the structures and have argued for changes on this basis. Even the United States Government considered in the mid-1960s that the Conference rates were set in such a way as to impose excessively high costs on many American exports; it argued, therefore, for reconsideration of the rates on the basis of equity, though not always successfully.

## Agreements on basic commodities

International agreements covering basic commodities such as wheat, coffee, cocoa, tin, rubber, etc., have been formulated or repeatedly studied in the postwar period, for the purpose of smoothing fluctuations in prices (and earnings) of raw material producers and of setting prices within a range that is equitable to both producers and consumers.

Most of the arrangements provide for a range within which the price is to be permitted to change according to demand and supply conditions. If supply is too great, the price falls to the lower (support) limit and consumer countries agree to buy a certain quota at that price. Conversely, if supply is short, and the price rises to the upper limit, producers agree to sell a certain quota to each participating country at that price. World prices can, of course, rise above or fall below the agreed range; the range applies to quota trade only.

Historically, the number of buying countries has been larger than the number of selling countries, and such agreements have been difficult to negotiate since the long-term prices seemed to be low. It was not seen as in the interest of the buying countries to set minimum prices, and there were too many to come to an agreement on the price range. Now, with prices rising and short supply appearing to be the long-term condition, there is more interest in such agreements from the demand side. Of course, the producers also see it differently now and are more likely to try to form selling cartels.

In the instances in which agreements were made, equity considerations were resolved implicitly, if not explicitly. In the instances in which agreements were not reached, equity considerations were also avoided, in favour of the purchasers, who were largely satisfied with the results of the market. In the short-supply situation, they will also be avoided, but in favour of the producers.

Another short-supply situation has given rise to interferences in the market for purposes of equity through export controls imposed by the United States Government. Under the Export Control Act of 1949, the Department of Commerce was given authority to restrict exports of any items which became in short supply so as to reduce the pressure of inflation and the results of foreign aid, which might increase the export demand for scarce materials or products.

Under this authority and the emergency powers of the President, short-supply controls were imposed during the Korean War in conjunction with the International Materials Conference established in 1950 to allocate critical materials equitably among the nations supporting the United Nations effort. Supplies were based on past uses and consumption, altered by the needs of each nation's military effort.

During the mid 1960s and the early 1970s, short-supply controls were imposed on, first, walnut logs and then lumber logs when American furniture manufacturers and lumber mills complained of the 'unfair' competition from foreign buyers. Controls were granted, for a short time, on the ground that it was inequitable for American buyers to sustain the adjustment, with the consequent drop in local employment and income. The aborted imposition of export controls on soybeans in the early 1970s also had equity connotations, attempting to protect United States purchasers. Foreign buyers complained, however, that it was inequitable for them to be pressured by the American Government to open their markets to American agricultural produce, for them to respond favourably to such pressure, and then to have the supplies cut off. They also were dependent on soybeans in their own agricultural programme. Consequently, the United States agreed to a scheme in which it fulfilled past contracts on a stretched-out basis.

These experiences indicate that the market mechanism will not be wholly acceptable in short-supply situations. Considerations of equity quickly come to the fore affecting both supply volumes and prices; mere ability and willingness to buy (demand) is an insufficient criterion as to whom should be served.

### The petroleum market

The Organization of Petroleum Exporting Countries (OPEC) has introduced the problem of equity into the world petroleum markets through its monopolization of a major portion of oil supplies. Given the high prices of gasoline and petroleum products in the consuming countries, the producing countries have long argued that the world 'competitive' prices they received were inequitable. They successfully imposed a 'reference price' that raised the tax revenue to the governments but left the world price alone; the companies argued against these artificial reference prices.

More recently, with the gradual takeover of the producing facilities by the host governments in the OPEC countries, they have raised the world price as well, increasing considerably their revenue. They have not yet stated what levels they consider 'equitable.' The price will be set between producing and consuming governments under considerations far removed from the simple criterion of the efficient use of the oil resources, as reflected in a free market.

The producing countries will argue that the price should be near the 'market' price, which will reflect the fact that substantial supplies are reserved (held off the market) and demand is steadily increasing. But the consuming governments are arguing that such market prices are 'ruinous,' 'unfair,' and 'inequitable.'

Though the lesson will not be very palatable, it is that the LDCs will use whatever power they have to re-distribute income in their favour, regardless of 'market conditions,' and that they will restrain the market to make it work in their favour when they can. To them, this is only equitable, given the inequitable treatment they have received in the commodity markets for so many years—at least as they see it.

Several observers have argued that copper is the next commodity to be handled in a similar fashion, probably with OPEC financing. There are only a few producing countries involved and supply is short compared to demand, and is likely to remain so—or, at least, it is likely to be reserved as a means of tightening supply and raising revenue in the face of relatively inelastic demand. The higher revenue will permit retention of the supplies without damaging the potential growth of the producing countries. They will—as with the OPEC countries—seek to 'sow the copper' by using the proceeds to accelerate diversified growth, reducing further their dependence on copper and thereby increasing their negotiating strength.

## Taxation of international companies

The division of revenue from taxation of international companies raises questions of equity—which country should get what revenue? The Indian Government employs the criterion of 'economic connection' to assert that a sale of coffee in jute bags by a Colombian to a Mexican warrants taxation of the Colombian income in India because it is the source of the jute. The United States Governments permits, through its tax credit, the foreign government to receive all of the taxes on foreign income earned by American-owned affiliates in the rate equals or exceeds that in the United States. If the rate is lower, the American parent pays only the difference between the foreign and the American tax and (normally) only when the income is remitted to the parent.

In addition, the IRS will assign prices at which intercompany transactions 'should have' taken place, altering the tax revenue. It will assign headquarters expenses to a foreign affiliate, at times, and even costs of transferring technology.

Each of these actions is based on some equity concept of the sharing of revenue. The concept of tax sparing is also based on equity considerations. The host country argues that it is unfair for the American Government not to spare the taxes it would receive if the host country cut its tax rate in order to attract United States investment. The present operation of the American tax credit merely shifts taxes foregone by the host country to the United States Treasury, if the foreign income is remitted to the parent company.

## Defence movement in NATO

The principle of equity has been taken to an extreme under the co-production schemes of NATO and several European co-operative ventures; costs and benefits were divided in rather minute ways. In fact, without a mutually acceptable solution to the problem of sharing, there would have been no such co-operative efforts. Though the projects undertaken had high priorities, they were not sufficiently high to be undertaken 'at whatever cost' or under just any division of costs and benefits.

The NATO co-production projects involved the transfer of technology from the United States to a consortium of American and European companies which allocated the production, assembly, distribution, and repair services among the customer countries in such a way as to divide the benefits equitably. The benefits included not only production and services but the accompanying employment, training in advanced technologies, balance-of-payments contributions through exports (offset by imports, of course), tax revenue, and potential future industrial ties. Each of these was allocated in such a way that all participants felt that the result was worth the costs, even if they rose higher than the United States export price for the same equipment [20].

There is little doubt that the production of the same equipment could have been accomplished 'more efficiently' in other ways, but it would not have been produced at all without the equity criteria employed. And, once the equity criteria were satisfied, the participants bent every effort to remove impediments in the way of production and distribution. Duties were removed, border taxes eliminated, domestic taxes rebated, non-tariff barriers removed, etc. Once equity was assured, efficiency was brought back to the fore as a primary operating criterion.

Similar efforts outside NATO have been attempted with the Concorde, the European Airbus, ELDO, ESRO, the MRCA, INTELSAT, and the SATCOM system. These have not always had the desired results because of the inability to determine the *juste retour* for the participating countries. Comparing the experience of INTELSAT with that under ESRO and ELDO, it appears that it is easier to solve the problem in commercial-oriented projects than those that either are welfare-oriented or do not have a commercial output. The problem revolves around the extent of integration of activities deemed acceptable to the member countries. Participants in ELDO and ESRO were unwilling to let their national programmes be melted into the co-operative one, reserving for themselves the right to design and build key parts of the system or to conduct their own national research. But mere dovetailing of national programmes and efforts was not sufficient. To function effectively, ELDO and ESRO required a fine meshing of functions and activities; and, therefore, a sharing of costs without a clearly delineated distribution of benefits. Joint (known) costs produced a joint product with unknown benefits.

INTELSAT avoided the necessity of dovetailing national programmes by dividing up the total into nationally-oriented pieces while requiring co-operation in the main effort [21]. The successful NATO projects did the same thing, providing co-operative programmes in which each country could see its national benefit. Programmes which require integration of a high order and which do not permit the distinguishing of national returns are likely to gain little support, despite the obvious benefit to the whole. This conclusion reinforces the argument that equity is a critical element of decision making in international economic policy. Increasing the total pie will not be seen as desirable unless each knows the size of his slice. The NATO projects and INTELSAT indicate that this can be done, under certain conditions, without unacceptable costs from inefficiency. These conditions include the recognition of a pressing need (military or other), of the inability to meet that need by national means (in an absolute or cost sense), of the ability to meet it through co-operative projects (producing the desired result at shared costs), and a clear and determined benefit to the nation participating (known beforehand so as to justify the expenditure).

## 'Complementation agreements'

Similar attention to the problem of equity has opened up the possibility of wider and deeper reductions of tariffs through 'complementation agreements' under LAFTA and the Andean Pact. The technique was given a high priority when it became clear that across-the-board duty reductions would not be accepted beyond the 50 per cent level under LAFTA because of the inequitable distribution of the benefits in trade. These agreements permit the selection of specific products to be traded among participating countries, subjecting them to mutual duty reductions but not extending these same duties to other members of LAFTA. The narrow selection permits more ready calculation of the reciprocal benefits to each party and, therefore, more ready agreement. A number of such agreements have been negotiated under LAFTA.

Under the Andean Pact, the complementation agreements are used also to allocate production. The mere reduction of duties in a given industrial sector would not necessarily distribute benefits equitably, for production might still be concentrated within a few countries—as with petro-chemicals, pharmaceuticals, rubber products, automobiles, etc.

Therefore, the agreements also stipulate that each country will be given a 'head start' in production of specific commodities within an industrial sector. (Governments are unwilling to match participation in one sector against another—that is, to permit specialization by sector rather than within a sector.) Each other member will accord duty-free access to its markets to this one country's products but will apply former high duties on the same item from the other countries. Each country has 'infant-industry' protection for its specialities throughout the region. Each country will have a number of such specialities within each industrial category. At the end of the 'infant-industry period' the markets of all are to be opened to all members in these allocated commodities and if any country cannot stand the competition, it will lose out in future development of that product. Thus, after a period in which equity is the prime consideration, efficiency will be given the priority.

The critical problem which the Andean countries have attempted to face up to, is that of determining ways to provide *reciprocidad* (balancing benefits among members) while at the same time avoiding purely uneconomic arrangements. A complementation agreement that was rigid could produce a wholly uneconomic structure within a short space of time, merely because of changes in demands or technologies. An inability to adjust supplies to demands will lead to large unused capacities, as has occurred in the steel industry in some Latin American countries. The problem of adjustments to a more competitive situation (both within the region and facing the world market) is met under the Andean procedures by the removal of the preferential treatment within a stipulated period of years [22].

The use of complementation agreements also runs into the problem of whether *any* component of a given industrial sector can economically be developed within one of the economies of the group. For example, it is conceivable that Bolivia or Ecuador would simply not be able to develop economical production of *any* component within an assigned industry (such as pharmaceuticals) or, because of their small economic size, would have to give up participation in one or more industry sectors in order to use its resources (human and natural) in more preferred sectors.

If Bolivia or Ecuador were assigned a component, they could not produce economically, and therefore, after the period of adjustment, lost the operations to others, it is likely that they would become dissatisfied and pull out of the Pact or insist on other benefits. A solution to this problem can be found in the use of the multinational enterprise to invest in several countries within the same sector, integrating the different operations. In this way, an uneconomic plant in one country could be offset by a more profitable operation in another. This solution would require acceptance of all parties to pay more than would otherwise be the case, but a price necessary to maintain participation by all the members in each industry [23]. The problem of equitable distribution of benefits of industrialization would be resolved through decisions of the international companies, made known beforehand to the participating governments.

Agreements similar to the complementation agreements are being made among private companies in producing and consuming countries. They are called compensation agreements—not to be confused with the older compensation (payments) agreements to clear currency balances among countries. The objective of these agreements is to 'clear' components and parts and to offer new production opportunities to participants. For example, if an aircraft company wishes to sell planes to a given customer, he will often find that the customer requests local production in his country of a given component (undercarriage, airelons, or whatever) so that the net balance-of-payments impact is reduced. This compensation will exist not just for the customer's planes but for all planes manufactured in that series by the producer. A substantial plus in exports can conceivably be created for the purchaser by such agreements.

Multiple customers create multiple allocations of production. A complex industrial product may thus be manufactured over several countries, assembled in one or more and sold back to the original countries plus others. To calculate the net balance of benefits and costs of such a system would not be easy—nor is it possible to assume that the total costs are higher than would have been the case without the repartition of production; they may, in fact, be lower as a result of economies of scale achieved in a more specialized operation producing similar items for several different aircraft companies.

The result of such agreements is specialization by agreement and a kind of barrier in trade. The effect is to achieve an acceptable level of efficiency with an acceptable sharing of the benefits, not guaranteed by the workings of free-market or comparative-advantage type specialization.

## Unilateral adjustments in balance of trade

The most extensive interferences in the market mechanism in the postwar period have arisen in the national efforts to prevent adjustments in the balance of payments and to achieve greater equity (of each nation) without coming to an agreement as to the criteria of equity *among* nations. The key to the understanding of the continuing crises in the international monetary system is that reduction of perceived national burdens has been placed above the efficiency criterion by each of the countries involved. The criteria of equity in burden sharing are set by each of the countries in its own interest; without first posing the question of sharing at the multilateral level, an agreement on an efficient method of achieving equilibrium in international accounts is not likely.

Almost any technique for achieving equilibrium will be efficient—in the sense of producing an equilibrium quickly, for instance, the gold standard, freely fluctuating rates, and most in between (though some are more complex and more difficult to administer than others). The problem is over the acceptability of the system, and acceptability has to do with equity, not efficiency. No significant group of countries (not even members of the European Community) can seem to agree as to the criteria of equity and the consequent sharing of the burden of a common monetary system.

In order to prevent an inequitable share of the burden of adjustment from falling on its economy, each nation has introduced measures that effectively prevent the achievement of payments equilibrium from either the deficit or surplus side of the accounts. The situation has to become quite serious (crisis) before one side or the other gives a bit.

The measures introduced in each country are aimed at protecting particular interests, or at preventing harm to specific groups in the country, or at preventing frustration of national policies (as outlined in the section on the 'new nationalism' above). In addition, a set of rigidities exists as a result of other international agreements which tie the hands of governments in altering their policies.

Looking at the policies followed in the United States which prevent correction of the deficit, one can find a fairly long list of factors which 'institutionalize' the deficit, that is, make it chronic. Reduction of the deficit is likely to come not from anything the United States does, but from acts of other countries—so ingrained are the policies outlined below.

On the domestic scene, the pursuit of high levels of employment means that correction of the deficit cannot be sustained at substantial costs in terms of unemployment; the 'politically acceptable' level of unemployment has already been raised by the Nixon Administration from 4.5 per cent in 1968 to 5.5 per cent. Even this rate has been exceeded at times, and the rate has been held down only by an unacceptably high level of inflation, which itself adds to balance-of-payments pressures (unless all other countries inflate faster, which is the case occasionally, temporarily pulling the United States chestnuts out of the fire).

Nor can costs of production be lowered significantly, because of the inflation and of other rigidities in the cost structure. One example is the *raising* of prices of electric power and heating fuels, as a result of the drop in consumption in response to the energy crisis. None of the cost elements faced by business (including taxes) is readily amenable to reduction, partly because each factor considers that its present share is inequitable and should be raised. With increasing political power in the hands of each interest group (and the concern for shares), pressure builds within each group to demand higher returns, wages, or prices.

Similarly, it is not possible to reduce prices of many individual items, even without inflationary pressure, because of the fact that key prices tend to be administered and respond only upwards. Witness also the increase in auto prices when demand fell off, so as to maintain profits. To let prices in particular sectors fall significantly might put some companies out of business, an adjustment equally unacceptable.

Nor has it been possible, politically and institutionally, to reduce military expenditures significantly—either at home or abroad—thus adding to the inflation at home and the plethora of dollars overseas. Despite the fact that the United States Government thinks it would be equitable for European and other countries to assume more of the cost of defense of the West, not all see it the same way. The United States Government has not been able to decide unilaterally to cut its commitments substantially.

On the international scene, the United States has refused to use its gold reserves as a means of reducing the deficit, despite the fact that such a refusal in effect means that it must adopt policies as though it has none. Not to be able to support the dollar with gold sales or sales of commodity exports means that it remains vulnerable to any shift in confidence, shaken by supply or demand changes. Therefore, any internal weakness adds to the external weakness of the dollar, although the United States seems institutionally unable to strengthen the dollar internally, reducing the options for adjustment. This inability, as stated, results from a desire to prevent the burden of adjustments falling on particular sectors or groups.

Because of international commitments under the GATT, the United States is basically stopped from raising restrictions against imports; by doing so it would probably induce an increase in barriers to its exports. Its trade is too significant to be used as a means of correcting its balance-of-payments difficulties, in any case, save by an expansion of its exports within a pattern of increase in total world trade, not by a significant increase in its share of world markets.

Other countries cannot be expected to make converse adjustments to ease the American deficits, such as accelerating inflation in their countries above the rate in the United States, though this may happen for other reasons. Similarly, they cannot be expected to stimulate wage increases merely to raise costs of exports, thereby easing the American deficit. And their reluctance to revalue currencies reflects their concern for burden sharing.

Nor can they be expected to remove their barriers to agricultural imports, placing the burden on their own rural sectors, which have been most capable of obtaining protection from both foreign and domestic pressures. Thus, foreign countries are operating, as does the United States, to attempt to place the burden of adjustment largely outside the domestic economy, if at all possible [24].

Similar comments can be made concerning the use of capital markets (long- or short-term) to ease adjustments in the balance of payments. These markets are too critical in the formation of investment capital and in the structure of interest rates and the maintenance of liquidity domestically to permit these functions being interfered with by outside influences. They also form institutional rigidities.

In sum, these comments lead to the conclusion that balance-of-payments equilibrium is not of sufficiently low concern to permit a merely *technical* solution; only a clearly equitable one would be acceptable—one that took into account all of the domestic and international priorities that have been built into increasingly rigid systems. But this rigidity is itself a reflection of a desire on the part of each country to achieve equity for itself, without concern for others.

The basic problem in the international monetary scene is that governments are not facing up to the need to share benefits and burdens. This omission underlies the opposition to technical solutions; governments are concerned with national burdens rather than international equity or burden sharing. This being the case, they have argued for, and largely adopted, the floating exchange rate system, which hides the distribution of the burden without eliminating it. When harm to some sector or interest is sufficiently identified, governments step in and interfere with the float, creating a 'dirty float.' Actually, there is nothing dirty about it at all—the adjective reflects more on the criteria of judgment employed than on the cleanliness of the operation. (It is by the use of such pejorative words that we are dominated, as Keynes said, by the defunct ideas of some long-dead economist.) Present efforts to manage the float have as an objective the creation of greater equity—in the eyes of the interferer—

than would exist without interference. It would, in a sense, be 'dirtier' for the government to permit the burden to fall on those least able to bear it (e.g., the poor, hit by rising prices of imported necessities) than to intervene in the exchange markets. Unless the governments are willing to focus on this problem and to seek solutions for it through common criteria and means of sharing the burden, we will be faced with repeated crises and repeated techno-economic nostrums aimed at making the adjustment mechanism more efficient—yet, *any* efficiency solution will work if deemed equitable and none will if deemed inequitable.

## Co-ordinating Intervention

Intervention must be co-ordinated so as to meet basic national requirements, not producing situations requiring traumatic adjustments, but permitting adjustments when they are needed. Such co-ordination can be achieved only by focusing on the primary problems of the international division of industrial and agricultural activities and how it is to be guided.

The place to begin is with a search for new principles of an international division of labour—not based on present (static) comparative advantage and free-market forces alone, but on a mixture of market forces (where they are applicable and acceptable) and co-operative action that leads to a wider participation of all countries in the benefits of economic growth.

If industry is located over the world under criteria of the market or of international corporate investors it will continue to be principally in advanced countries (unless stifled by pollution or ceilings placed on growth). This one-sided pattern of world industrialization will simply not be acceptable. Japan is, in some ways, ahead of our thinking on this issue, for it is now planning a redistribution of industrial activity out of Japan to neighbouring countries and a redirection of its own activities to 'future' industries. Such planning at the national level is better than none, but it would be still better to have effective co-ordination at the international level, to reduce the costs of adjustments and the stresses on the international monetary system. Planning, which has moved from the level of the giant corporation to that of national governments, must now move on to the international level. Negotiations on trade and the monetary system that do not include considerations of the structure and goals of the international economy and the division of labour (distribution of industrial activity) will leave us exposed to still more crises to be met by temporizing methods. The alternatives are to build a set of agreements that guide the distribution of the sacrifices, sharing them among the deficit and surplus countries in particular ways, or to establish new institutions providing some automaticity under accepted criteria of sharing.

# A co-operative world order?

Over the past years, and during each monetary, trade, or other crisis, there have been strident calls for greater international economic co-operation and accommodation of diverse interests. The United States Government has repeatedly tried to obtain agreement on the formation of a new international monetary system and has tied the new solution to acceleration of moves toward freer trade. Its goal of building a worldwide system of freer trade and payments remains unchanged from the mid thirties. But its competitive approach to international co-operation is unacceptable to many others [25]. Even if the United States were capable of forcing its view on the rest of the world, the system would soon be disrupted again, for it treats last things first.

The likely rejection of the American concepts arises from different views of the world's problems and their treatment. First, from the viewpoint of many developing countries, the problem of efficiency is not one of finding the least-cost combination to meet demands in a market but of making the most effective use of resources to meet given needs, often determined by governments. Second, for developing countries and many in Europe, the problem of least-cost production is not to reduce total costs absolutely, but to distribute them so that those borne by each nation are less than would otherwise be the case; co-operative solutions are desirable if they reduce the national burden, even if they raise costs above 'free market' levels. Third, it is often seen as more desirable to have a larger portion of the benefits for the nation than to provide a larger gain for the world economy, with the distribution of benefits uncertain. Fourth, many countries of the world have not rejected the mediaeval concept of a 'fair price' and employ it in agricultural programmes especially. Regardless of its nebulous basis, it remains a desired measure of acceptable transactions. Even the United States is employing the concept in respect to oil prices, though it has long refused to do so in the purchase of other raw materials from abroad. Finally, many countries will trade off some benefits for an increase in certainty, so as to be sure of maintaining their position relative to others or to enhance planning possibilities.

These attitudes toward fairness and certainty are likely to be strengthened by increasing pressures on international resources and on governments to assume greater responsibility for economic and social welfare [26]. With increasing long-run costs and the uncertainty of substitutes (and their costs), a premium will be placed on negotiating long-term arrangements under 'fair' prices. Concepts of fairness will also arise as a result of the shift in economic gains to oil-rich (or resource-rich) countries in the form of requests for aid from them to lesser-developed countries.

The United States solution of freeing trade and payments and of permitting the adjustments to be made by the 'impersonal and a-ethical' forces of the market will not be acceptable to other countries, few of which have a social philosophy similar to the one that has dominated the United States in its development. The alternative is establishment of criteria for the distribution of the costs and benefits of the adjustment process and of then describing the mechanism for accomplishing that division [27].

If the world rejects a worldwide free market and is also unwilling to face the problem of equity on an international level, we can expect continued crises and mini-chaos until the evil of the day is intolerable—at which point we will *have* to face the problem of sharing the costs and benefits of a new international economic order. But it would seem more desirable to take thought now as to what might be an acceptable new approach so as to shorten the time span of the prediction of an Austrian foreign minister that 'Governments do adopt the best solutions, after all others have been tried.'

There is an argument for holding up for attainment principles that will be honoured more in the breach than in compliance—if such a goal is desirable and will be pursued in some degree even if not reached. If the goal is itself unacceptable, it is better to adopt principles consonant with the goals which nations and peoples do seek. Multilateralism is violated repeatedly—not just with and among the socialist states but also among and with the developing countries and among the industrialized countries. Long-term barter agreements are arranged for reasons which are good and sufficient in the eyes of the parties involved, and even the United States has pressed on Japan the settlement of specific industrial problems and its balance-of-payments deficit on a bilateral basis—an accommodation it refused to accord Japan in the early 1960s when she was in substantial deficit to the United States [28].

Out of bilateralism comes discrimination, both in trade and in investment relationships. Governments discriminate against the foreign seller in their procurement policies; 'buy national' regulations are rife; non-tariff barriers are set to discriminate against certain countries' products (such as large cars); quotas are inherently discriminatory, if not among countries, at least among potential suppliers; investment restrictions sometimes are applied against applicants from selected countries or in specific sectors; and multiple exchange systems or controls permit repeated discrimination against certain currencies, commodities, or buyers and sellers. Not to recognize the usefulness of discrimination is to maintain a hypocrisy that is harmful to future co-ordination in the international economy. For so long as the domestic goals sought have top priority, these discriminations will not be removed. Only when the underlying reasons for the discriminations are removed, or the goals for which they are used are fulfilled or achievable by other means, will they be dispensed with. These goals relate to *national* interests in the growth and distribution of wealth and power over the world.

## Criteria of co-operation

The criteria for judging whether or not any given economic policy will serve the national interests do not stop with *efficiency*. Consequently, the 'first-best solution' of the economists is unacceptable by itself. In addition, the market definition of efficiency is unaceptable because of a lack of full costing of all factors and affects of market decisions. But, even if efficiency were to encompass all relevant costs, nations are also concerned with the extent to which costs and benefits are *equitably* shared in the system. They are also unwilling to let that distribution be at the hands of others—those who might create wealth and then graciously pass it around. They will insist, therefore, that they *participate* in the process of wealth-generation and in the decisions as to how it is distributed [29]. To gain self-respect, they will insist that such participation be on a basis which provides for a *creative* role—not one of hewers of wood and drawers of water. Finally, the process of participation should not be such as to require that all nations and peoples fit the same cultural and social mould but one that permits sufficient *autonomy* to retain desired diversities in national ways of living [30]. These five criteria—efficiency, equity, participation, creativity, and autonomy—require means of achieving a sufficient degree of unity to solve basic problems co-operatively but also means of maintaining diversity and differentiation. To achieve these will require international co-ordination—harmonization in some areas—with local control in matters affecting vital national interests.

These criteria have been employed in several different types of international arrangements, as mentioned in the preceding chapter. The non-efficiency criteria which have been applied in various co-operative situations include both an equitable distribution of the returns and an equitable participation in the processes of production and management. These same criteria will be required in future co-operative efforts to form a new economic order.

The increasing interdependency of industrialized countries and those holding the resources will force a negotiation more of equals than has been the case in the past. It is doubtful that the more wealthy countries can continue to disregard either the environmental impact of their industrial growth or the pressures created by over-population in the rest of the world. If an 'environmental conscience' is in fact developed it will force a concern for the rates of growth in the advanced countries and for the effect on poorer countries of slowed rates of growth for the world. Once again, negotiation is the means of resolving the trade-offs—not a free market—for problems of sharing are resolved either at the political level *or* automatically within an acceptable *system of allocation*. The free-market system has been found wanting for this purpose.

But what will be the criteria for success of such negotiations? By what measures will the parties determine that they are 'satisfied'? At the extreme, each nation will want a solution which both increases its absolute wealth and improves its relative position. Each will want an acceptable level of participation in the distribution and production of benefits in the decision processes as to what shall be produced and where. It is, of course, patently impossible for all to be made better off relative to all others. The issue remains, for many of the LDCs have considered that they have been worse off than they should have been, relatively, because of the behaviour of the more advanced countries. They want this injustice redressed.

The specific criteria for redressing it will include the following: (a) a more equitable distribution of the location of industrial activity, (b) a more equitable distribution of the use of advanced technology and of the opportunities to generate advanced technology, (c) a more equitable distribution of employment in diversified industrial activities (or agribusiness), and (d) a pattern of production and trade that does not make a few countries highly subject to the vagaries of international demand. This last can be translated to mean less wide swings in balance-of-payments positions and less dependence on a few critical commodities.

The free market cannot make these kinds of decisions. These have to be made in the political arena, through direct negotiation, for the free market will respond to what *is* (or what is *thought* to be) and not to what *ought* to be. The market permits only those to participate who have 'earned' the income with which to participate; it will not redistribute benefits or opportunities to help change the system. The shift from market criteria to a negotiated international division of labour will be acceptable to the advanced countries as well as to the LDCs if each sees the desirability of ceasing to treat men as means, and considers them as ends—not just *some* men, who are producers in the system, but *all* men. At that point, goods and labour will be used for all men's satisfaction—not solely material—rather than using men to produce material goods for some men's satisfaction. It will not be satisfactory merely to alter the system to produce *more material* goods for everyone, rather than for just a few; improvement in the quality of life in terms of freedom, participation, self-respect, and community involvement should also be sought.

This shift in attitudes is on the horizon, partially forced upon us by ecological and growth constraints, but also by the growing power of the developing countries in the international economy. To enter the new situation reluctantly, with feet dragging, will be to spoil the development of co-operative attitudes at a time when we can certainly afford to be co-operative, for their problems are ours, and ours theirs. (The necessity for international co-operation to solve the problem of drug abuse in the United States is but one poignant evidence of this interdependency.) To solve these problems co-operatively will require the attention not just of economists, who must give up their 'first-best' solutions, but also of sociologists, politicians, lawyers, and scientists of many types. The process does not require the complete abandonment of the market system but does mean that it would be used for its limited purpose, to produce evidence of economic efficiency, within the constraints imposed by society. But the efficiency would itself be judged by the achievement of goals other than purely economic and by production of public goods, and services (those which would be rejected in the market but chosen by other decision processes).

## Implications of blocs

Although the American Government opposed the formation of regional blocs after World War II, its policies since the late 1950s and especially in the early 1970s have strongly encouraged the formation of economic blocs. It saw the creation of the European Common Market, the EFTA and the LAFTA not only as a means of bolstering world economic development but also as a bulwark against the spread of Communism.

Although it did not desire to strengthen these groups against itself, actions of the American Government in the early 1970s have had this effect. The unilateral devaluation of the dollar in August 1971, the efforts to tie trade negotiations to a new international monetary system, and the rapid spread of private investment gave rise to defensive moves by others. These acts appeared to others as a return to pre-World War II 'beggar-thy-neighbour' policies, putting the burden of adjustment on others, and as economic penetration potentially similar to colonial dependence.

These unilateral acts helped undermine the roles of the IMF and the GATT, which were the cornerstones of postwar policy in exchange rates and trade. In order to protect themselves both from economic dominance and from idiosyncracies of a world free market, countries have sought some haven in the tighter alignment of economies on a regional basis. The African countries have an association with the expanded European Community, the Andean Pact group has welcomed Venezuela, the Association of Southeast Asian Nations (ASEAN) group is progressing, and nascent groups expand (and contract) in North, East, and West Africa. The Council for Mutual Economic Assistance (Comecon) faces the same problems as other economic groups plus some peculiar to its ties to the Soviet Union, involving Soviet dominance of industrial policies, absence of real prices, and lack of convertibility of currencies. Japan has been trying to strengthen its ties with the countries of Southeast Asia, without formal success. One can envisage a set of regional blocs over the world, of which the United States is itself a major one. Some countries would not fall readily into any such grouping, however, and they would pose a problem in negotiation: for example, South Africa, Canada, Israel, Australia, New Zealand, Taiwan, Brazil, and others.

The implications of the formation of blocs are to change the priorities, membership, and structure of negotiations but not to alter their content significantly. That is, the policy issues remain the same, but their priority will be different within the various blocs, and the parties to the negotiations will, of course, differ. Four sets of negotiations would take place under a bloc system: one within the bloc, among the members; a second between two or more blocs; a third between a bloc and one or more non-bloc countries; and a fourth among nations and blocs at the international (or supra-bloc) level. (These do not necessarily preclude agreements also between nations which are members of blocs but have common interests not shared by other bloc members.)

The pattern of agreements sought would run the gamut of rules for competition and market behaviour, long-term contracts between blocs or among members in interbloc trade or investment, barter or compensation agreements between two or more blocs, interregional institutional arrangements, and finally international institutions or agreements covering multi-nations or multi-blocs and including the non-bloc countries.

These arrangements could relate to rules of the game, to permanent or *ad hoc* institutions, to projects, co-operative efforts in research and development, or mechanisms for clearing payments—in fact, to any of the policy issues in international economic relations. Despite the fact that the issues are not really altered by bloc formation, the shifts in the structure, number, and priorities of negotiation are important. The number of participants alone is an important constraint of the success of international agreement—the more members, the more difficult to find agreement and the lower the 'least common denominator.' And the necessity to find agreement within the bloc will delay inter-bloc or international agreements.

## Policy areas

There are seven keys in international economic relations that require new patterns to achieve this unity with diversity among nations or blocs. All will require distinct new institutional initiatives, but they are linked. Once the first are accomplished, the remaining should fall more easily into place. Trade and monetary relations are last in sequence, for they are not ends in themselves but merely means to *other* objectives. They can be treated successfully only after the others are adequately handled; this demonstrates again the futility of the present United States approaches on international trade and monetary negotiations.

The seven policy areas include: raw materials and energy; agriculture; industry, and technology; foreign investment; rules of competition and the role of the free market; international trade; and exchange rates [31, 32].

## Raw materials and energy policy

All other trade and monetary problems will fade into insignificance in the face of increasing demands for raw materials and energy resources, their rising prices, and the difficulty of paying them.

In recognition of the critical nature of these problems, the UN Economic Social Council (ECOSOC) received in May, 1974, a series of resolutions urging co-operative action [33]. A resolution offered by France began by 'Recognizing that it is vitally important that the changes taking place in the relations among States should be effected in accordance with the requirements of greater justice and greater international solidarity, so as to ensure equitable and stable social and economic development for present and future generations,' and recommended formation of a committee to begin dialogues among producers and consumers to the end of obtaining 'satisfaction of world needs in conditions which are reasonable and equitable for all.' [34]. Others called for information gathering, discussion groups looking toward new international agreements, and a fund for acceleration of exploration.

The problems facing the Conference on the Law of the Sea involve the same issues of exploration of the seabed for the benefit of all and an equitable distribution of the benefits in terms of rights to exploitation and use. Nations are in disagreement as to the extent of territorial rights over the continental shelves, and private companies are proceeding to take resources off the ocean floor despite UN resolutions to the effect that they should be reserved for 'all mankind.'

The only factor of production that faces rapidly increasing costs is land (resources); labour, capital, and management are reproducible at relatively constant costs compared to resources and basic materials. Few countries in the Northern Hemisphere are adequately supplied with the materials needed for continued industrial progress. Those in the Southern Hemisphere which have such materials need to sell them to permit purchase of capital goods and equipment for their own industrial progress. But the balance of need is likely to tip toward the advanced countries, handing to the LDCs a negotiating position that will alter significantly the balance of benefits from trade.

## Rules for trade?

In an effort to prescribe rules for trade in raw materials, Richard Gardner has urged acceptance of the 'principle of equal access' [35] in order to 'de-politicize' international trade in minerals and materials [36]. And as a counter-offer to the developing countries, he suggests a guarantee of 'equal access to markets' in advanced countries [37]. The LDCs are unlikely to be satisfied with the principle of 'equal access' to their materials by others or to an offer of trade opportunities. They will not be seen as *quid pro quos* [38].

Access through a market involves allocation of supplies by *exclusion:* those unable (or unwilling) to pay the price are left out. The concept of 'equal access' is applied, therefore, to a process which excludes some claimants, rather than including all. It is assumed that there is some process of determining 'equality' that is acceptable to all claimants—a process whereby some have adequate purchasing power and others (appropriately) do not. It is precisely this principle of exclusion that is under attack, and for political reasons—that is, that the result has been unequal or inequitable. For the past two decades the developing countries have been attacking the principle as it has applied to industrial development. Now advanced countries are attacking market equality as applied to petroleum; they do not want to pay the 'market' *or* the political price *. Distribution via the market would give the supplies to those willing (and able) to pay the highest money prices—which is precisely what the Arab countries (and now Venezuela) are doing with oil—merely raising their 'reservation price' (a perfectly acceptable market technique). Yet this has brought on the cries for 'equal access'—a rather curious result, especially when no criteria of equality are proffered **.

## Criteria for equality

Some criteria of equality are available, such as per capita, per volume of industrial output, per historical use of each commodity, etc. But there are gross injustices in giving each person a pound of copper, or a coupon entitling him to buy it, or a gallon of gasoline, *unless* one assumes that the mineral and material wealth of the world is appropriately owned by *each and every* person jointly and severally and should be equally divided per capita once separated from its source. This would be a curious concept of property for neo-classicists to adopt.

Use of a criterion of industrial output to allocate materials would fix in concrete form the present distribution of industrial activity over the world, leaving the less-developed countries in the backwash that they are now seeking to avoid. Their reservation of materials is an attempt to have some for their own later processing and use, and for export for future imports. The expressed Arab concern to assist developing countries with petroleum supplies reflects also a desire to alter the worldwide industrial pattern, even if indirectly and slowly.

Similarly, a criterion of equality based on historical usage would continue the inequalities already built into the international economic system. To achieve equality in the eyes of many developing countries, it would be necessary to

* The difference between "paying the price" in money or in support for political objectives of the seller lies, of course, in the concepts of equity and justice.

** Is the United States ready to apply the same principle to soybeans, logs, and wheat?

restructure not only the patterns of trade and the use of materials but also the location of related industrial activity over the world.

LDCs will most likely insist on participation in the industry sector using the materials (e.g., petrochemicals, aluminium, iron and steel) so as to upgrade their industrial activity. Even Canada is concerned that it is an exporter of nickel and platinum but a net importer of items processed from these materials, and suggestions have recently been made that it should use its resource-bargaining power [39]. LDCs will eventually want to enter the international arena through some sharing of ownership of the various stages of processing and distribution. In the case of petroleum, for example, the Arab countries have gained a majority share of ownership in the development and production stage. They will press further for shares in the processing stages (located within their countries) and probably later for shares in the distribution stage. The petroleum companies will become partners to Mid-East governments and consuming governments, if they are to remain as a significant player on the scene [40].

If the advanced countries are to retain ready access to the raw materials supplies in the LDCs, they will have to permit sharing in the entire process of exploration, processing, and distribution so that the producing countries can participate equitably not just in the revenues but in the decisions affecting the industry worldwide. The welfare of the LDCs is too closely tied to market shifts, prices, taxation, development of substitutes, etc., for them not to use their increasing power to alter policies and outcomes. Among the initiatives which will likely appear desirable from the standpoints of both advanced and developing countries will be an international stockpile for critical commodities, helping to smooth prices and supplies.

The mere smoothing of price fluctuations in raw materials and energy sources will not be sufficient, however. Equity will require a more acceptable relationship between these prices and those of industrial goods [41]. Fluctuations in terms of trade of raw-material-producing countries *vis-à-vis* industrial products are more predictable than is any long-term improvement or deterioration of one against the other. Although raw materials and energy are likely to be relatively more scarce over the coming decades, cyclical swings in advanced countries can depress the prices of materials for some years at a time. (If, for example, the Western countries cannot solve their immediate problems and there is a drive for liquidity on a worldwide basis, prices of all commodities will fall significantly. This event would intensify problems of distribution along with those of economic and political stability.) But in the short run, rapid variations in prices of industrial goods, reflecting both monetary changes and shifts in the nature of the products themselves, will continue to upset the 'balance' between raw materials prices and those of industrial goods.

If the producers of energy and raw materials remain dissatisfied with the distribution of income (as determined by the relation of industrial prices to their exports), they will seek to alter it in their favour by restricting further the supply of materials. Without longer-run agreements to maintain price and supply, the advanced countries will have to turn to more sophisticated means of obtaining minerals and energy from readily available sources—the oceans, the sun, and less-rich resources within their borders. The cost will be high, but even if they succeed, and in doing so cut out the participation of the LDCs, the result would not be satisfactory, desirable, or equitable [42]. Suppose, for example, that the advanced countries made a breakthrough in energy technology and found it feasible to tap the earth's core or the sun's rays at costs competitive with petroleum. Would it be acceptable for them to cut off purchases from producing countries, leaving them in the industrial backwater? Would it not be better to consider now ways of making adjustments so as to keep the petroleum countries in the picture in the longer run but to prepare for the day of substitution by 'sowing the petroleum' in other activities? This is much better resource management than we have been accustomed to, but it is feasible, and certainly desirable [43]. Within such an approach, policies toward investment, trade, and capital flows resulting from these operations would fall into place and adjustments would be eased.

## Co-operation in raw materials

The problems brought to a critical heat in petroleum are no less significant in other raw material supplies. And the principles and procedures finally adopted in petroleum will likely be urged for others. Certainly the embryonic conference of copper-producing countries (Zaire, Zambia, Chile and Peru) will find the tactics of OPEC quite enticing, and there are indications that OPEC may be willing to finance the $1-2 billion buffer stock necessary to maintain current production yet hold supplies off the market to raise prices [44]. Bauxite is produced only by a few countries (Guyana, Surinam, Jamaica, Australia, Yugoslavia, and Guinea), and a BAUPEC is seen by some observers as the next most likely arrangement [45]. Tin is largely from Thailand, Malaya and Bolivia. Nickel from Canada and Norway. Manganese from Brazil, Gabon, South Africa, and Zaire. And lead and zinc are largely from a few producers, headed by Canada, Australia, and Mexico.

At present, the demand pressures are not severe, and new processes can stretch the present volumes of production, as is occurring in tin. But restriction of supply could easily raise prices and incomes to producers in several of these commodities, and substitutes do not readily exist for each. Alternative sources such as in the seabed are yet unproven and development would probably require international agreement on the rules—though some exploration and exploitation is beginning without formation of the rules.

From the standpoint of the most effective use of the world's resources and avoidance of waste in the use of capital and technological expertise, it would seem advisable to begin co-operative efforts in major minerals and metals not only at the level of exploration and development but also at the processing stages. Without such an effort, waste and frustration (if not conflicts) will arise simply from each nation trying to protect itself against monopolistic or excessively competitive pressures of others.

It is only a step away from the metals and minerals to the use of food as a political or economic weapon. The United States could certainly have employed it during the postwar years and in emergencies in other countries, but to have done so would have sown a legacy of intolerable power and intervention. Smaller countries using such tactics would be less criticized, on the ground that they are only obtaining redress for past slights and exploitation, but withholding food is not seen as a feasible monopolistic tactic. To exact conditions for its provision in an emergency would not be seen as 'fair' and *would* be seen as exploitative or imperialistic. Again, the pressure of high prices will undoubtedly lead to discovery of protein and vitamin substitutes on a large scale. But the world will face then another adjustment in production.

These observations raise to a critical level the question of what is 'fair' in pricing and distribution of scarce commodities—and capital is not different. Concepts of fairness underlay the low-interest, long-term extension of loans and the provision of grants in the postwar period. Willingness to continue these will be altered if raw materials suppliers act in ways considered 'unfair.' The issues are not resolved and are intertwined. Not to recognize them as inextricably meshed is to seek isolated solutions that will not hold for long.

## Agricultural policies

Agricultural problems are only slightly more complex than energy and materials policies in that the products are renewable annually. Their solution also requires co-operative arrangements in order to prevent undesirable disruption from market forces. To date, agricultural policies have been solely nationally based (save for the European Common Agricultural Policy), and most of them divorce cost of supply from income and price for the purpose of achieving an equitable system. No government wishes to leave its farmers subject to an unbridled market (domestic or international) nor to leave its economy dependent on foreign supplies of food if it can be helped.

But, as a result of a lack of international co-operation, we have large areas of the world near starvation and in famine conditions during bad weather or emergencies, while others are subsidizing farmers *not* to produce surpluses. A more crazy set of policies could not be devised than exists in agriculture—not because we do not use the free market, which has an insanity of its own in this sector, but because we have adopted policies with a view to *national* objectives rather than to the *world* needs in the relief of hunger and to *world* capacities to produce foods. As far back as Adam Smith, it was recognized that the world population could be fed adequately only if world resources were used for all. World food and nutritional needs require a systems approach not reachable through merely national or agribusiness planning.

If we did extend agricultural policy into the international economy, areas in the United States, Canada, Argentina, the Soviet Union, and sectors of Europe, North Africa, and Asia would become highly efficient suppliers of much of the world's grain; marginal grain-growing areas would be turned into other kinds of farming and meat production, or into recreation or conservation areas. The existence of several grain-producing centres over the world would prevent unsettling weather conditions in one region from drastically curtailing world supplies, and adequate stockpiles would be developed to prevent shortages. Presently emerging problems of food crops in the Northern Hemisphere and famine in South Asia and Africa are likely to test our ability to co-operate in food distribution in the near future. (For example, will the American people be willing to pay $5.00 for wheat and $1.00 for bread in order to send wheat to famine-ridden India in 1974-75?) The more difficult test, however, lies in food production—its location, levels of productivity, and prices.

The improvement of agricultural productivity would induce greater investment in agribusiness, including the processing and distribution of exotic foods from many corners of the world. Pricing of agricultural products is itself a matter of equity, for purchasers in extreme circumstances (a large portion of the world) are in no position either to pay or to argue about the price. Producers, on the other hand, have long been subject to wide variations in income without reference to effort and frequently inverse to productivity. The price mechanism does not, therefore, elicit appropriate responses on the part of farmers to meet the needs of the population. These problems are recognized in food-grant programmes, but they will also require resolution over the longer term. Means will have to be found of keeping prices down but farm income sufficiently high to keep production up. Any such policies will involve a sharing among countries, as well as within them.

Investment policies, trade policies, and national farm-support policies would fall into line within an overall policy toward world agriculture, as would the various international commodity agreements, such as that on coffee and the repeatedly aborted one on cocoa. The world has not lacked for ideas on how to improve the agricultural picture. What it has lacked are appropriate criteria of sharing and pressure to develop or use them. But a vision of a co-operative agricultural policy would be facilitated by an understanding that sharing criteria exist and can be implemented in both production and trade.

## Industrial policies and technology

Industrial policies are needed, complementing those in resources and agriculture, to guide the international division of labour. Criteria of comparative advantage (being static and historical) are unacceptable to countries seeking to improve their status in the world. They will seek, at considerable cost, to alter the existing comparative advantages. The more successful they are, the less significant will differences in industrial comparative advantages become. The differences will also be narrowed by the continued transfers of technology, managerial skills, and capital by progressive increases in wage rates in LDCs, and by the reduction of transport costs relative to values of goods traded. The precise location of industrial activities over the world will become a matter almost of indifference to international (direct) investors, for markets will be close and supplies of materials readily transportable from almost any distance.

Though investors may become indifferent among a variety of locations, governments will not remain so. Nor will shifts in location of industrial activity (from advanced to developing countries) be a matter of indifference to the companies adversely affected or to labour. What is needed are guidelines which will assist developing countries in the selection of industrial activities and which will help advanced countries make the adjustments appropriate to a new structure and location of industrial activity over the world.

For co-ordination of industrial policies, a new institution should be established examining the movement of industry and the costs and adjustments required—an Organization for International Industrial Integration [46]. It would undertake studies of key industrial sectors at first—such as electronics, communication, aeronautics, autos, textiles, and iron and steel—which are already sources of tension among advanced and between advanced and developing countries. First steps would be simply information gathering; second would be projections of demands and supplies; third would relate to industrial locations; fourth to governmental policies of adjustment to new production and trade patterns; fifth to technological developments for continued improvement [47].

Such information would not only help governments direct their promotional activities, but it would also support programmes of foreign aid and development lending, plus facilitating private investment decisions. These, in turn, would affect the patterns of trade and the adjustments necessary in international payments.

Even after the specific industrial sectors to be developed are selected, there remains the question of what technologies to use—those requiring large numbers of low-skilled workers or fewer high-skilled? And can a continuing upgrading of skills be built in so as to increase productivity through creativity, adding to self-respect and a pride of accomplishment? Can these choices be made without the continuing assistance of the international companies or international centres for technical assistance?

Since creativity would be one of the primary objectives of the new order, how can the development of new technologies be spread equitably among nations so that all can share in the process? Decisons should be co-ordinated as to where particular kinds of research would be undertaken, for it will not be possible for smaller and less advanced countries to duplicate the entire range of research and development undertaken in the advanced countries.

Some of the projects are so expensive that duplication among many countries is highly undesirable. At present, some important research projects are simply not being financed because of the 'lack of resources,' while others are pursued in a quite competitive manner, wasting valuable manpower and equipment. For example, after a quick push, oceanographic research has fallen off considerably. Research in aerospace is too costly not to be co-operative, and even aircraft can no longer be left to a few countries to develop—witness the problems of the Concorde and Lockheed's F-1011—without the risk of very costly errors.

Yet to ask many countries how they would respond to new technologies or employ them is to expand the problems of technology assessment, which has only recently appeared on the national stage. Regardless of the complexity, such assessment will be required in many areas. And when these assessments involve several countries, each will insist on a 'piece of the action' if it is to use or be affected by the adoption of innovations. It will want to participate in the design, innovation, and development stages—if not in production! Or, if it does not participate in invention and innovation of one system, it will insist on being in on others. Thus, one can anticipate that the OPEC countries will soon see that the future of petroleum is intimately tied to development of substitute sources of energy and will want to insure a future income from and participation in these through financing part of the research—and where better to put a research centre on solar energy than in the desert areas of the Arab countries?

Is it not now possible to harness the energies of man to create complex techniques for macro-engineering and social development in the gestation of integrated techno-socio-politico-economic systems for man's progress rather than weapons systems for his destruction? If the vision is large enough, it may be possible. Control of ourselves could conceivably be recognized as more important than control over others.

Given the fact that smaller countries will have to specialize in order to make any contribution to technological advance, the international companies could be expected to distribute their efforts in a fashion that would permit research activities among various national locations. National research institutes could be set up that would specialize in one area—insecticides and their environmental effects, tropical diseases, nutrition from tropical foods, natural drugs, architectural impacts on living styles, electronics, urban ecology, facets of parapsychology, development of communication to replace the need to transport people (encouraging small-town development), impacts of mobility, etc.—but linked into wider systems for the dissemination and cross-fertilization of knowledge. Monopolies of knowledge by others will not be acceptable to any nation with the power to prevent such monopolization; but duplication of effort to prevent technological dominance is too costly and reduces the ready transfer of information. Better systems of development and transmission are required, which are less costly, sharing both the burden and the benefits. Tentative efforts along these lines are being made by the regional organizations and under the International Institute for Systems Analysis, but much more needs to be done.

### Foreign investment

Foreign investment policies of host countries have moved from the non-discriminatory 'right of establishment' extended under the bilateral FCN treaties and the GATT 'Code of Liberalization' to increasing interference on both entry and operations of foreign-owned affiliates. These restrictions are directed at making certain that investment activities are consonant with the national interest as seen by the host government. The regulations include screening procedures for entry, which both deter acquisitions as compared to new establishments and impose some requirements as to ownership and operations; they also constrain the movement of funds among affiliates or back to the parent. They are imposed over technology transfers and royalty payments for know-how. Restrictions are imposed over intercompany allocations of expenses and intercompany pricing and some are aimed at inducing greater exports and creation of local R&D facilities.

But nationally-oriented restrictions will not necessarily obtain the most effective or efficient use of the international companies, whose special capabilities are the use of world resources in serving national or multi-national markets. When company objectives coincide with those of governments, the latter should encourage or permit international companies to operate under their own criteria. However, such coincidence will likely occur only after governmental goals are made more explicit and guidelines for companies are detailed. In addition, not all international business forms are appropriate for meeting 'worldwide efficiency' criteria, nor are worldwide criteria primary in national development programmes. Some development projects require multinational co-operation among industries, and international companies can be used effectively in them.

What is needed in the field of international investment are two different approaches. One would codify the types of constraints which national governments could acceptably impose on international investment activities, including an agreement on harmonized constraints to be imposed by all governments. The other would be an institution to faciliate use of the international companies in co-operative projects which require the participation of many governments and the international companies for their completion, such as exploration of the seabed, de-pollution of the Rhine river, regional developments such as the Mekong Delta, the Choco Valley, the Sahara, etc., not to mention supersonic transport [48]. The code would require a new agreement and would involve governments, companies, and labour groups. Gestation of the multinational projects could be assigned to the World Bank, which would develop appropriate consortia (and sharing arrangements) among state and private enterprises and financial institutions.

These agreements, in turn, would depend on prior agreement among countries as to the roles which private enterprises (and the free market) will be permitted to play within each country and among them. They also are affected by the industrial policies implemented by each nation or regional grouping. And, of course, the role of private investment in petroleum and minerals will depend significantly on the decisions as to energy and materials policies mentioned above.

The primary objective, however, would be to make certain that foreign direct investment supported and accelerated the achievement of developmental goals in the national and international economies, which themselves are no longer dependent on market decisions and will not be permitted to depend solely on corporate decisions at the hands of the giant international companies. The criteria of effectiveness or efficiency which are employed by governments are different from those employed by companies, and a resolution can come only through governments establishing the limits of behaviour and then letting the companies operate in the most efficient manner to pursue the goals established within and among governments.

## Competition policy

Competition policies should explicitly signal the role to be played by the free market in domestic and international transactions and the extent to which corporate entities would be permitted to dominate any given sector. A variety of approaches are now taken by national governments toward monopoly, mergers, concentrations, acquisitions, and conglomerates. Some nations are encouraging concentration of particular industrial sectors, while encouraging competition in others. A few governments are encouraging cross-national mergers; others are discouraging them while encouraging mergers on a national scale.

The merger/concentration movement in Europe is said to be a response to the rise of the American multinational enterprises and not an anticompetitive move. It is argued that the competitive scene has changed, so that one can no longer think in terms of national market dominance but must consider international competition as well. Undoubtedly, more mergers at the national level will enhance international competitiveness of the resulting group, but they may stifle competition locally, changing radically the nature of the industry (this is the fear of small manufacturers and shop owners in France).

Competition policy also requires determination of the extent to which government-owned enterprises will dominate key sectors. This determination will affect not only the nature of economic growth, but also its rate and its cost, and will alter the reception to foreign investment. Equally, the eagerness of foreigners to invest will reflect the treatment of local enterprises. This is not to say that the developing countries should adopt the patterns in the advanced countries—certainly there are fewer companies to merge into large-scale enterprises—but it does stress that the policy issue cannot be avoided except at considerable cost because of greater uncertainty.

Competition policy is addressed not only to the structure of business but also to its actions in the market. Governments themselves frequently interfere in the market on behalf of national companies so as to gain production and selling opportunities for them. Or, they set rules such that foreign-owned companies cannot bid, as with government procurement. Sometimes they support industrial compensation agreements which divide production among several international companies, and at other times they strengthen a contract offer from a favoured company to another government with diplomatic representations or sweeten it with favourable credit terms or grant assistance.

Competition policy involves determinations as to the nature and extent of discrimination in the market—that permitted among companies and that injected by governments. The approaches taken by all countries other than the United States involve considerably more discrimination and anticompetitive behaviour than supposedly permitted under American law. The pattern in Japan includes consultation among companies within an industry on major industrial developments and investments projects, with the participation at critical junctures of government officials and banks. German policy permits collusion among potential competitors, especially as to exports, and many instances in the domestic market are overlooked when not considered harmful. The European Community criteria of anticompetitive action are based on *abuse* of dominance—not on dominance itself, as under American law.

Establishment of a European incorporation statute potentially involves a different kind of discrimination, that against the foreign-owned firm. It is not yet determined whether foreign-owned companies can be incorporated as 'European companies.' If not, some competitive disadvantage will arise for the international companies of the United States and Japan.

To achieve a new economic order will require an intergovernmental understanding as to the competition policies to be employed, so that the area of free-market determination will be well defined. This does not mean that harmonization must be achieved in competition policies. It simply means that the various constraints on the free market are surfaced and examined to determine their continued desirability, especially in the light of proposed initiatives (and results) in the areas of energy, investment, and commodities discussed above. Without such a broad agreement, continued disputes will arise over the application of discriminatory measures and the extent to which adjustments should be made through the market. Such disputes would hamper the pursuit of the other four objectives stated above.

## Trade policy

Neither the advanced nor the developing countries want to make the adjustments in the direction and volumes of exports and imports that would be required by a policy of free trade. Despite the fact that several billions of dollars of world production are lost as a result of lower productivity resulting from trade barriers, no country is willing to let the free market decide how the added income and employment would be distributed for fear that its national income might fall while world income rose. Rather than a progressive movement toward freer trade, at present, we find a regression in the form of increasing impediments (such as non-tariff barriers) and cartelization of trade. Where there is movement to freeing trade, as in the LAFTA complementation agreements, it is highly selective. The European preferences to imports from LDCs are selective and limited and further duty reductions among advanced countries are likely to be selective.

A major reason for the reticence toward removal of tariff- and non-tariff barriers is that these restrictions are used to soften the impact of the world market and to make certain that the country imposing them has an appropriate participation in agricultural and industrial development. The reluctance is a question not merely of income distribution but also of employment levels, employment diversification, industrial patterns, technological levels, international dependence, and costs of adjustments to worldwide changes.

If the structure and location of industrial activity over the world can be directed so that all nations feel that they are treated equitably; if technological participation can be dispersed appropriately; if a world food bank could be created, assuring adequate supplies to all; if sharing can be achieved in energy and raw materials; and if adequate control over the flow of direct investment can be gained—then, much of the reluctance to adopt freer trade will be removed, for the objectives of the restrictions will be achieved by other (more appropriate) means. If such agreement cannot be achieved, little will be gained by pushing hard along the lines of past negotiations; new approaches in the trade field are needed.

The new initiatives should be based on sectoral negotiations. There are some specific sectors in which progress can be made toward reducing barriers to trade without other prerequisities. The elimination of all barriers is more likely if sought first on specific categories of goods among a group of countries. Some entire industrial sectors may be ready for open international competition, such as aluminium, paper and pulp, some processed foods, automobiles, etc. Such an agreement is possible only if each participating country considers that its industry could survive and participate in worldwide growth. In other sectors, intergovernmental agreements covering agricultural or industrial policies would help assure participation of individual nations that would lead to operations efficient enough to survive (as under the Andean complementation agreements), at which point reduction of barriers would not only be easier but would probably be sought as a means of reducing costs and raising productivity *within* the agreed structure of production [49].

No country would be willing to sign an industry's death warrant through such sectoral free trade. And LDCs would certainly not participate until they had a suitable entrant in the industry. This point indicates the pre-conditions for further reductions of tariff and non-tariff barriers; assurance of a continued participation in particular sectors. With the increased evidence that the only major limitation on industrial diversification is country—not peculiar—resources, each country will want assurance that it can obtain a significant diversity of industry so as to provide a variety of employment opportunities, to share in technological advance, and to reduce reliance on fluctuations in a single industry.

Trade negotiations, therefore, will depend on the ability to insure each country involved that it will continue to participate in the particular industry sector under negotiation through production of some significant portion or component. For example, the United States has been unwilling to let production of mushrooms be swamped by foreign imports; it has shown considerable interest in saving footwear, various sporting goods, tiles, etc., to say nothing of the 'voluntary agreements' imposed on Japan and others in the sectors of textiles and iron and steel. Acceptance of the shifts indicated would be more easily obtained within overall policies guiding industrial development and technological change.

Further moves toward freer trade will be contingent, therefore, on guarantees that industrial structures will not be radically altered by the resulting trade pressures and that changes which are needed are made palatable through adequate *prior* adjustments. Again, what is needed are means of determining an equitable, as well as efficient (i.e., based on dynamic comparative advantages and least-cost production) distribution of industry internationally.

### International monetary system

There are two basic ways in which the international monetary system could be restructured to be consistent with the objectives proposed in this essay. The system could be designed to assist in the attainment of greater equity in the international economy through injections of new money (reserves) in the required places and at the required times. Or, it could be designed to function 'neutrally,' letting equity be achieved by the other policies discussed above. No one system is necessarily 'better' than the other, if the objective of justice in the world economy is achieved. The first requires a managed money system; the second would lead to a more automatic system. But both require creation of a system in which confidence in the monetary unit is generated (by an acceptable valuation procedure), appropriate liquidity is provided, and equity in the distribution of monetary reserves is fostered.

The present scheme for SDRs falls into the first category. The proposal for a Commodity Reserve Currency falls into the second [50]. Both have been discussed at some length, but much more attention has been focussed on the SDR schemes. A careful comparison of the objectives and advantages of the Commodity Reserve proposals would highlight some of the inadequacies of the present SDR proposals. The SDR schemes provide no sure valuation of the currency unit, no agreed way of controlling worldwide inflation, no way of assuring less-developed countries of the opportunity to earn monetary reserves, and no means of spreading the costs of maintaining the international monetary system [51].

The costs of maintaining any given international monetary system are borne not simply in terms of 'out-of-pocket' costs of operation (printing bills or certificates, clearing balances, communication, administration, etc.) but also in the real economic impacts of changes in the money supply—i.e., inflation or deflation. A higher 'production cost' of money may be justifiable if the economic cost of unstable systems is reduced. The more automatic Commodity Reserve system would produce a more stable price level even though at the higher cost of storage of commodities. However, it achieves stability at the price of a loss of freedom in handling problems of domestic growth [52].

Obviously, it would be better to have greater stability in international price levels without high operating costs in the system. This could be achieved if the governmental parties were more interested in equitable results than in so-called efficiency results. The SDR scheme at present is aimed more at the liquidity objective than that of equity, providing reserves for the advanced countries to hold when they want more liquidity; this is a device for correcting imbalances of payments among *advanced* countries.

As a creation of the advanced countries, the SDRs leave the LDCs out of the determination of the distribution volume and of liquidity and involve a distribution of money claims on real assets without real production by the recipients. The value of the SDRs is also a result of fiat rather than of production of real values; confidence in the system would still rely on the behaviour of each major country in terms of maintaining the value of its own currency. The SDRs will not themselves become an international currency so long as they are denominated in gold or United States dollars.

If governments can operate without a real-value numeraire, they still must face the *means* of distributing it and when to do so. The equity objectives proposed in the present essay would be served by the distribution of SDRs to the lesser-developed countries or through an international aid agency. To maintain price stability, their issue could be tied (as suggested by Pierre Uri) [53] to an index of raw material prices—those entering strongly into industrial production or directly into consumption, such as petroleum, wheat, coffee, cotton, rice, gold, silver, platinum, molybdenum, copper, tin, bauxite, iron ore, etc. When this index fell, SDRs would be issued to the lesser-developed countries on a distribution pattern agreed upon in advance to rectify some of the inequities in the international economy. They would be a form of aid, admitting that the LDCs do not have the same opportunities as do the advanced countries. The pattern of distribution could be shifted from time to time, through decisions by the aid agency, for example, reducing that to countries that become more advanced and able to create opportunities of their own (such as Brazil and Mexico). And temporary shifts could be made to meet emergency situations in countries such as those in Central Africa facing a drought. (The volume of such emissions would not necessarily be sufficient to meet emergency problems or the needs for long-term economic development; additional resources would undoubtedly be called for from the more advanced countries as at present.)

Present proposals surrounding the SDRs are deficient in three major respects: there is no provision for determining the value of SDRs save in terms of gold or dollars, leaving us with the same problems as before as to the source of confidence in the system; there is no provision for using the monetary system as a means of achieving equity in the international economy; and there is no means of sharing the burden of maintaining the international monetary system. The answer to the third can be coupled with the second; the first remains unanswered by any approach to the SDRs that does not tie them to real asset values.

# Problems of a co-operative system and next steps

Solutions to one set of issues are seldom problem-free [54]. Unseen problems will undoubtedly arise from an effort to create a just international economic order—one that achieves equity, efficiency, participation, creativity, and unity with diversity. Some can be envisaged beforehand; they include frictions arising from increasing interdependence, tensions from a lack of institutions for settlement of disputes over inequities at the international level, rigidities introduced through the search for certainty, reduction in innovation and technological change resulting from these rigidities, an expansion of bureaucratic decision making, and a potential reduction in the amount and relevance of information flowing to the public. But there are also pressures arising to encourage us to take the next steps toward a more co-operative and just order.

## Problems

The co-operative integration of economies implied in the solutions to the issues discussed above means that there will be a substantial rise in the recognition of interdependence of nations and thereby in interdependence itself. What the world has faced over the past century has been a high degree of dependence of one set of countries on another. In the absence of a sense of community, in which the more advanced countries also looked after the interests of the less advanced, such dependence was found unacceptable and was rejected as soon as practicable.

Interdependence implies a sense of community, in which the interests of nations are inextricably tied and mutually acceptable solutions are found to pressing problems [55]. Each member (person, group, or nation) of the community has some ability to affect the selection of criteria of acceptability, to determine the distribution of rewards for efforts or contributions, to assign tasks, and to participate in creative activities. Thus, each is *needed* and is an integral part of the whole, with each relying on the other. When inequities arise, a means exists of adjusting them without the use of force.

At present, however, there are no institutional means either for assigning tasks or of adjusting inequities that arise. New arrangements will have to be made. None of the existing institutions is suitable for these tasks—not the OECD, the World Bank, NATO, UN, or any of the functional agencies. Though criteria exist for determination of whether equity will be gained in any given arrangements, means will have to be found of determining who plays what roles and for whose benefit. For example, will the rise in the price of oil be for the benefit of LDCs other than OPEC members? Or will they suffer disproportionately from not having their basic needs covered or being able to create substitutes for energy? Will greater international equity be at the cost of reduced living standards in the United States? Or will it merely mean a relative slowing of the increase of its consumption of materials and final products in comparison with others? And what will be the impact of an overall slowing of world industrial growth on developing countries without basic resources, as costs of resource development increase?

Unless carefully formulated, answers to these questions are likely to introduce greater rigidities into the system than now exist. Countries will want to increase employment and maintain it in the face of changes in technology or industrial developments. Planning agencies will wish to project their plans for several years and not to have to alter them when avoidable. Long-term arrangements for development and sale of raw materials (such as present arrangements for oil and iron ore) will force adjustments downstream or in other areas when changes in conditions of supply or demand occur; alternatively, rigidities will be created in these sectors to pass the adjustment on elsewhere.

Such rigidities can be reduced by designing production structures to provide goods and services for *systems* rather than mere products for finite demands. Better planning would bring more effective use of resources as well as a reduction in the loss of capital assets from business and project failures. But this assumes, of course, that planners use the greater certainty provided by the policies proposed to make long-range decisions that provide for careful adaptation to shifts in needs and demands.

Although greater certainty will tend to increase rigidities and reduce the attractiveness of innovation in the system—both technological and managerial—the high cost of inability to provide adequate solutions to new problems should be a safeguard against stagnation [56]. There is little evidence that the private sector has been any more capable of seeing long-run changes—viz., the shortage of energy, the need to shift to smaller automobiles, or the need to substitute communication for transportation of people—than would be a co-ordinated effort on the part of governments and companies. The market simply does not reflect *future* or long-run supply and demand in *present* prices.

Offsetting the slower innovation would be a longer period in which to assess the desirability of technological changes, rather than merely adopting each new technology simply because it exists. Rapid changes have undoubtedly been costly and wasteful of resources and manpower, to say nothing of confusing to the consumer when he is provided with more variety without functional improvements, or improvements only at excessive costs.

Still another problem will be the proliferation of governmental bureaucracy that arises from passing decisions into the realm of intergovernmental arrangements or rule-setting. The energy shortage is but the most recent example of such expansion of bureaucratic decision making. If spread over wide areas, these arrangements can lead quite readily to the 'planning state,' with the government involved in all major decisions along with private interests.

Labels are not important unless they carry meaning, and it is conceivable that a kind of corporate state is needed to produce an appropriate and acceptable sense of community while reserving an optimum degree of personal freedom. Freedom is not achieved only in a market but also in the exercise of responsibilities to the society which nurtures and protects the individual. Some co-operation is undoubtedly necessary also at the international level. 'The planning state' is rejected by those who see the free market as the *only* appropriate organizing mechanism for the world economy. Once that mechanism is seen as inadequate and the alternative to private planning is seen as public planning, the choice becomes one of how much planning and under whose authority. Both private and public domination must be constrained.

Whether under the 'planning state' or merely an expanded bureaucracy, a singular danger is that the people will not be provided the information necessary for them to make careful decisions as to their role in the political economy. This is not to say that they have had adequate information on the operations and activities of oligopolistic firms operating in the market (private corporatism). Under either a free-market or a co-operative system, individual freedom and choice must be based on adequate information. And bureaucratic systems (whether in public or private institutions) tend to withhold such information. New systems must be devised, therefore, for the prompt release of all relevant information to the public [57], and the media must be prepared to interpret the information properly.

Without adequate information, even a co-operative system can be readily corrupted. It would be impossible to determine whether equity or efficiency exists; participation and creativity would be reduced and stunted, while autonomy would be lost in the maze of inadequately explained and understood regulations. With information, freedom can be retained through the decisions of informed electorates and consumer groups. Greater participation by individuals at the local and national levels in political and economic decisions, therefore, becomes a prerequisite to protection of freedom at the international level.

## Next steps

The first step is to recognize that the underlying problem in the tensions and disagreements among nations both politically and economically is the perception of injustices—the plight of the Palestinian refugees, the ghettos over the world, famine, the prices of necessities, unjustifiable income disparities, the presumed exploitative power of the large corporations, boredom in or dehumanization of work, the advantages of the dollar-exchange standard for the United States [58], loss of pride, and various forms of imperialism (territorial expansion, cultural invasion and economic penetration). Of course, the correction of one injustice (e.g., raising the price of crude oil to redistribute the benefits to the producing countries) may create another (e.g., the burden of higher prices of crude on the lesser-developed countries).

But once justice is given high priority, solutions to specific issues or conflicts will not likely be proffered without an effort to determine the equity conditions of co-operation [59]. This will be a signal step forward and a move to greater stability in political and economic relations. Take for example the question of non-tariff barriers, which would appear to be a relatively simple and technical problem: it cannot be resolved until the underlying problem of equity in the distribution of industrial development is approached. Nor can that of international monetary reform.

Not all issues require resolution simultaneously. An attempt to do so would imply revolution. Such broad changes do not occur within a system; only by its rupture. It is doubtful that the leading factions will seek to alter the system too radically. But they can be induced to do so step by step [60].

The selection of the areas for co-operation will probably be made on a 'spur of the moment' basis, reacting to emergency situations, such as the energy crisis. But some longer-run pressures exist which show the ways in which tensions are likely to build pressures which will alter policies. The first is that of technological development; a second is environmental impacts of continued growth; a third is the shift in power toward the LDCs; and a fourth is the rise of the multinational enterprise.

As recognized by Jefferson, de Tocqueville, and more recent observers, the continuing rapid proliferation of technological advance both ties nations together in new forms of interdependency and creates problems in the use and allocation of the world's resources. The necessity eventually to spread the development of technology and the responsibility for selecting the technologies used (technology assessment) will require intergovernmental agreements.

The environmental impacts of continued growth, the spread of industrialization, the transnational impact of pollution, the necessity for co-operative efforts at de-pollution of common rivers, seas and the oceans, and the problems of radioactive wastes with greater use of atomic energy will all create pressures for intergovernmental agreement. They will be resisted for a time, and probably for too long but the move will eventually be toward accommodation and co-operation.

## New international forces

The increasing power of the LDCs is shifting the balance of negotiating strength away from the advanced countries. Though history shows few instances in which the rich voluntarily gave up their perquisities in favour of the poor, it does reveal instances of 'enlightened self-interest' arising from perception of the rich of changing circumstances, as well as instances in which the poor forced reversals of the basic conditions. We will probably see both again in the coming decade. The rich are bothered by the 'inhumanitarian' conditions of life around the world—aid continues, and some nations are still increasing their contributions. 'Humanitarian motives' in redressing inequities should not be downplayed. In addition, the willingness of the major countries to lead has shifted. The United States seems less willing to bear the burdens of leadership, and though no other country has taken up the mantle, it is unlikely that it will pick it up again in this decade. Conversely, though others see the United States as both strong and wealthy and entitled to a leadership role, they are looking elsewhere for leadership also—the Soviet Union, Japan, China, and a united Europe. The absence of the use of force for economic advantage will also change the bargaining positions, leaving the LDCs in a position to exert strong pressures on the economic policies of the advanced countries through the ability of LDCs to open or close lucrative markets, through their ability to withhold critical raw materials, and through their treatment of the investments of the advanced countries in LDCs. On the last point, the debtor tends to have the upper hand, unless he is expecting to be a future borrower; constraints apply to both debtor and creditor. Direct investment is a two-way sword, also, providing a hostage to the LDCs in the form of existing investment.

Finally, the rise of the multinational enterprise is a source of tension which will lead to increasing co-operation among governments *. The international companies which operate as multinational enterprises are tying the world more tightly together, integrating the industrial economies and pulling the LDCs into the industrial orbit. At the same time they are potential channels for a more equitable distribution of the benefits of industrialization and of economic integration [61]. These companies can be used not only to achieve greater equity but also to undertake a number of co-operative (intergovernmental) projects that are currently side-stepped for lack of efficient and equitable means of accomplishment.

## The need for leadership

If governments are induced to focus on the primary question of equity in international economic relations by these pressures, they will find that there are ways of reducing injustices in the world economy. But if they continue to think that equity will fall out of mere technical solutions, the underlying tensions will not be removed or the inequities redressed.

* The recent hearings by the Group of Eminent Persons under the aegis of the UN-ECOSOC are likely to lead to recommendations for co-operative action in gathering information and in guiding the activities of the international companies.

Given the ability of the world to produce ample goods, through the careful use of technologies, husbanding of resources, and development of human resources, the primary challenge is that of distribution of benefits and burdens. It is a challenge that tests not only our will, but our maturity, political acumen, and our morals. 'Indeed, it is amply clear that, if man wills it, a world community can be created in which human beings can live comfortably and in peace with each other. But it is equally clear that the achievement of this condition will require the application of intelligence, imagination, courage, unselfish help, planning, and prodigious effort. And it is equally clear that the time for decision is the present [62].'

The present lack is that of leadership. It appears that each of the major players is looking to the others to take the lead; otherwise, only marginal managerial decisions will be taken [63]. Governments seem to rely on companies to take initiatives in 'correcting the system'; businessmen, in turn, assert that the rules must be set by governments. Labour seems to be taking some initiative, at least toward bargaining with the multinational enterprise, but not toward any of the other problems [64]. And the public—voter and consumer—is still not as active as would be necessary to take leadership; various groups are pointing up problems but not asserting themselves enough in formulating solutions to be considered the decision makers.

Yet there are evidences of awakenings among each of these groups. Consumer groups and community associations are becoming more active, and much counsel is being given that government must be returned to 'the people' at the local (neighbourhood, city, provincial) levels. Labour is torn between handling specific problems of unemployment and achieving 'fair labour standards' over the world. Businessmen, from the United States through Europe to Japan and Latin America, can be heard espousing a greater social responsibility on the part of the corporations (both domestic and international) for meeting the problems of unemployment, lack of necessities, environmental degradation, and dehumanization of work. Governments seem the least capable at present of coming forward with programmes clearly directed at reducing injustices without at the same time going so far (as in Denmark and probably the United Kingdom) as to remove substantial incentives to continued economic progress.

What seems lacking is a sense of responsibility to match the entitlements which each group or person seeks—and is taught that are his under the world view of industrialism and material progress. To achieve that sense of responsibility will require a new world view, recognizing that man is a part of all nature, that all persons (and their actions) are affected directly by all others, and that social institutions can be altered to reflect the underlying values of the society, removing its hypocrisy [65].

To move in this direction requires more information, honestly and relevantly communicated, to those involved. Toward this end, all major actors can and should move simultaneously, clearly displaying their acts and motives.

Governments must be more open than they are—not only with their citizens but with each other—reflecting the values of the society. Business must recognize that both market decisions and planning require all relevant information to be available to decision makers and that this information must be as accurate as possible—i.e., honesty and truth are required for the *system* to achieve its objectives (even though it might pay an individual or group to flout these rules). Business can start by discussing openly and fully its actions and motives in helping to solve social problems and to direct each company to the goal of human development of those associated with it [66]. Business cannot hide behind the assertion that 'the business of business is business,' for the social impact of business is critical and it can be altered; it must be altered either by business or society: society will do the altering if that impact does not accord with the changing values of the society.

Business cannot abandon the leadership to governments, but it should not be left to lead alone [67]. Governments are responsible for representing the will of the people and should be attuned to their highest values. Co-operative action by business, government, labour, and consumers (or the public) is required, reflecting the changing goals of the society, including the increasing concern to remove the injustices in the present system. The first step is to recognize the significance of the changes in values which are placing equity and justice on a par with efficiency and material progress. By this action every policy toward reforming the international economy would be aimed at achieving not only efficiency but also equity, which alone can gain acceptability for the new system.

## Notes

1. Quoted by Carl Madden, *Clash of Culture: Management in an Age of Changing Values* (Washington, D.C.: National Planning Association, 1973), p. 61.

2. One third of the world's population presently consumes three quarters of the total harvested crops, overeating while the remainder goes hungry.

In his study of *The Food and People Dilemma,* George Borgstrom concludes that the widening gap is an ominous feature of our days and one which poses the greatest challenge mankind has ever faced, overshadowing atom bombs, continental missiles, microbial toxins and nerve gases. The relentless greed of the 'haves' and the 'have mores' is not only highly calamitous but indicates perverted goals in a world where parsimony, moderation, and responsibility should be our guides. (Series on the Man-Environment System for Duxbury Press, North Scituate, Mass., 1973, p. 59.)

Borgstrom concludes further (page 63) that the inequities are not removed by the pattern of foreign trade ; rather, the poorer countries are using their resources to feed the more well-to-do.

3. Quoted by Joseph A. Kohl, 'Latin Americans Turn Again', in *World View,* March 1974, p. 38.

4. Borgstrom notes that several of the more advanced countries 'show an annual increase in fuel and energy consumption far greater than the total used in most nations, below the world's poverty line'. (Borgstrom, *The Food and People Dilemma,* p. 95.)

5. The Japanese consider that a contest among unequals is uninteresting, and Americans and Europeans also accept such a constraint when they classify entrants by weight or age (as in weight lifting, boxing, wrestling, etc.). But Americans take the greatest pleasure in the 'unlimited' class, reserving for these champions their highest praise and honour.

The drive to win in the top classes is warping the concepts of the game, causing individuals and coaches to seek to win, even if they have to cheat.

Concentration of the rules and the result (winning) voids adequate consideration of why the game is played in the first place or at all!

If the economic system is not to provide justice, what is it for?

6. In commenting on the Nairobi monetary conference, Philippe de Weck concluded that '...too little attention is being paid to the human and political elements; the problem is viewed in a purely technical sense. Experience proves that if an excessive deficit appears... no technical device can put things right. The problem is basically political, rather than technical.' *Vision,* January 1974, p. 17.

7. The French economist Pierre Uri stresses this point in arguing that our fundamental responsibility is 'to work out policies which will base growth on the reduction of inequalities rather than accepting that inequalities should increase with growth.' Pierre Uri, *L'Europe se gaspille* (Paris, Hachette, 1973), p. 34.

8. Nationalism at present is of two sorts: the 'old' nationalism of the consolidation of tribes, cities, or regions into a nation state, creating necessary loyalties and linkages, and the 'new' nationalism of the increasing responsibility of governments for economic growth and stability and for social welfare. Both nationalisms require greater national cohesion and regard for national interests at the same time that there are strong pulls towards international interdependence. (For a description of the 'new' nationalism, see Theodore Geiger, *The Fortunes of the West,* [Bloomington, Ind., Indiana University Press, 1973], pp. 49-53).

9. That all economic policy proposals have an implicit welfare objective is stressed by Robert Z. Aliber in a recent essay: 'Most analysts have an implicit world-welfare function in mind when discussing reform proposals.' But he also emphasizes that '...the objective function—the welfare function to be maximized—is ambiguous.' 'National Preference and the Scope for International Monetary Reform,' in *Essays in International Finance,* No. 101, Princeton University International Finance Section, November 1973, p. 2.

10. The lack of acceptance of the postwar orientations in Asia is stressed by Ernest H. Preeg: 'The highly legalistic and rather abstract concepts embodied in the IMF and

most particularly in the GATT are largely alien to economic intercourse in Asia. To some degree, this reflects the historical absence of a truly *laissez-faire* economic concept, the central principle underlying the Bretton Woods system.' *Economic Blocs and United States Foreign Policy* (Washington: National Planning Association, Report No. 135, January 1974), p. 130.

11. Eric Wyndham White, formerly Director General of the GATT, has suggested that sectoral trade negotiations will probably be more successful than across-the-board reductions and that greater reductions can probably be obtained with a smaller number of countries participating. *Negotiations in Prospect* (Washington, Brookings Institution, 1972).

12. See Walter Laqueur, 'Europe—Run out of Gas,' in *New York Times Magazine,* January 20, 1974.

13. Preeg, *Economic Blocs and United States Foreign Policy,* p. 146; for the next 40 pages on future policies Preeg does not once address the problem of equity.

14. Preeg, *Economic Blocs and United States Foreign Policy,* p. 139.

15. *Survey of Current Business,* December 1972 and January 1973.

16. Not all international business takes the ME form, and not all MEs have identical characteristics, since they are found in different industrial sectors and are operated under different management styles. For a detailed characterization, see my monograph *Some Patterns in The Rise of the Multinational Enterprise* (University of North Carolina School of Business, 1969), and for a comparison with other forms, see my monograph *Decision Criteria for Direct Foreign Investment in Latin America* (New York, Council of the Americas, 1974), Ch. 1.

17. Professor Richard N. Gardner has argued for acceptance of the principle of 'equal access' so as to avoid the injection of politics into raw material supply. (*Hearings* before the Joint Economic Committee of the United States Congress, December 1973).

But one cannot urge the 'equal access' principle without considering the concept of equality which is implicit in it, and that concept is itself highly political (ethical, and even theological). Urging 'equal access' will not de-politicize the issues; rather, it will raise to a high power the concept of equity, which can be resolved only at the political level. It is not possible to ask questions concerning the equitable distribution of materials without also asking the same question about the distribution of final products and, therefore, about the international distribution of incomes—the OPEC price increases are a substantial redistribution of income among nations. To assume that the market will provide 'equal access' is to presume that the distribution of 'money chits' is also equal (or is seen as equitable) and that people or nations will spend them in different ways according to their tastes. To assume this is to assume further that the present distribution of incomes and industrial activity is seen as 'just.' Therefore, one cannot suggest a principle of 'equal access' through the market without at the same time asserting that the rest of the system which produces the structure of claims behind the market is acceptable or 'just.'

What is needed, instead, is a recognition that any economic system or economic means of allocation is predicated on ethical constructs (usually no longer visible or questioned) and that criteria of 'equality' or 'equity' will require a reconsideration of the ethical foundations. From this recognition will come a further realization that proposals for 'equal access' are efforts to do some mending on the patchwork quilt we call the 'international economic system' where what we need is a new design—one increasingly based on principles of co-operation in allocation (i.e., sharing) rather than on market competition.

18. Professor Eugene Skolnikoff of MIT has observed that 'The old belief that growing interdependence among nations would breed at least a sense of common purpose, and more hopefully a genuine community of values, has proven a weak reed at best. Unexpectedly rapid growth in the relations and dependencies across national borders hasn't reduced strife, but rather sharpened divisions and distinctions.' Alan L. Otten, 'Politics and People' [column], in *The Wall Street Journal,* January 17, 1974.

19. See Samuel Pisar, *Co-existence and Commerce* (New York: McGraw-Hill, 1970), for the Soviet techniques.

20. See Jack N. Behrman, *Multinational Production Consortia: The Lessons of NATO Experience* (Washington, D.C.: Department of State, Bureau of Intelligence and Research, 1972).

21. A study of INTELSAT concluded that 'Commercial objectives, traditional practices, and a desire to exercise financial and political controls have created a condition in which the key national secondary groups and national governments have learned how to apply pressure, control gates, and negotiate agreements which minimize the potential for the integrative process to occur within the organizational decision-making process. Nevertheless, accommodation of these political realities has not impaired the technical quality and functional efficiency of the organization's operation.' Joseph N. Pelton, *Global Communications Satellite Policy: INTELSAT* (Mt. Airy, Maryland: Lomond Books, 1974), p. 47.

22. An alternative procedure would be the use of differentiated exchange rates to reduce imports and stimulate exports within a sector, as proposed in the book by Pierre Uri, Nicholas Kaldor, Richard Ruggles, and Robert Triffin, *A Monetary Policy for Latin America* (New York: Praeger for the Atlantic Institute, 1968), pp. 67-74.

23. For analyses of the problems and prospects for using the international companies in the auto and petrochemical sectors, see my study of *The Role of International Companies in Latin American Integration* (Lexington, Mass.; Lexington Books, for the Committee for Economic Development, 1973).

24. Italy provides an interesting case of adjustment through export subsidies (*Vision,* January 1973). The Government has been subsidizing exports in order to avoid a devaluation and to prevent unemployment which would result from reductions in wage rates or deflationary measures. Devaluation is avoided because it would raise import prices and feed inflation. Cuts in employment are avoided because of the high costs of severance of workers. The editor of *Vision* urged the necessity of cutting wages, restricting the right to strike, and reducing 'sick leave' permissions as means of cutting costs and raising productivity. But he admitted that these seemed impossible of acceptance by the Italian government.

Pursuit of the technique of export subsidies was, of course, possible only with the acceptance (tacit if not explicit) of the other members of the European Community. They apparently preferred this 'solution' than alternatives facing them—such as the revaluation eventually forced on them by the United States and which Italy did not follow. In effect, the lira was devalued against major European currencies.

25. For example, the comment of Abderrahman Khene, Secretary General of OPEC: 'If the international community really wants to concern itself with its global future, it will certainly have to pool its resources and ensure an equitable distribution. But you cannot do anything limited to a single sector.' In *Vision,* December 1973, p. 52.

26. In an article on 'The Struggle for the World Product: Politics between Power and Morals,' Helmut Schmidt (Chancellor of the Federal Republic of Germany) argues that '...the main problem then is to define the laws which determine the distribution of this enormous output; it might be added: which determine the 'fair' distribution, the 'equitable' price, the 'proper' value.' In *Foreign Affairs,* April 1974, p. 442.

27. In discussing United States trade policy, William J. Diebold concludes that 'Perhaps the most important long-run question is whether this new mix of producers and consumers... will be able to discover a broad enough area of common interests to accept arrangements that can be seen to give all parties a reasonable share of the continuing benefits of co-operation...' 'But if, instead of trying to find some new rules to live by, governments act as if the conduct of international economic policy is a zero-sum game, they may prove themselves right.' In *Foreign Affairs,* April 1974, pp. 492 and 496.

Despite these observations, neither Diebold nor several other writers in the same issue addressing foreign economic policies focus clearly on the implications of a co-operative system which would be sufficiently equitable to be acceptable to all nations involved.

28. These actions fly in the face of the principle of 'neutrality' which is espoused by American officials in international conferences on economic policies—a principle stemming from economic theory. 'Neutrality' is sought to avoid interferences in markets that alter decisions of specific actors; macro policies are permissible but not micro policies, since the latter would alter the relative positions of particular participants in a single market.

It should be noted that, when it appears that this principle rebounds to the disadvantage of United States interests, it is readily voided by these same American officials.

This principle, along with that of 'national treatment' and 'nondiscrimination,' presumes that the underlying economic situation is just, and therefore acceptable to all involved. For this reason, the United States is against 'incentive and disincentive' systems for altering the flow of international investment. But it is precisely the unacceptability of the market-determined allocation of investment in industry around the world that causes governments to employ such systems.

29. A useful insight into the relationship of equity and participation comes from Morgan Doughton: 'A democracy can survive imbalances of income and wealth, but it cannot survive a crushing imbalance in capacity that leaves substantial numbers of its citizens atomized without responsibility to one another, and, therefore, powerless.' *Harper's Magazine,* March 1974, p. 8.

A study by Irma Adelman and Cynthia Taft Morris concludes that 'participation' does not necessarily produce greater equality, being linked to other factors than growth and the power to force re-distribution. *Economic Growth and Social Equity in Developing Countries* (Stanford: Stanford University Press, 1973).

30. Raoul Prebisch has stressed this last criterion in his study of *Transformación y Desarrollo:* 'Where the Latin American countries are concerned, the intention to develop their economies is closely linked to a consideration whose importance is beyond question: the compatibility of international co-operation with an unequivocal sense of autonomy in decision-making.' *Change and Development: Latin America's Great Task* (Report to the Inter-American Development Bank, Washington, D.C., June 1970, p. 135).

31. A number of other governmental policies will directly and indirectly affect these seven, but they will remain the preserve of national ministers for much longer: wages and prices, employment, housing, monetary and fiscal, regional development, social welfare, science and technology, education, manpower development and training, population, and immigration.

There is another group of policies that will increasingly move into the inter-governmental realm, but they are more of the facilitating than of the restrictive type: patents, standards, taxation, unemployment compensation and social security, transport, exploration of space, labour unions, etc.

The mere enumeration of these policies—all to be set by governments and some to be implemented by them—emphasizes how different the present world economy is from that in 1945, when we were still debating whether 'full employment' was the responsibility of governments.

32. In an examination of 'The Hard Road to World Order,' Richard Gardner includes among the policies to which the United States should commit itself in assisting the LDCs the following: 'More multinational aid, more market access for developing countries' exports, more transfer of technology, a world food reserve, more private investment on mutually satisfactory terms, revenue sharing from seabed exploitation, the issuance of special drawing rights to multilateral lending agencies, and a new look at commodity agreements in those special situations where they may be practicable.' In *Foreign Affairs,* April 1974, p. 569.

He argues for the removal of politics from foreign economic policies, which is to argue for either avoiding the problems of equity or of building equity into the system itself; however, he makes neither of these points nor seems to recognize the implications of this omission for the acceptability of his proposals.

33. These resolutions were pursuant to the resolutions of the General Assembly adopted May 1, 1974 (Nos. 3201 [S-VI] and 3202 [S-VI]) entitled 'Declaration on the Establishment of a New International Economic Order' and 'Programme of Action on the Establishment of a New International Economic Order.' The latter charges all organizations and conferences associated with the UN with implementation of the programme, submitting progress reports to the ECOSOC.

34. Draft resolution A/AC.166/L.45 reported in Doc. E/5496, May 3, 1974, of the UN ECOSOC.

35. The principle of 'equal access' was point 4 of Atlantic Charter of August, 1941, drawn up by Roosevelt and Churchill as the 'Common principles' for conduct of their international relations after World War II: '(4) They will endeavour, with due respect for their existing obligations, to further the enjoyment by all States, great and small, victor or vanquished, of access, on equal terms, to the trade and to the raw materials of the world which are needed for their economic prosperity.' This principle was predicated on the international operation of free markets (or at least considerably freer than during the inter-war years).

The problem behind this provision in the Charter was the attempt before the war to pre-empt supplies of materials or to embargo their sale to certain countries. 'Equal access' meant that the materials or goods available would be allocated according to supply and demand, under the basic postwar principle of 'non-discriminatory, multilateral trade and payments.'

36. Gardner, 'The Hard Road of World Order,' in *Foreign Affairs,* April 1974. This view reflects again the desire to separate the inseparable. Policy makers shy away from political economy at the price of frustration. They need to focus on the political aspects of foreign economic policies more clearly than they have in the past. The continuing frustration in the negotiations on international monetary reform and on trade are a reflection of the unwillingness of officials to grasp the nettle of politization firmly enough. Consequently, 'technical economic nostrums' are proposed which do not adequately meet the political and social aspects of the problems.

37. William Diebold, *United States Trade Policy in Foreign Affairs,* April 1974, p. 485-486 and 490, demonstrates the irrelevancy of the principle of 'equal access' in the present world situation.

38. To offer the developing countries, in return, 'equal access' to markets will not avoid the problem of politization. Equal access to markets is not produced by the removal of barriers—not even equal *opportunity* for access to markets and certainly not equality of *results* or benefits. The removal of all trade barriers gives greater benefits to those with an early start (an advantage recognized long ago by Adam Smith), who have been fortunate enough, or better endowed, or aggressive enough, or smarter, or sufficiently dominant so as to get ahead of their neighbours. The fact that removal of barriers will benefit the more advanced countries *more* than the less advanced is a conclusion readily drawn from the regional integration movements of the past few decades. To achieve greater equality of access to markets would require discrimination in favour of the developing countries *and* a more selective discrimination in favour of the *least* developed among them (as with Bolivia and Ecuador in the Andean Pact under LAFTA). Therefore, under this prescription also, the concept of 'equality' is not clear and will require specification under some new criteria, for past criteria are not now acceptable.

39. Max Saltsman, 'A National Plan,' in Abraham Rothstein (ed.), *An Industrial Strategy for Canada* (Toronto: New Press, 1972), pp. 99-109.

40. In a speech in Tokyo, J.K. Jamieson, Chairman of the Board of Exxon, called for co-operation among the companies and the producing and consuming countries, but he did not specify its form (April 24, 1973).

41. The criterion of equity or fairness proposed by Abderrahman Khene (*Vision,* December 1973, p. 52) is that of an oil price matching the percentage increases in wheat or industrial products—that is, 'parity' as in agriculture. Since 1972, wheat has risen from $1.50 to $6.25/bushel or over 400%, and oil from $3.00 to $11.50 or under 400%.

42. Bernard Nossiter raised the spector of a glut of oil arising from the successful drive for additional and alternative energy resources. (*Washington Post,* January 30, 1974.) What then would the Arab states do with their unwanted oil—reduce the price, making alternative investments uneconomic and wasteful? Who would bear the costs of readjustment?

43. The present situation in petroleum has, of course, created an emergency in which the guidelines for co-operation will be rather different from what they might be under less strategic pressure. But the seven-point co-operative programme proposed by Secretary of State Kissinger is worth noting for its creation of a potential precedent.

As presented to the 13-nation Conference of Consumers, it included:

1) Conservation through reducing consumption and other means, with sharing of costs;
2) Alternative energy sources to be tapped from known resources;
3) Research and development of additional sources, particularly nuclear, through co-operative efforts;
4) Emergency sharing of supplies among consuming countries;
5) International financial co-operation to meet soaring prices;
6) Less-developed countries to be given 'special understanding' in facing their critical needs;
7) Consumers and producers to recognize that their 'enlightened self-interests' are not in conflict.

The mere calling of this Conference of Consuming Nations raised the question in the minds of producing countries whether a conflict situation was not being created, and some argued that if the move was really to be conciliatory, *all* consuming (e.g., LDCs) and producing countries should be included in a conference, under the auspices of the United Nations.

44. See *Forbes* (February 15, 1974) and Bension Varon and Kenji Takeuchi, 'Developing Countries and Non-Fuel Minerals,' *Foreign Affairs,* April 1974, pp. 497-510.

They conclude that CIPEC for copper is less likely to succeed because supply elasticity outside of the cartel is likely to be substantial, but nine minerals will be subject to increasing monopoly pressures by developing countries: 'the chance of their resorting to such drastic measures could depend, in the last analysis, on the overall state of relations between rich and poor countries' (p. 510).

45. Somewhat in desperation as a result of rising costs of fuel imports, Jamaica's Prime Minister requested an eight-fold increase in bauxite taxes without waiting for other countries to act in concert. (*Business Week,* May 25, 1974, p. 57.)

46. I have detailed this proposal in 'Sharing International Production Through Sectoral Integration and the Multinational Enterprise,' in *Law and Policy in International Business,* v. 4, no. IV, 1972, pp. 1-36.

A different proposal for an International Industrial Institute to prepare the groundwork for industrial policies is made by the National Academy of Science, *Meeting the Challenge of Industrialization* (Washington, D.C., 1973).

47. As needs were pinpointed and particular projects developed, based on multinational co-operation, a foundation would be built for including Communist countries in joint programmes. Out of particular projects, a basis for wider co-operation would arise. Gradually, they could be included within the new institutions, thereby integrating their industrial development with those of the West.

48. For examples of such projects in the military field see *Multinational Production Consortia: Lessons of the NATO Experience* (Bureau of Intelligence and Research, United States, Department of State, 1971).

49. A move to free trade under the NATO co-production arrangements occurred *after* all sharing techniques were agreed upon. See *Multinational Production Consortia* (Bureau of Intelligence and Research, United States Department of State, 1971).

50. Most recently proposed by Jan Tinbergen and Nicolas Kaldor before the First UNCTAD Conference, but earlier by Benjamin Graham, *World Commodities and World Currency* (New York, McGraw-Hill, 1944); Frank D. Graham, *Social Goals and Economic Institutions* (Princeton, Princeton University Press, 1942); F.A. Hayek, 'A Commodity Reserve Currency,' in *Economic Journal,* LIII, 1943, pp. 176-184; Milton Friedman, 'Commodity Reserve Currency,' in *Journal of Political Economy,* LIX, 1951, pp. 23-32; and Elmer M. Harmon, *Commodity Reserve Currency* (New York, *Columbia University Press,* 1959).

51. The importance of the distribution of costs is stressed by Robert Z. Aliber in his essay on 'National Preferences and the Scope for International Monetary Reform,' *Essays in International Finance,* Princeton University, International Finance Section, No. 101, November 1973.

52. This loss is a critical issue underlying the present reluctance of governments to agree on a new international monetary system; it is reflected in Ted Geiger's report on the 1972 negotiations: '...a kind of resignation permeated every speech—even by those paying lip service to the principle of domestic discipline—that there was little to be gained by relying on a system that counted on countries to adapt their domestic policies to the dictates of their external payments situations... Canada, France, Germany, and Japan all objected very strongly to the adoption of any kind of rigid criteria or to any 'automatic mechanism' for determining when or by what means exchange rates should be changed.' *The Issues in International Monetary Reform: Looking Ahead* (Washington, National Planning Association, February 1973).

53. Pierre Uri, *Développement sans dépendance* (Paris, November 1974), Ch. 7.

54. The problems facing the world at present are a result of the success in meeting past problems, as pointed out by Willis S. Harmon (Stanford Research Institute) in his paper on *Planning Amid Forces for Institutional Change.* He counterposes the following successes and resulting problems:

1) prolonged life span
2) national defense weapons
3) labour-saving machines
4) advances in communication and transportation
5) industrial engineering efficiency
6) growth in power of knowledge
7) affluence; pile-up of goods
8) ascendancy of "need-level" hierarchy
9) expanded wealth of advanced countries

1) overpopulation; problem of the aged
2) mass world destruction
3) technological unemployment
4) urbanization, increasing complexity, and risk of societal breakdown
5) dehumanization of work
6) threats to privacy and personality gap
7) environmental degradation; risk-poor/energy shortage
8) revolution of rising expectations; rebellion against meaningless work
9) widening gap between them and LDCs

(as cited in Madden, *The Clash of Culture,* p. 102).

Madden and Harman agree that the new problems 'are ultimately unsolvable under the present world view because their origin and cumulation lie in the very success of that view.' And that a major risk of continuing in the present world view is 'its difficulty in achieving the appearance of a more equitable distribution of power, health and justice.' (P. 102.)

55. Kenneth Waltz argues that Europeans have long recognized and lived with interdependence while the rest of the world has been faced with dependence or a myth of independence. 'The Myth of National Interdependence,' in Charles Kindleberger (ed.), *The International Corporation* (Boston: MIT Press, 1970), ch. 8.

56. In presenting 'A New Rationale for American Business,' Michel Crozier asserted that '...American business will be led to reconsider some of its basic thinking about economic and social rationality. Especially at stake will be the balance between human relations and economic rationality, between the demand for participation and the necessity of innovation.' In *Daedalus,* Winter 1969, p. 154.

57. Andrew Shonfield emphasized this necessity in his analysis of *Modern Capitalism* (London: Oxford University Press, 1965, Part 4), and proposed several changes, including an information ombudsman.

58. In the words of Helmut Schmidt, 'Bretton Woods benefited some countries more than others—particularly the strong more than the weak—and above all it burdened the international monetary system with the payments deficits of the superpower.' In *Foreign Affairs,* April 1974, p. 438.

59. Although the issue is raised, it is not given a high priority even in the research agenda proposed by Fred Bergsten in *The Future of the International Order* (Lexington, Mass: Lexington Books, 1973).

60. The *ad hoc* functional approach is proposed by Gardner, in 'The Hard Road to World Order,' pp. 559-562, *Foreign Affairs,* April, 1974.
information and in guiding the activities of the international companies.

61. This result is suggested in my examination of *The Role of the International Companies in Latin American Integration* (Lexington, Mass: Lexington Books, 1972).

62. Written 20 years ago by Harrison Brown (geochemist, and more recently Foreign Secretary of the National Academy of Science in the United States), in *The Challenge of Man's Future,* quoted by Madden, *The Clash of Culture,* p. 62.

63. This, as I read him, is the thrust of C.L. Sulzberger's *An Age of Mediocrity,* (New York: Macmillan, 1973), in which he argues that men such as Nixon, Heath, Brandt and Pompidou are 'technocrats,' 'efficient,' 'men of man's dimensions,' but certainly not leaders to a new world view: 'Our age of mediocrity is marked not only by an absence of outstanding men, but also by an absence of vigorous new ideas' (p. 2).

64. One observer of economic ills has concluded that ultimately, the only cure for unemployment is a complete rethinking of the goals of society... We must substitute for efficiency' the broader goal of finding productive occupations for the entire labour force.' Kenneth E.F. Watt, *The Titanic Effect* (Conn.: Sinauer Assoc., 1974), p. 111.

Labour does not seem to be thinking so broadly—at least not in the United States—though this may be the result of co-determination moves in Europe.

65. On the need to change social institutions, Carl Madden writes that, within this new world view, 'Our social institutions would be changed so that they would seek, more than before, the self-fulfillment of the individual, equality of justice before law (rather

than official or managerial indulgence), human dignity and meaningful work, honesty and trust in dealings, and responsibility for humanity and for the planet.' (Madden, *The Clash of Culture,* p. 108.)

66. Neil Chamberlain has urged a similar shift in company orientation: 'It may be worth experimenting as to whether we cannot make ours a livelier, more creative, more daring society by invigorating the private corporate centres of power. We may, in time, develop new standards for judging the effectiveness of such institutions, but I should not want to postpone our experimenting until we have done so. The pace of change is matched too closely by impatience with the lack of change. The corporation is one resource we can not afford to waste by chaining it tightly to the profit stake, while searching for another more suitable stake to which to anchor it.' 'The Life of the Mind in the Firm,' in *Daedalus,* Winter, 1969, p. 144.

67. For a number of policy areas in which business and governments should take the lead, see Madden, *The Clash of Culture,* pp. 109-111.

# About the Authors

JACK N. BEHRMAN is Professor of International Business, University of North Carolina at Chapel Hill.

ROBERTO CAMPOS is former Planning Minister, Brazil.

LOUIS CAMU is President, Banque de Bruxelles.

GUY DE CARMOY is Professor at the European Institute of Business Administration, Fontainebleau, France.

CURT GASTEYGER is editor, Atlantic Papers (Atlantic Institute for International Affairs) and Professor at the Graduate Institute for International Studies, Geneva.

DR. WALTER GUMPEL is Professor at the University of Munich.

WOLFGANG HAGER is a Senior Research Fellow at the German Council on Foreign Relations, Bonn.

HISAO KANAMORI is Chairman, Japan Economic Research Center.

JÜRGEN PONTO is Chairman, Dresdner Bank.

ROBERT V. ROOSA, former Undersecretary of the U.S. Treasury, is a Partner in Brown Brothers Harriman.

MASAO SAKISAKA is President, Institute of Energy Economics Tokyo.

NATHANIEL SAMUELS, former Undersecretary of State for Economic Affairs, is Chairman, Louis Dreyfus Corporation.

MARCEL TOUSSAINT is Managing Director, Business Asia, Hong Kong.

EMILE VAN LENNEP is Secretary-General, Organization for Economic Cooperation and Development (OECD), Paris.

# About the Atlantic Institute

The Atlantic Institute for International Affairs is an independent international organization based in Paris. Its purpose is to assist in solving problems which are common to the Atlantic countries and, to an increasing degree, countries with similar political structures and levels of development, such as Japan, Australia, and New Zealand. Through basic research and regular programs of conferences, the Institute deals with three types of issues: the relations of its member-countries among themselves; their relations with developing countries; and their relations with communist countries.

The Board of Governors of the Institute, under the chairmanship of John H. Loudon, is composed of 60 eminent men and women from 21 nations. Under the guidance of the newly formed Research Advisory Council, consisting of 10 leading international scholars, the Institute's work has been increasingly oriented toward today's major international economic problems and their political implications. Whether it be in the form of books, periodical reports, or informal recommendations to governments and international organizations, the emphasis of all the Institute's activities is toward policy-orientation and action.

The Institute and its international staff are directed by John W. Tuthill. Curt Gasteyger is the editor of the Atlantic Papers, a bimonthly series of papers reflecting the Institute's areas of interest.

# Related Titles

Published by
Praeger Special Studies